# The Faith of

# Robert Louis Stevenson

By

John Kelman, Junr., M.A.

PUBLISHED BY

OLIPHANT ANDERSON AND FERRIER

EDINBURGH AND LONDON

1904

# PREFACE TO THE SECOND EDITION

*I CANNOT send forth a second edition of this book without a few further words with my readers, and the first word must be one of heartiest gratitude. The cordiality of its reception by the great majority of reviewers, both in Britain and America, has surprised me; while many letters from friends, known and unknown, have touched me very deeply. If the book has braced the courage of some readers and quickened their belief in life, one of its main ends has been accomplished. For several criticisms revealing errors of detail I also thank my critics, and have gladly made the necessary changes.*

*With regard to more important matters, the main attack has been so direct and uncompromising as to exhilarate and delight me hugely. He would be but a dull fellow whose sense of humour were not touched by the sweeping announcement that, good or bad, his book should never have been written. 'Schweig Hund!' ('Silence, you dog!'), cries Fritz der Einzige; and Andreas can only say 'Das nenn' ich mir einen König' ('There is what I call a King!'). Yet, with all possible deference, Andreas still ventures to think that his book, or a better one to the same effect, should have been written. Both these opposite opinions are absolutely dogmatic, but I think that my critics are 'dogmatic and wrong.' I can see no reason at all why the faith of a novelist and artist should not be selected for special study. It is true that a man's faith is a matter between himself and his God, but when he has published it in some twenty-seven volumes, he has made it also a matter between himself and his readers.*

*But much exception has been taken to the word* Faith *as here understood. Obviously it is not synonymous with* Creed *in the conventional meaning of that term, for it includes many phases of the man's life and art which are generally reckoned among things secular. All I can say is that this use of the word Faith was emphatic. A man's real faith is not a thing that can be shut off in a department of so-called religious views and interests, far from the world and aloof from life. That is a view of faith which has already cost us dear. It has impoverished the sacred and exiled the secular. My protest was deliberate, and I stand by it.*

*One other point has been raised by many reviewers. Is the faith here expounded really the faith of R. L. S.? What would Stevenson have said could he have read this? My answer is that this is what he did actually say. Some of his most serious work is as yet accessible only to readers of the Edinburgh Edition, but even those of his books which have been published in popular form contain the message which I have sent forth as his. Since I did not know him personally, I waited with some anxiety for the verdict of certain of the friends who were best acquainted with his mind and heart, and few things have gratified me more than the fact that these consider that I have interpreted him justly.*

*But though I believe 'without capitulation' in his faith and in my task, no critic has come near expressing my own sense of the inadequacy of my performance. Robert Louis*

# PREFACE TO THE SECOND EDITION

*Stevenson is greater than his contemporaries yet know, and his message is more helpful than they realise. My hope for this new edition is that, with all its defects, it may spread yet more widely the acquaintance of English-speaking men and women with one who has very much to say to them which will be both wholesome and heartening for them to hear.*

JOHN KELMAN.

*June* 9, 1904.

# PREFACE TO THE FIRST EDITION

*No apology is needed for another book concerning Robert Louis Stevenson. It would be impossible to have too much of him ; and while his faith has been touched upon in passing by most of those who have written about him, it has never yet been selected for special and detailed study. But a large, and for the most part a very excellent, literature has for the past nine years been gathering round his personality and his work, so that the difficulty grows ever greater for a new writer. How much may be taken for granted ? How much must be explained ? It may be expected that some will read this book who are intimately acquainted with the subject, and others to whom it is almost wholly unknown. It is an arduous task that lies before him who would offer anything of even the slightest value to both these classes. Yet I venture to hope that what I have written may tempt some to enter one of the richest and most delightful regions in modern English literature, and may interest others to whom that region is already familiar.*

*I have to thank Mr. Graham Balfour for his generous and cordial permission to make use of his Biography—a permission of which I have availed myself with obvious freedom. To Miss E. Blantyre Simpson, for her 'Edinburgh Days' and for other help given with her characteristic good-will, I am also indebted ; to the books and articles of Professors Colvin, Raleigh, Baildon, and Genung ; and to those of Mr. Gosse,*

# THE FAITH OF R. L. STEVENSON

*Mr. Cope Cornford, and Mr. Chesterton, besides many others.
It has often happened that passages which I had chosen for
quotation turned out to have been already selected by one or
other of the writers named. I have not discarded these
passages on that account; but in no instance (except one or two
where the debt is acknowledged) have I quoted from Stevenson
anything which I had not found for myself in his works.
From him I have quoted incessantly, weaving his words together
with what skill I could command, that I might thus induce
him to tell his own tale. Abundance of quotation is a feature
in every book which has been written about him, and no one
would wish that this were otherwise. But the excess of
quotation-marks grew alarming as the work advanced. I
had a long battle with inverted commas, as the printer knows
to his cost. Fearing to irritate even the most forbearing
reader, I drove them from their possession of many words and
phrases, and allowed them to remain only in the longer
extracts. The incorporated fragments will be easily recognised by all lovers of Robert Louis Stevenson; and if any
phrase should strike the uninitiated as suspicious, I would
respectfully invite them to search for it in Stevenson's books—
it will be a most profitable exercise.*

*My claim to write is not that of one who was personally
acquainted with Stevenson. I have seen him in Edinburgh,
but have never spoken with him. There is, accordingly, no
reference to personal and private facts of his life except such
as are already public property. An immense number of his
writings, and unusually full and sympathetic accounts of his
personality, have been given to the public. My endeavour has
been to gather from these, so that any one may verify or*

xiv

*dissent from my contention for himself, the faith which appears
to me manifest and precious. And yet I cannot allow that I
have felt myself writing quite as an outsider. Like him I
spent the Saturdays of my boyhood among the ships at Leith:
I knew all about ' 1d. plain and 2d. coloured': and I too bore
a lantern at my belt. These memories alone, to say nothing
of the student days in the old Quadrangle, are enough to
establish an intimacy of some sort. 'Et ego in Arcadia vixi.'
But there is a stronger claim in the love I bear him and the
great debt I owe him for help of the most vital kind If
gratitude qualifies a man for such work, none could be better
qualified. Indeed it has often been necessary to restrain the
book from becoming a monotonous panegyric—a kind of
appreciation which he would have despised, and a kind of
book which has less than no value.*

*What I have tried to do is to estimate his thought justly,
and to pass it on, that its quickening message may go still
more widely abroad. It is only beginning to be generally
realised that Stevenson had a message to his times and that
his faith is to be taken seriously. I have felt myself
advocating this against a considerable body of common
opinion, and that is one reason why so much of the book
is written in his own words, and why certain sayings of his
have been repeated in it so often. It is with what he has
said, and not with the opinions of others on either side, that
we have to reckon.*

*The type of faith which his own words declare is peculiarly
valuable in the present time. There is around us much
unconscious Christianity. There are strong men whom God
has girded though they have not known Him, and quiet men*

*who do not seem to be following Christ, and yet unquestionably are casting out devils. These are the men who will best appreciate Stevenson's faith. Its unconventionality, its freedom from dogmatic expression, and the inseparable weaving of it into the warp and woof of his life's various activities, must appeal to many who have found themselves out of sympathy with the external forms of modern Christianity, though in heart they have remained true to its spirit.*

*I only wish that the task I have attempted had been done more worthily of him for love of whom it was undertaken. Beside the rare sparkle of his wit, and the swift and irresponsible flight of his imagination, any systematic analysis may well seem pedestrian. It comforts one to remember that he was fond of walking tours. At least I may claim to have drawn him into much brilliant conversation by the way, and it is never dull when Stevenson is speaking.*

JOHN KELMAN.

EDINBURGH, *April* 28, 1903.

xvi

# CONTENTS

# THE FAITH OF
## ROBERT LOUIS STEVENSON

# CHAPTER I

## RELIGION AND THE MAN

IT is not the purpose of this volume to attempt to force
words or actions of Robert Louis Stevenson beyond-their
real significance, or to clothe him with religious garments
not his own. A large collection of extracts might be made,
which, if taken apart from his other work, would seem
irreligious enough. At the sectarian side of Scottish church
life, and at the conventional respectabilities of some common
types of religion, he sneers openly. These, of course, are
but local matters, but the question becomes more serious
when he tells us that he has been a 'youthful atheist';
when he sees behind the King of Apemama, busy at his
futile devil-work, 'all the fathers of the Church'; or when he
makes us shudder with the bitter sarcasm of his fable of the
yellow paint which was to set men free from the dangers
of life, and the bondage of sin, and the fear of death for
ever. All this, and much else more pointed still, may
strike many readers as disconcerting in a man who is also
the friend of missionaries and the humble and devout
worshipper, and who holds that all freethinkers 'are much
under the influence of superstition.' Here, certainly, it
will be necessary to avoid the preponderance of single
elements, and to consider the wide stretch and whole
purpose of the man. It must be again confessed that at
the outset this task seems a sufficiently perplexing one.
The numberless apparent incongruities and conflicting

A                                                    1

aspects of Stevenson's life might at first sight tempt one to take a cynical view of the situation, and to count him among those who smile at faith. Yet no one who knows the spirit of his work could permanently accept that easy but impossible solution. Even after a slight acquaintance the religious element is apparent, and further study serves only to show it more deep and clear.

The explanation is, after all, not far to seek. This man, both by constitution and by experience, was so complex a personality that there is no possibility of defining him in a sentence or of expressing his faith in any set of articles. There are always many—and especially is this the case in an age strong in criticism—who are essentially men of the museum. They look out upon the world as a place of phenomena demanding to be catalogued. To get a definition of a new man—to find a pigeon-hole for him, fit him into it and label him—that is the duty that appeals first to their consciences. Either he is Elias, or else that prophet, or if not these, Who then is he? Such questioners have forgotten that life is greater than many pigeon-holes, and that every soul of man eludes the subtlest definition. For indeed this rage for defining is often a more dangerous thing than it seems. Apparently the desire for clearness and logical accuracy, it is often but a phase of that deadly worship of antinomies which does such havoc to the search after truth. If a man be not *this* he must be *that*; and it is prearranged that if he be this I may approve of him and admire him, while if he be that I am in duty bound to hate and frustrate him. It never occurs to the inquirer to leave these and all other antinomies alone, and ask apart from them, What manner of man is this? Yet surely it were wisdom to let the man reveal himself in his own right, as he is, apart from any such labels and divisions. It is the method of synthesis by which we construct about us a

2

world of living knowledge, as contrasted with that dreary analytical method which makes our world but a collection of classified specimens.

All this applies with special force to such a character and mind as Stevenson's. So complex to begin with, so vitally changeful in his moods, so catholic in his appreciation of apparent opposites, so fascinated by the idea which for the time being is most absorbing,—you may define him (to parody the words of Socrates) if you can catch him. Epithets like 'Optimist' or 'Pessimist' are inapplicable to him, and fall off as soon as they are considered—how much more the epithets of religious sect or party! He felt the mystery of life. He travelled fast in thought and in sympathy across the whole field of human experience, and saw 'the beauty and the terror of the world,' but he found no easy formula which would express them. Nor did he demand such a formula. He did not think that

> 'It's strange that God should fash to frame
> The yearth and lift sae hie,
> An' clean forget to explain the same
> To a gentleman like me.'

The mystery of things remained and even deepened:

> 'O, I wad like to ken—to the beggar-wife says I—
> The reason o' the cause an' the wherefore o' the why,
> Wi' mony anither riddle brings the tear into my e'e.
> —It's gey an' easy speirin', says the beggar-wife to me.'

In a memorable passage in the *Inland Voyage* he tells us that 'it is not at all a strong thing to put one's reliance upon logic'; and thirteen years later he speaks of himself and the poet Fergusson as 'born in the same city; both sickly, both pestered, one nearly to madness, one to the madhouse, with a damnatory creed.' Accordingly we find throughout his work that the distinguishing mark of this most dogmatic of men is the absence of dogma in the theological sense. The faith of Robert Louis Stevenson could never be expressed in any formal creed.

And indeed it were the worst sort of folly to demand this of such a man. To present to him the blunderbuss of conformity, and bid him stand and deliver, were an attempt at intellectual highway robbery. Nor, supposing him to yield, and to state his convictions in formal terms to the best of his ability, would we have gained anything. It is a transparent fallacy that the creed a man may find it possible to formulate will exactly embody his real religious thought and life. 'Almost every person,' says Stevenson, 'if you will believe himself, holds a quite different theory of life from the one on which he is patently acting.' In estimating the position of many men of our time—such men as Carlyle, Matthew Arnold, and certainly also R. L. Stevenson—it may be taken as an axiom that they will invariably understate their faith. In their formulations there will always be expressed less than they are actually working from. That deeper, inner, inexpressible faith may at times find words in a poem or in a sudden outburst of poetic prose; but the moment it tries for exact expression its light fails, the mystery closes in once more, and words ring cheerless and inadequate.

We shall not, therefore, attempt to construct any creed for Stevenson out of words of his that bear reference to religious doctrines. The uniting principle of the many elements of his thought must be found in his personality itself. Yet we shall retain and insist upon the word religion. 'Religion,' by etymology and by common usage, is the connection of the soul of man with God, that which *binds* the finite with the infinite and eternal. The bonds may be of various material. There are the steel chains of dogma—great bonds which have knit great men with their

4

Maker in every age. There are also the flexible and yet strong cords of sentiment; and there are those other cords which we call character. It is at religion understood in the latter senses that we must look directly in this study.

The Religion of Sentiment is a term easily misunderstood. It may be confused with sentimentalism, and for that we shall look in vain in Stevenson. Whatever else he is, he is robust and healthy; nor would it be easy to find a writer equally voluminous and imaginative in whose works so little of the sentimental is to be found. He himself has condemned it with the word 'splairging'—a word so expressive as to justify the prophecy that no Scot who had ever used it would dare to sentimentalise again. In a higher vein than the sentimental is the saying of David Balfour in *Catriona*: 'Indeed there was scarce anything that more affected me than thus to kneel down alone with her before God like man and wife.' Of the same order is his description of the New Year in Edinburgh : ' For at this season, on the threshold of another year of calamity and stubborn conflict, men feel a need to draw closer the links that unite them ; they reckon the number of their friends, like allies before a war; and the prayers grow longer in the morning as the absent are recommended by name into God's keeping.' Another passage, from *Vailima Letters*, may be classed with these : 'Did you see a man who wrote the *Stickit Minister*, and dedicated it to me, in words that brought the tears to my eyes every time I looked at them—"where about the graves of the martyrs the whaups are crying. *His* heart remembers how." Ah, by God, it does !'

Such quotations might be multiplied, but there is no need. In a still higher form (though this is far more delicate, and hard to express in words) the religion of sentiment appears in that *spirituality* which is so constant a quality of his work. His nickname 'Sprite' was prophetic of more than freakishness. 'He gave,' as his biographer strikingly says, 'the impression of something transitory and unreal, sometimes almost inhuman.' At times this reminds one of Kipling's Mowgli, where he personifies and, as it were, humanises Nature—as when in Silverado the evening breeze blows 'right down the canyon, fanning it well out, airing it as a mother airs the night nursery before the children sleep'; or when 'the dark woods below were shrill with that noisy business of the birds' evening worship.' At other times we think rather of such uncanny creations as Undine or Maeterlinck's *Melisande*—'divine or human, or both mingled'—'I seem to have been born with a sentiment of something moving in things, of an infinite attraction and horror coupled.' A man does not write like that for nothing; there is more in it than the words express. All through his life the thing he most prizes in himself is soul. The horror of deadening or of losing that is vivid,—the loss would be veritable damnation. The worst of the invalid time in Mentone, immortalised in *Ordered South*, is that 'my soul is rarely with me here.' But how splendidly his soul *is* with him at other times, and how brilliantly it thinks and speaks! Of no man of our time do the great words seem more appropriate: 'Revere the Maker, lift up thine eye to His style and manners of the sky.' When Stevenson's spirituality assumes this *grande manière*, it touches the highest level of what may be honourably called the religion of sentiment.

Spirituality takes its most definite and highest form in the instinctive sense of God. His biographer tells us that this was at the root of everything, that it filled his soul with strength and patience for his awfully difficult task, and opened his heart in self-sacrifice; and it is not too much to say of him that, in his own way, 'in God he lived and moved and had his being.' No doubt some caution is needed here. The Name of God is the most picturesquely symbolic of all names, and is capable of poetic as well as literal interpretation. Joubert has well said that 'It is not hard to know God, provided one will not force oneself to define him.' Probably there are very many thinkers in our time to whom these words appeal strongly, and we may grant that Stevenson was one of them. Yet the very darkness that is round about Him may be in such a case the guarantee of His divinity. If pressed for definitions Stevenson would have answered that there still are some whose God no house of words that men have builded can contain.

It is noteworthy how constantly the Divine Name keeps recurring in his later work—too often perhaps, too casually and lightly. Yet it shows how familiar this thought was to him; and if one test of the irreligious man be that 'God is not in all his thoughts,' we have here a good certificate. If there are references whose faith is a very doubtful quantity—'God, let us say,'—there are others where the realisation is genuinely deep and instinctive. When he speaks of God as 'the master of our pleasures and our pains,' when in the Samoan troubles he prays God his *Footnote* be in time to help, and hopes that by His help he may succeed, he is evidently meaning what he says in its simple acceptation. The same is surely true also of the description of the night in Vailima, when 'we must sit in the dark, the wind would not suffer any light, and so loud was the roar of the rain and the beating boughs on the roof, that we must sit in silence also . . . in such hours . . . there is a communion impossible in any chapel of ease, even in any cathedral. You are alone with God: with one face of Him, that is: which he who blinks, blinks at his peril.' And there is a note of unmistakable reality in the words he speaks to the Sisters of Charity, weeping quietly as they are rowed shorewards to Molokai with a

7

company of lepers—'Ladies, God Himself is here to give you welcome.'

But though the Religion of Sentiment is thus finely and worthily represented, we draw nearer to the inmost truth of the man when we turn to the Religion of Character. In two of his weirdest fables he shows how noble action excels and may survive orthodox faith. In the saddest and the bravest song he ever wrote, he turns from the bewilderment of a life which for the time had lost faith and almost lost hope, to strenuous and courageous action as a last resort and citadel:

> 'God, if this were faith?
>
>          ,      .        .        .
> To go on for ever and fail and go on again,
> And be mauled to the earth and arise,
> And contend for the shade of a word and a thing not
>     seen with the eyes:
> With the half of a broken hope for a pillow at night
> That somehow the right is the right,
> And the smooth shall bloom from the rough:
> Lord, if that were enough?'

It was in this fashion, though not often so sadly, that he turned from the speculative to the practical side of religion, and his life bore witness to his right to do so. 'To be the writer that he was, amounted to a great exploit and service to humanity; to become the man that in the end he became, seems to me an achievement equally great, an example no less eloquent.' He is well aware that 'faith is a more supporting quality than imagination,' but faith was often as difficult for him as imagination was easy. He is content with such speculative faith as he can get: 'If I from my spy-hole, looking with purblind eyes upon the least part of a fraction of the universe, yet perceive in my own destiny some broken evidences of a plan, and some signals of an over-ruling goodness; shall I then be so mad as to complain that all cannot be deciphered? Shall I not rather

8

wonder, with infinite and grateful surprise, that in so vast
a scheme I seem to have been able to read, however little,
and that little was encouraging to faith?' In the last of
his published songs he reaches a calmer and more assured
point still:

'So far have I been led,
Lord, by Thy will:
So far I have followed, Lord, and wondered still.

.        .        .        .        .        .

I hear the signal, Lord—I understand
The night at Thy command
Comes. I will eat and sleep and will not question more.'

The transition from theory to practice in the matter of
religious faith could hardly be stated more explicitly than
in his address to the Samoan students : 'The meaning of
religion is a rule of life; it is an obligation to do well; if
that rule, that obligation, is not seen, your thousand texts
will be to you like the thousand lanterns to the blind
man.'

This leads us to the most important fact of all in connection with Stevenson's religious thought, for it turns our
attention away from a man's formal faith to his whole life
of character and personality. It is in this that we must see
and judge of his religion—in the life, in which a faith of the
theoretical sort is involved and, as it were, understood,
whether it have found fuller or less full doctrinal con-
sistency and expression. Of Stevenson this is truer than
of almost any man one can remember. With an altogether
exceptional number and variety of interests, he combined a
vitality which flung him into each as if it were the only
one. He was of that order of beings which 'moveth all
together if it move at all.' His work was so much himself
for the time being, that it is utterly impossible to separate
his human characteristics from his religious message. He
did much preaching, but it is his whole life, his thoughts and

9

deeds, his writings, and his experiences—it is these that he gives you to be better or worse for. With a difference, and yet with the same profound truth, his words about the French peasants may be applied to himself: 'It is not a basketful of law-papers, nor the hoofs and pistol-butts of a regiment of horse, that can change one tittle of a ploughman's thoughts. Out-door rustic people have not many ideas, but such as they have are hardy plants, and thrive flourishingly in persecution. One who has grown a long while in the sweat of laborious noons, and under the stars at night, a frequenter of hills and forests, an old honest countryman, has in the end a sense of communion with the powers of the universe, and amicable relations towards his God. . . . His religion does not repose upon the choice of logic; it is the poetry of the man's experience, the philosophy of the history of his life.' So with Stevenson there is no separation of life into departments of secular and sacred. He even scorns the general type of the 'novel with a purpose,' in which 'we see the moral forced into every hole and corner of the story, or thrown externally over it like a carpet over a railing.' His religion was as wide as his human life: 'I feel every day as if religion had a greater interest for me; but that interest is still centred on the little rough-and-tumble world in which our fortunes are cast for the moment. I cannot transfer my interests, not even my religious interests, to any different sphere.'

Surely this is in itself no small gain. It approaches from the other end, as it were, that ideal of Christian men in every age, the ideal of a wholly consecrated life, which has fascinated or tormented so many of the fathers. Nay, it fulfils Christ's own demand for a life in which saying and doing shall not be held apart—a fatal separation which is at the root of all hypocrisy. But at this stage it is more to the point to notice that the identification of

10

life and religion sets for us the only possible line along which a study of Stevenson's religion may proceed. It will be absolutely necessary for us to get a clear view of the man as he was, and that will be our only necessity. If we can construct for ourselves the image of his manhood, from the physical powers and characteristics up to the inmost spiritual aspirations—we shall need nothing more. For much of what was most characteristically *himself* in Robert Louis Stevenson reveals itself sooner or later in a religious form.

The successive chapters of this book, then, will be devoted to the study of the man, with the quest of religion for a more or less subconscious principle of guidance. They will not be confined to any one class of his books, but will look across the whole range of his work and interest, since no part of that can be excluded where the message and the movement of life are one. Nor must we confine our attention to any one period of his life. There seems to be an impression in some quarters that his religion was a late phase, developed almost entirely in the Samoan years, and cutting him off entirely from the Robert Louis Stevenson of early days. This, we take it, gives a quite mistaken idea whether of the late or of the early time. In Samoa he is indeed mellowed and sometimes pathetically aged before his time; yet no one can mistake the identity even in respect of the wilder and more freakish characteristics. In some of the early years he is wild enough, no doubt, and often to all appearance daringly and rudely irreligious; yet, as may be easily shown, even then there is a hidden life very different from the exterior.

It is quite true that the religious life of the Samoan period is a most impressive fact. Sometimes indeed, in an hour of depression, we hear a cry *de profundis* whose desolation is tragic. Yet in spite of such cries these years

11

are years of faith, and even in its outward expression their aspect is conspicuously religious. He attends church. It is true that sometimes it is for the love he bears the native preacher, as in that notable service in the Gilberts when 'The congregation stirred and stretched; they moaned, they groaned aloud; they yawned upon a singing note, as you may sometimes hear a dog when he has reached the tragic bitterest of boredom.' Yet he tells us of other services in which he found refreshment to his spirit; and at an earlier period, when in the Adirondacks he first discovered the broadminded and manly sermons of Robertson of Brighton, he could not find words to express his appreciation. Still more impressive is the family worship in Vailima, for which he wrote prayers, some of which are masterpieces in the literature of devotion. But the climax is reached when, in his account of a Sunday in Samoa written to Sidney Colvin, the words occur 'teaching Sunday-school (I actually do).' He actually did: and it makes one remember his saying that Dumas was 'no district visitor.' Yet Robert Louis Stevenson was, for several months, a Sunday-school teacher in Samoa.

All these are, no doubt, very outward and conventional facts—inadequate beneath contempt as final tests of a man's religious life. Yet it is just their conventionality and outwardness that make them significant in the biography of so extremely unconventional a man. Had any one been asked beforehand as to what form a religious life would be likely to take in Stevenson, the last answer that would have suggested itself would have been enthusiasm for foreign missions and teaching a Sunday-school class. Yet so it was, and it surely counts for much.

Hardly less surprising are the records of family worship, conducted morning and evening in his Vailima household. The low-born precentress and her Samoan hymn with five

12

verses and five treble choruses; the interruptions of unsympathetic animals from the curiously assorted live-stock of the estate; the attendance at the functions of 'folk of many families and nations'; all this might seem a sufficiently incongruous and fantastic manner of religious service. Yet it was for these gatherings that he wrote the prayers which are now happily so widely known. Of them nothing more need be said than to quote two of them, which may serve as typical of all.

### PRAYER FOR SUNDAY

(Used by Rev. Mr. Clarke as part of the burial-service at the grave of Robert Louis Stevenson)

'We beseech Thee, Lord, to behold us with favour, folk of many families and nations gathered together in the peace of this roof, weak men and women subsisting under the covert of thy patience. Be patient still; suffer us yet a while longer; with our broken purposes of good, with our idle endeavours against evil, suffer us a while longer to endure and (if it may be) help us to do better. Bless to us our extraordinary mercies; if the day come when these must be taken, brace us to play the man under affliction. Be with our friends, be with ourselves. Go with each of us to rest; if any awake, temper to them the dark hours of watching; and when the day returns, return to us, our sun and comforter, and call us up with morning faces and with morning hearts—eager to labour—eager to be happy, if happiness shall be our portion—and if the day be marked for sorrow, strong to endure it.

'We thank and praise Thee; and in the words of Him to whom this day is sacred, close our oblation.'

### FOR FRIENDS

'For our absent loved ones we implore thy loving-kindness. Keep them in life, keep them in growing honour; and for us, grant that we may remain worthy of their love. For Christ's sake, let not our beloved blush for us, nor we for them. Grant us but that, and grant us courage to endure lesser ills unshaken, and to accept death, loss, and disappointment, as it were straws upon the tide of life.'

13

# THE FAITH OF R. L. STEVENSON

In the life that grew to so rich and beautiful a close there was no supreme crisis such as those which cleave many lives asunder into parts wholly distinct. There was nothing violent or sudden in his inner experience, though there were, indeed, some points of definite crisis and change. Two of these, characteristically unlike the usual records of religious experience, may be quoted here. The first is that in which the 'youthful atheist' passed out of his atheism, under the influence of the late Professor Fleeming Jenkin. He had met with a scepticism deeper than his own, a distrust of scepticism itself: '"Certainly the church was not right, but certainly not the anti-church either," he would argue— so that the very weapons of the fight were changed to swords of paper.' The other passage is an extremely interesting fragment of autobiography which occurs in the *Reflections and Remarks on Human Life*, many of which are written very directly from experience: 'I remember a time when I was very idle; and lived and profited by that humour. I have no idea why I ceased to be so, yet I scarce believe I have the power to return to it; it is a change of age. I made consciously a thousand little efforts, but the determination from which these arose came to me while I slept and in the way of growth. I have had a thousand skirmishes to keep myself at work upon particular mornings, and sometimes the affair was lost; but of that great change of campaign, which decided all this part of my life, and turned me from one whose business was to shirk into one whose business was to strive and persevere,—it seems as though all that had been done by some one else. The life of Goethe affected me; so did that of Balzac; and some very noble remarks by the latter in a pretty bad book, the *Cousine Bette*. I daresay I could trace some other influences in the change. All I mean is, I was never conscious of a struggle, nor registered a vow, nor seemingly had anything

14

personal to do with the matter. I came about like a well-handled ship. There stood at the wheel that unknown steersman whom we call God.' Mr. Graham Balfour quotes this passage and says that there were several periods to which it might equally relate; it would be impossible to say which of these, or whether any of them, should be singled out as the spiritual turning-point of his life. Indeed, we seem to be warranted in holding that the later years were not so much the beginning of religious interest as the choice of religion for an emphasis which it had not had before. It had been often so neglected or abused as to become a mere picturesque background for the more inviting but less creditable play of immediate pursuits. Yet it had a real interest for him at every stage, and had been a dormant but genuine element in his nature, which broke out into memorable expression at unexpected times. When it took command at last, it was indeed marked with the scars of early conflict and defeat, but it was no new thing; it had been there through all. It is quite possible that some of his early friends saw little or nothing of this, and that from some of them he may have studiously concealed it. Such reticence is characteristic of the turbulent period in all such lives as his. Yet we catch glimpses of the hidden life in many passages, of which the following extracts may be taken as typical examples.

With the days of childhood we shall deal in a later chapter. Suffice it here to say that, susceptible to these influences as all natural childhood is, it would be difficult to find a record of nursery days more wholly saturated with religious thoughts than his. The influence of his parents' faith and character, and the tender faithfulness of his nurse's piety, filled his earliest years with religious thoughts.

In the wild time of revolt, about 1870, we have this entry in his diary: 'Decline of religion: I take to the New

15

Testament: change startling: growing desire for truth:
Spencer: should have done better with the New Test.'

About 1878 he wrote of the 'unknown steersman.'

In the same year he wrote to his father from Paris: 'Still
I believe in myself and my fellow-men and the God who
made us all. . . . I am lonely and sick and out of heart.
Well, I still hope; I still believe; I still see the good in the
inch, and cling to it. It is not much, perhaps, but it is always
something. . . . There is a fine text in the Bible, I don't
know where, to the effect that all things work together for
good to those who love the Lord. . . . Strange as it may
seem to you, everything has been, in one way or the other,
bringing me a little nearer to what I think you would like
me to be. 'Tis a strange world, indeed, but there is a
manifest God for those who care to look for him.'

From the next period, that of his California life, we may
choose from many possible quotations the verses in which
he, like his own David Balfour, kneels before God with the
woman he loves. In that well-known song of praise the
closing lines of the verses name God 'the great artificer,'
'the mighty master,' and 'the august father'; and the
whole is carefully planned, so that these three names give
the key to the entire thought of each verse.

## MY WIFE

'Trusty, dusky, vivid, true,
With eyes of gold and bramble-dew,
Steel-true and blade-straight,
The great artificer
Made my mate.

Honour, anger, valour, fire;
A love that life could never tire,
Death quench or evil stir,
The mighty master
Gave to her.

> Teacher, tender, comrade, wife,
> A fellow-farer true through life,
> Heart-whole and soul-free
> The august father
> Gave to me.'

In 1883 he writes at the close of a letter to Mr. W. E. Henley :—

> 'Sursum corda :
> Heave ahead :
> Here's luck.
> Art and Blue Heaven,
> April and God's Larks.
> Green reeds and the sky-scattering river.
> A stately music.
> Enter God !  R. L. S.

'Ay, but you know, until a man can write that " enter God," he has made no art!  None!  Come, let us take counsel together and make some !'

Two years later, in the beginning of 1886, appeared *Dr. Jekyll and Mr. Hyde,* the book which before many months gave him world-wide celebrity as a serious writer.

From the South Sea voyages no finer example could be given than his words to the Sisters of Charity already quoted. And this has brought us to Samoan days.  It is a curious combination of extracts, but it serves at least to prove that the religious element in Stevenson was not a thing of late growth, but an integral part and vital interest of his life.

# CHAPTER II

## SUBJECTIVITY

If it be granted that the religion of Robert Louis Stevenson is to be sought, not so much in any formal creed as in his general life of thought and action, our chief task must evidently be that of considering the individuality of the man. It may be hoped that even those readers who had little previous acquaintance with Stevenson's work have already found themselves in contact with a very distinct and conspicuous personality. Such he was, and felt himself to be. To him the world was full of striking phenomena, but for interest none of them all was comparable with that strange being who was impressed by them. He may have learned his habit of writing in the first person singular from his favourite Montaigne; but, if so, it must have been a congenial lesson, a permission to follow his bent rather than a mere fashion of style. His own thoughts, experiences, likes and dislikes; the things he saw and heard, and felt and did; his memories, his impressions, his forecasts; even his personal appearance and the condition of his health and spirits; these were to him matters in which he was frankly and strongly interested. Such highly developed self-consciousness is no doubt often a painful gift, if it goes with a nature sensitive to criticism and appreciation; but it has the huge advantage of providing a field of keen interest near home. To find oneself very interesting is to guarantee life at least against dulness.

And though he was indeed sensitive, yet he had the compensating power of counting his own experiences in with the general spectacle of the world; of sitting off, as it were, and viewing the situation as a fine matter for reflection, as an excuse for laughter or for tears.

In every department of his work this fact appears. Romance is usually objective, though there is no apparent reason why objectivity should be demanded of it. Yet it is unquestionable that those of his romances are the most successful in which his own individuality is most present. *The Black Arrow* he considered a failure, and a considerable proportion of his readers have agreed with the verdict. *Prince Otto*, in spite of his own fondness for it, the delicacy of its character-work, and the infinite care bestowed upon its style, can hardly be counted a success. From both of these he is conspicuously absent. Of them it may be said, as Arnold wrote of Racine, 'The talent of Racine is in his works, but Racine himself is not there.' They are perhaps the only books of his which you feel might possibly have been written by some one else. On the other hand the David Balfour novels, in which he seems to live in the personality of his ancestor, have attained a success which, if we discount the personal element, is surprising—no doubt a bold statement, but one which will stand consideration. The tales themselves are good, but that which is excellently good about them is the reader's converse with the teller. Again, while many of the *Poems* reveal a rare and delicate poetic quality, it is not that alone, but our communion in them with the soul of the poet, which is the secret of their altogether unusual appeal to the heart. The *Essays* and *Letters* are of course the most intimate of his self-revelations. Regarding the latter, one able and friendly critic wrote, among other astonishing things, that 'these letters, except for occasional touches, are indistinguishable

19

from the myriads of letters which are exchanged between young men every day of the year.' The only interest of a statement such as this is the psychological puzzle as to how it ever came to be made. The explanation which suggests itself is, that the critic was on the outlook for work and not for the man. As finished literature, the letters are of course fragmentary and unsatisfying. As brilliant and delightful revelations of one of the most fascinating personalities of our time, they are beyond praise. Again, the volume entitled *In the South Seas* has not been received with at all the amount of favour which its author anticipated for it, and which its immense store of information vividly imparted deserves. Probably the reason is that which Professor Colvin has assigned—that he tried to make it too impersonal. Consciously or unconsciously his readers had learned to look for and to welcome himself in all his writings, and in this volume they are kept in the outer court for the most part—discussing subjects in themselves very fascinating, but seldom crossing the threshold and conversing on intimate matters with their friend.

One of the ways in which he impresses himself on his readers—coming on them at unawares throughout his work —is in the recurrence of favourite figures and ideas, which in themselves are casual and of little intrinsic value. Just as Jean Valjean, lying on the night of his great temptation in Father Myriel's chamber, sees continually the checked pattern of a fellow-convict's knit cotton suspender, so certain details haunt Stevenson. The idea of a heavy piece of sculpture left upon the artist's hands or travelling aimlessly about the world is one such recurrence. Another is that of the bather lingering stripped upon the water's edge, eager to take the plunge and yet fearful. A third instance is that of the cathedral, which does metaphorical service in so many of his books, sometimes with a

20

curious irrelevance. The main interest of these and many other such allusions is that *he* was interested. The images had captivated his imagination, and we feel more intimate with him every time we meet them.

This kind of intimacy reaches its keenest in the snatches of verse which recur—snatches which have evidently caught his ear and sung themselves into his heart. Sometimes this happens with a verse which occurs but once. Sailing, for instance, in the Dangerous Archipelago: 'As I lay in the cockpit and looked upon the steersman, I was haunted by Emerson's verses:

> "And the lone seaman all the night
> Sails astonished among stars."'

—lines which haunt those to whom he has repeated them, and recall that night near Raraka when 'the heaven was a thing to wonder at for stars,' as if one had actually seen him there in the starlit ship. Still more haunting are the verses which repeat themselves at intervals through a story or a play. The brown old seaman holds us like the Ancient Mariner he is, with the unhallowed spell of his rhyme:

> 'Fifteen men on the Dead Man's Chest—
> Yo-ho-ho, and a bottle of rum!'

Then there is that provokingly unforgettable lilt of Pew's:

> 'Time for us to go,
> Time for us to go,
> And when we'd clapped the hatches on
> 'Twas time for us to go.'

Above all others, there comes back to us the memory of Stevenson's own version of 'Wandering Willie.' It would be difficult to find anywhere a more intimate and poignant pathos than that which lies in the lines:

> 'Home no more home to me, whither must I wander?'

and

> 'Home was home then, my dear, full of kindly faces,
> Home was home then, my dear, happy for the child.'

21

We meet fragments of the last-named song in the *Master of Ballantrae, The Wrecker,* and other books. Obviously they haunt and strike home to our hearts because they come from the depths of his own heart. In his *Critical Kitcats* Mr. Gosse tells us that Walter Pater, to guard from infection that style of his which has become the very type of the elaborately exquisite, found he had to abstain from reading Stevenson. Nothing could have been further apart than the styles as such: the danger must have been in the irresistible personality.

More obvious, though hardly less appealing, are the personal reminiscences that appear everywhere in his books. A quite unusual proportion of his work is directly and avowedly autobiographical. Many of the essays are simply chapters or collections of incidents from his private life. All the life of childhood, boyhood, student days, and growing manhood is there—his life, told by an artist, yet without glorification or belittling. In the poems we naturally expect the same thing, and we find it. The travel-books are but pages from his own experience of travel. Even the novels have sometimes Robert Louis Stevenson rechristened for their hero; or, if not, they have him for chorus moralising and explaining things. Even if the *Letters* and the *Life* had never been published, we would have known him and his friends, and when we read these later volumes we recognise many an old acquaintance. There are parts of *John Nicholson's Misadventure* which are evidently memories, exaggerated but unforgotten. There are other parts of that, and of many another writing of his, which must be only dimly intelligible—if indeed they are even that—to any reader who has not been a boy in Scotland. Did any town elsewhere, for example, use the classic word ' Leerie ' of its lamplighters? From Hunter Square there went forth of old a procession of nightly illuminators, with

22

black cloth caps and white linen jackets, and little tin lamps swung a-dangle at their fingers by hooks only known to dairy-men and them. Does anybody who then lived elsewhere than in Edinburgh *quite* understand the inwardness of:

> ' My tea is nearly ready, and the sun has left the sky,
> It's time to take the window to see Leerie going by ;
> For every night at tea-time and before you take your seat,
> With lantern and with ladder he comes posting up the street ' ?

In the *Family of Engineers*—a fragment which carries the family history down to the building of the Bell Rock Lighthouse—there are many recognisable traits. It is here that we understand what gave the cue to the inimitable description of domestic economy in the house of Weir of Hermiston : ' My grandmother remained to the end devout and unambitious, occupied with her Bible, her children, and her house ; easily shocked, and associating largely with a clique of godly parasites. . . . The cook was a godly woman, the butcher a Christian man, and the table suffered.' Nothing, again, is more characteristic of Stevenson than the frequent introduction of trivial incidents or everyday allusions, evidently reminiscences of his own life, which few writers would dare to use in so *naïf* a fashion. Finally, there is a favourite phrase of his, which every lover of his work will recognise, so frequently is it repeated. It is the phrase ' dying daily,' which he has borrowed from St. Paul. It is a striking combination of words ; but that which made it so familiar to him, and so ready for his use, was its tragic aptness as a description of many days of his invalid life.

It might be expected that a man so conscious of himself would in times of depression let his subjectivity sink into morbidness. In the last days of crowding anxieties and broken health there are such seasons of morbid self-examination and depression, but these are not the real man, the soul of him, at all. Occasional outbreaks of the overstrung nerves, they may be, and ought to be, entirely discounted. There is also an uneasy, ill-conditioned stage through which most boys pass on their way to manhood—the 'troglodyte' stage, in which they sulk and dwell apart each in his particular cave. How dark and disagreeable was the cave of Stevenson may be judged from certain of the personal reminiscences in *Memories and Portraits*. 'The interests of youth are rarely frank; his passions, like Noah's dove, come home to roost. The fire, the sensibility, and volume of his own nature, that is all that he has learned to recognise. The tumultuary and gray tide of life, the empire of routine, the unrejoicing faces of his elders, fill him with contemptuous surprise; there also he seems to walk among the tombs of spirits; and it is only in the course of years, and after much rubbing with his fellow-men, that he begins by glimpses to see himself from without, and his fellows from within.' And again: 'The ground of all youth's suffering, solitude, hysterics, and haunting of the grave, is nothing else than naked, ignorant selfishness. It is himself that he sees dead; those are his virtues that are forgotten; his is the vague epitaph. Pity him but the more, if pity be your cue; for where a man is all pride, vanity, and personal aspiration, he goes through fire unshielded. In every part and corner of our life, to lose oneself is to be gainer; to forget oneself is to be happy; and this poor laughable and tragic fool has not yet learned the rudiments.' Through such a stage of unpleasant and aggressive morbidness Stevenson passed in his young Edinburgh days. The Holy Land of this perverse and unlovely worship of sorrow is the grim old Calton Cemetery in Edinburgh, where he nursed the mood and at the same time watched a certain overlooking window

24

for the vision of a pretty face. The Calton Cemetery reappears in later books—that cemetery 'by some strange chance immured within the bulwarks of a prison; standing, besides, on the margin of a cliff, crowded with elderly stone memorials, and green with turf and ivy.' It was, however, but a phase, this youthful melancholy. His life passed out, like one of the wakeful nights of his childhood, from the miserable silence and fear of the dark into the 'wholesome noises' of the morning, and the bright stir of day.

A less tragic, but perhaps more objectionable, form of his self-consciousness is that of affectation and egoism, which appears to have been the impression he made on all his friends at one period. Miss Simpson, among the many vivid pictures of her *Edinburgh Days*, has left him before our eyes in a drawing-room, sitting in his shirt-sleeves that he might attract attention to himself. Stevenson in all his glory was certainly not arrayed like anybody else. As we see him in all the fantastic absurdity of attire and mannerism which he cultivated in these early days, the words of Milton's chorus come to mind:

> 'But who is this? what thing of sea or land? . . .
> That, so bedeck'd, ornate, and gay,
> Comes this way sailing.'

Of that young time he tells a story at his own expense. Salvini had visited Edinburgh, and Stevenson wrote to the *Academy* a notice of his first performance of *Macbeth.* Fleeming Jenkin opened the paper, read so far, and then flung it on the floor. 'No,' he cried, 'that won't do. You were thinking of yourself, not of Salvini.' Yet the article, as one reads it now in the *Edinburgh Edition*, certainly does not justify that criticism. All the more plainly do we read between the lines, and note the egoism for which his friend was on the outlook, and which he

25

found. For in those days he must be king of his world,
or else a conscious and wretched failure—*aut Cæsar aut
nullus*:

> 'This was the world, and I was king :
> For me the bees came by to sing,
> For me the swallows flew.'

But then, he had the saving grace of knowing it all the
time. Your unconscious egoist, whose vanity is so serious
a business that he does not know how vain he is—who
likes to be the centre of attention, but thinks you have not
noticed that—he is indeed in a bad case. It is not so with
Stevenson. At an early age he left off keeping diaries, he
tells us, ' finding them a school of posturing and melancholy
self-deception.' While still president of the Speculative
Society at college, he sums himself up in his valedictory
address : 'Mr. Stevenson engaged in explaining to the other
members that he is the cleverest person of his age and
weight between this and California.' Later on he notes
how a man who lives apart from society becomes both
weak and vain. From Vailima he writes to his American
publisher: 'I hope my own little introduction [to the
*Family of Engineers*] is not egoistic ; or rather, I do not care
if it is.' To Professor Colvin he speaks of ' Milton and I,' and
with refreshing impudence he writes to Mr. Gosse : ' You
know what a wooden-hearted curmudgeon I am about some
contemporary verse. I like none of it except some of my own.
(I look back on that sentence with pleasure ; it comes from
an honest heart.)' In yet another place he speaks of something he has said as ' honest, for a man naturally vain ' ; and
there is a twinkle in his eye as David Balfour hears in
*Catriona* the plain words : ' Ye 'll have tae supple yer back-
bone, and think a wee pickle less o' yer dainty self.' A
man who disarms criticism in so frank a fashion takes an
almost unfair advantage of his critics, and puts them on

26

their honour as gentlemen to say no more about a vanity
so openly acknowledged.

It were truer to say that he is more deeply *interested* in
himself than any other writer of our time. In a very
remarkable passage of his *Lay Morals* he describes 'man,
a creature compact of wonders, that, after centuries of
custom, is still wonderful to himself.' He describes him as
if he were some natural curiosity found unexpectedly upon
the seashore—the hair on him, growing like grass; the
sight, 'which conducts him, which takes notice of the
furthest stars, which is miraculous in every way, and a
thing defying explanation or belief, yet which is 'lodged
in a piece of jelly, and can be extinguished with a touch';
his savage energies, his inconsistent emotions and thoughts.
Of course in all this he is thinking first of himself. In
Mr. Barrie's *Sentimental Tommy* he recognises himself
beyond the intention of the author, and asks (propheti-
cally) whether he is to be hanged! 'I am one of the few
people in the world,' he tells us, 'who do not forget their
own lives,' and the words have a deeper significance than
merely that vivid power of living in the past, which has
given us the *Child's Garden of Verses*. He did not forget the
value of his own life any more than he forgot the facts of it.
Loyalty to oneself, treated in a very searching and suggestive manner, forms the burden of *Lay Morals.* Conversation with one's own soul is among the highest of human
employments. Thus is Stevenson much occupied with
himself. Body and soul, take him for all and all, it would
be impossible to find any object of consideration at once so
intimately known and so vastly impressive. He is puzzled,
shocked, delighted, and repelled by himself, and full of
curiosity about himself every way.

Nor does he conceal, or in any way desire to conceal, this
interest. On the contrary, after the manner of the shirt-

sleeves episode already quoted, he often makes a direct attack upon the attention of his readers by some pointedly personal allusion. You feel that he somehow likes you— likes you well enough, at least, to be unable to let you alone. Half the pleasure of a walk, he considers, lies in sharing one's sentiments and impressions with another; and the reader often seems to feel the friendly shoulder-tap, to see him face to face, and to be taken into his confidence, until it is not reading a book so much as meeting with a friend. This is true even of the novels. The David Balfour of *Catriona* is the Robert Louis Stevenson of *Memories and Portraits*. He has the sentimental weaknesses of youth, but he has also the grace to see them, and the frankness to discuss them with the reader. He discusses himself more directly in such writings as the Essays and the Poems. That is the phrase—'discusses himself'—as the most interesting subject he can think of, to himself, and no doubt to you also.

Yet there is nothing offensive in all this. He is the very opposite of the blatant egoist, differing from him by the whole width of the difference between 'I' and 'we.' Self-centred persons of that type he utterly condemns: 'Irvine had come scatheless through life, conscious only of himself, of his great strength and intelligence; and in the silence of the universe, to which he did not listen, dwelling with delight on the sound of his own thoughts.' Nor does he wear his heart upon his sleeve, garrulous talker though he may be. It would be a gross mistake to imagine that because he has not spoken on a subject he has no views on it. He knows the value of reticence, and has highly appreciated in one of his characters a reserved and old-fashioned precision of manner as 'an excellent thing in woman, since it sets another value on her sweet familiarities.' He believes, with his own Mackellar, that there is no distinction 'which is worth acquiring or preserving

28

at the slightest cost of dignity'—not even the distinction of making oneself conspicuously interesting to a friend. He never makes you ashamed or uncomfortable by telling you more than you feel you ought to have heard. In this respect every man who has published his diary has been a greater offender against reticence than he.

This, by the way, raises an interesting side-issue. He has often been compared with Scott, by injudicious admirers and others. There is much excuse for the comparison, for the *Letters* contain many passages in which Scott and he are coupled by himself. His nickname for Vailima was 'Subpriorsford'—a title whose very humility may sound arrogant. Yet surely the seeming arrogance of the collocation is abundantly atoned for by the reverence in which he always held the Master, and the unquestionable fact that they had certain qualities and aims in common. To place him, in respect of general greatness, above or on an equality with Sir Walter, is the most unfriendly kind of friendship. It is appreciation run into fatuousness, and serves no other end than to challenge just antagonism. Yet one point, it may be safely asserted, must be given in his favour in the comparison. Scott is objective from first to last—often boisterously objective, and always healthy. But subjectivity is not necessarily morbid, though there is great danger of its becoming so. Stevenson has solved the very difficult problem of *healthy subjectivity*. This personal presence, these passing notes of confession, are wayside wells where we often find more refreshment than in all the gloriously objective current of Scott's far broader stream. This is one of the few points in which a comparison in favour of Stevenson is anything but absurd. Yet to some of us this is so great a matter, that if condemned to choose between them—say as the one author for the traditional desert island—there are those who would take Robert Louis

29

Stevenson. Of one thing at least there can be no question
—it is this healthy subjectivity which accounts more than
any other quality of his for the altogether unusual tribute
of personal affection which he has gained from a public who
know him only in his books.

And he is worthy of it. We do not want to know all
about most people. Nothing could be more unnecessary
than much of the interview-literature of which our
magazines are so full. There are plenty of men who
have come before the public with work which is interesting and valuable, and yet have awakened no further
curiosity, and have flung no spell of personal affection
over their readers. But of the man who has written
such things as these of Stevenson's, we do want to know.
The things are too significant, too important and suggestive,
in some cases too surprising, to be accepted as the *ipse dixit*
of anybody. And then the glimpses we have of him reveal
a personality of which it would be difficult to have too
much revelation. Professor Colvin's Introduction to the
*Letters*—one of the most masterly essays in appreciation
ever written—bears out the truth of this. Mr. Barrie's
words bear it out: 'R. L. S., which initials are, I suppose,
the best beloved in recent literature; certainly they are the
sweetest to me.' Mr. Graham Balfour describes him in
one phrase which could hardly be made more perfect:
'So lovable and so brilliant.' Besides, he is so fresh
and in every way so unusual, that the very surprises of
acquaintance with him are enough to enlist and keep our
curiosity by the mental excitement in which they hold us
on the strain. And again, the character is so complex as to
tempt us by its variety and subtlety. In one sense his
was a very simple nature, and nothing is more characteristic than the unguarded frankness of his confidences.
His mind dwelt among a few central persuasions, though

30

his interests wandered all up and down the world. Thus there are few real contradictions or inconsistencies in his work; and it says even more for the wealth and vitality of his mind that there is no monotony nor sense of wearisome repetition, though there are things which he tells us a hundred times over. But his spirit was manifold in its movement, and his heart was open to the world. From the children dancing on the wet streets of Edinburgh to the South Sea beachcombers, there was something akin to every man in him, and this fact alone makes him one to whom most of us will gladly listen when he chooses to be communicative about himself.

It may be noted in passing that all this is by no means so remote from religion as it may appear. A strong sense of personal identity is but the philosophical counterpart to what the religious man calls a sense of the value of the soul. In such an essay as the *Lay Morals* the two points of view are combined, and one hardly knows whether one is reading a treatise on the Ego or a sermon upon the text: 'What shall a man give in exchange for his soul?' Religion, in one aspect of it, is self-denial; in another aspect it is self-assertion—the realisation of the infinite worth and preciousness of the soul. The deadliest doubt of all is the doubt of one's own value. It may be the cynical doubt which questions the worth of life and things in general; or the hypochondriac fear that the individual soul is not worth God's while. In either form it is the most irreligious of all phases of thought; and he who has entrenched himself against it in a strong sense of his personal importance, has not indeed achieved a religion, but has made a preparation without which no religion can be secure.

Before we turn from this subject one point further must be considered, viz. the strong element of sense and the sensuous in all his thought, even the most spiritual. By a

31

thousand passing hints and touches his work discloses this. The Homeric directness and vividness of physical impressions is everywhere. A buckle found in deep water calls up the image of its drowned wearer: 'the very foot that had once worn that buckle, and trod so much along the swerving decks—the whole human fact of him, as a creature like myself, with hair and blood and seeing eyes.' Delaunay the actor so modulates his voice as 'to make you feel the cold night air and the moonlight.' *The Wrecker* abounds in such passages; as its description of the man steering the *Norah Creina* through the storm: 'as the seas ranged up behind us, black and imminent, he kept casting behind him eyes of animal swiftness, and drawing in his neck between his shoulders, like a man dodging a blow.' A book still nearer, in places, to the crude sensations of the flesh is *The Misadventures of John Nicholson.* Who can forget the physical realism of the description of his despair after the scene with his father?—the smell of horse-hair on the chair at which he knelt, the jangling church-bells, the hard floor that bruised his knees, and the salt taste of tears in his mouth; or that little touch, with its infinitude of dreary suggestion of the hospitals of former days, when he prefers the disgrace of imprisonment to death 'in the gas-lit wards of an infirmary.'

Still more significant are the sudden descriptions of the body itself and its sensations. The 'sharp settle of the springs' while driving swiftly round a corner of the road; the air of the forest that 'penetrates through your clothes, and nestles to your living body'; the hunger of Rahéro when 'the water sprang in his mouth with a sudden desire of meat'; the chill that 'deepened and struck inwards' when the wanderer returned to the estranged house—such flashes as these come upon us continually. And there are broader and more deliberate passages which plainly reveal his sensuous keenness. The lad, stripped and ready to dive among the horrors of sunken wreckage in Sandag Bay, hesitates until 'the strong sun upon my shoulders warmed me to the heart, and I stooped forward and plunged into the sea.' Rahéro with frowning eyes sees and judges the woman in his boat:

'Broad of shoulder, ample of girdle, long in the thigh,
Deep of bosom she was, and bravely supported his eye.'

That these are the expressions of deep-set characteristic features of Stevenson, and not merely selected examples of his general power of description, there can be no doubt. No man in whom the physical was not developed to the utmost point of thrilling sensitiveness could possibly have written *Olalla*—a story which many of his admirers place at the highest level of his work. There, in a horror not second even to that of Ibsen's *Ghosts*, the tragedy of heredity, and the degeneration of human nature to that of the wild beast, are depicted with most terrible convincingness. The inhuman element which lurks within the loveliness of Olalla like a suspicion, and breaks out in her mother and her brother into terrific savagery, is animalism depicted by one who knows. That story recalls the remarkable words of Mr. Graham Balfour describing Stevenson: 'In all his movements he was most graceful: every gesture was full of an unconscious beauty, and his restless and supple gait has been well compared to the pacing to and fro of a wild forest animal.' There are times when this faunlike, hardly human element is suddenly revealed. In such times the interplay of flesh and spirit produces an effect of strangeness which for the moment shatters our sense of intimacy with him. At all times he is a spirit very deeply embodied in flesh. His senses are strong within him and their impressions are intense.

C

33

In this characteristic fact we find a guiding principle for our study. He is, as we have said, a man of clear and lofty spirituality, but it is a spirituality always reached through sense. In understanding him the progress must be continually repeated from sense to spirit. Neither element can be considered without reference to the other. In the flesh, as he depicts it, you constantly discern the spirit breaking through; in the spirit, you seem still aware of the red tinge of flesh. Each of his spiritual truths has its roots in the ground of the sensuous; and on the other hand every bit of physical work runs up into spiritual suggestion and symbolism. How far-reaching and deep a principle this is for the critic and appreciator of Stevenson, we shall have abundant opportunity of noting in later pages.

# CHAPTER III

## ACTOR AND PREACHER

### I. *Actor*

OUR main purpose is, as we have said, to follow out the various developments of Stevenson's nature, working outward from physical to spiritual. But there are some other matters which must first be considered. One of the most important of these emerges directly out of that interest in himself which we have found to be so strongly marked a feature of his character. It is obvious that a personality at once so vivid and so interesting to himself and others might easily run off into acting, and this is a view which has been taken by some critics. It has, not unnaturally, been supposed that he did his writing and even his thinking, for effect and with an eye on the audience. In regard to religion this becomes a serious accusation. If the religious side of Stevenson should turn out to be mere posturing, and not in any sense a part of his real self, then the less said or written about it the better. And, in fact, this charge demands all the more serious examination because there was one side of his character, which it is very easy so to misunderstand and exaggerate, as to leave the whole religious life and work valueless because unreal. Of his prayers in Vailima we have already written, of his intercourse with missionaries and their work we shall write in a future page. No doubt such situations offered him a

35

picturesque attitude, such as he dearly loved from first to last. Yet, though they may reveal the complexity of his nature and his love of picturesqueness in all things, they bear the very hall-mark of sincerity upon them.

But before we come to these more serious questions, let us glance at the theatrical element in his general taste and disposition. That there was such an element need not be denied. Nothing is more evident than the frequent consciousness, the delight in the spectacular, and the deliberate search for the effective. It might be said without fear of contradiction that all his books were conceived by him more or less as theatres, and that all his characters, real and fictitious alike, appear before the footlights. The *Master of Ballantrae* will leave his relatives alone if they will beg him to do it on their bended knees—'he thinks in public, too!' His Japanese hero of real life has a presentation sword three feet long, and too heavy for him to wear without distress, yet he would always gird it on when he went to dig in his garden. Similarly his own surroundings are a stage and he the player. He loves romantic and picturesque situations. He cannot help striking an attitude upon all possible occasions. He is self-conscious in the midst of all his energies, aware of himself and seldom forgetful of his appearance.

His style abounds with metaphors drawn from the stage, concerning scenes, acts, players, *et hoc genus omne*. He constantly makes allusions figuratively or literally drawn from the same source. In one of the college papers he chuckles over the medical student of 1824 who 'wore a white waistcoat and consequently talked loud.' He tells of a Marquesan chief that 'he wore gravity like an ornament'; and of King Tembinok he goes into great detail to show how well Nature had equipped him for the profession of an actor. 'You will never change; and the words of your

36

part on this stage are irrevocably written down,' says the
mysterious visitor to Markheim. Doctor Desprez 'was a
connoisseur of sunrises, and loved a good theatrical effect to
usher in the day.' Even when he himself was on board a
burning ship off Auckland, the main cabin, incarnadined
with the glow of fire, reminded him of the last scene of a
pantomime.

His fondness for the stage was so great as to give credi-
bility to the story that on the Continent he once joined
a company of strolling players and acted with them. An
opera, he writes to his mother, is far more *real* than real
life to him. A toy theatre was among the chief delights of
his childhood, and the favourite recreation of his student
days was acting in Fleeming Jenkin's theatricals. He is
said to have been but a poor actor, yet his critique of
Salvini's *Macbeth* is an excellent piece of dramatic sympathy
and understanding. In the plays which he wrote in collaboration with Mr. Henley we perceive a workman who
thoroughly enjoys his work. He throws about his stage
directions ('aside,' 'business,' etc.) with an amusing appreciation of their technicality. It is true that he does not
take them quite seriously, but sometimes lets the fun of the
thing carry him off. 'Goriot,' says Macaire, 'noble old man,
I grasp your hand'; but the astonishing stage direction is
—'(*he doesn't*)'! In fact the plays hardly appeal to the
reader as plays at all, but as racy bits of novel-writing
which sometimes gain, but more frequently suffer, from
having been put in dramatic form. But in the *Treasure of
Franchard* and the *New Arabian Nights* we see the true
actor's instinct. In the former the character of Dr. Desprez
allows the author to get upon the stage and perform comedy
to the top of his bent. Desprez reminds one of that strange
creation of Meredith's, the father of Harry Richmond. A
combination of egoist, mountebank, and little child, he is

excellently well conceived and firmly executed. The same thing is true of Prince Florizel in the *New Arabian Nights*. To many readers he is the very type of fantastic imagination, in which the theatrical has run to wearisomeness; and yet it is evident that the Prince represents an actual side, and that no small one, of Stevenson's genius.

Such being his bent, it would have been strange indeed if there had not been a certain theatrical element in his thought and life. It was, indeed, in his blood. His grandfather had it, though under restraint. It was he who laid out the eastern approaches to Edinburgh in such fashion as to make Cockburn write that 'the effect was like drawing up the curtain of a theatre.' That same grandfather established patriarchal relations with the servants of the Northern Lights, which reappear in the feudal establishment of the grandson in Samoa. His father's childhood had adventures which show that he too had the actor in him. Masquerading in a piece of iron chimney-pot for helmet, or labelling little parcels of ashes 'Gold dust, with care,' and leaving them in quiet streets, we find him the authentic father of his child, who nearly died because, in the character of shipwrecked sailor, he had eaten buttercups in dangerous quantities. 'Pretending' was the favourite amusement of Robert Louis Stevenson's boyhood, and it remained a favourite amusement to the last. It was his mother's secret also, and it stood them both in good stead. 'We agree to look upon it as an adventure,' is her magic spell for all manner of unpleasant situations; and no one can tell how much that one trick did for him through life. His freakishness, and his susceptibility to the charms of the unusual, made him something of an impression-hunter. Like Disraeli's Vavasour, 'His life was a gyration of energetic curiosity. .. He was everywhere, and at everything; he had gone down in a diving-bell and gone up in a balloon.' At least he

38

had gone down in a diver's dress, and if there is no record of an ascent performed in his own person, he sent his hero up in a balloon at the close of *St. Ives.* From Saranac he jokes with Mr. W. H. Low about getting himself painted in a buffalo robe and leggings as a wild man of the woods. In Samoa he is photographed standing side by side with the native chief Tui Malealiifano. Altogether he does a great deal of attitudinising, and seems constantly aware of a cloud of witnesses. Even when he himself has to stand for witness, in default of other audience, the play goes on. Recovering from illness in Mentone he writes, ' I burn two candles every night now ; for long, I never lit but one.' In the Cevennes journey, waking after a night's sleep in the open air, he is in high spirits, and views the green earth in the light of the best of inns: ' I had been most hospitably received, and punctually served in my green caravanserai. The room was airy, the water excellent, and the dawn had called me to a moment. I say nothing of the tapestries, or the inimitable ceiling, nor yet the view which I commanded from the windows ; but I felt I was in some one's debt for all this liberal entertainment. And so it pleased me, in a half-laughing way, to leave pieces of money on the turf as I went along, until I had left enough for my night's lodging.'

Life is not divided into compartments so that a tendency which shows itself strongly in one portion can be entirely absent from any of the rest. It may at once be admitted that the theatrical element entered to some extent into the whole of Stevenson's work. Even in the most serious writings a fantastic touch at times reveals some straining after effect. It is seen in several sentences of his prayers : ' Our guard is relieved, the service of the day is over, and the hour is come to rest.' ' Let not our beloved blush for us nor we for them.' ' Accept us, correct us, guide us, thy guilty innocents.' After all allowance for the habitual use of unexpected words, some slight consciousness of the human audience remains in such petitions. The same tendency does, occasionally, distract for the moment his usual directness and insight in moral situations. In Beau Austin, for example, one feels this. In the particular instance of Dorothy Musgrave, an appeal to honour and to pity happens to strike Austin at the right psychological moment. But the picturesqueness of the *dénouement* obliterates too lightly a long career of vice, and its victims are forgotten as if they had never existed. This is a criticism which may sometimes be applied even to his principle that a man should not brood over his failures, but should strenuously make the most of what is left. Every repentance has its picturesque aspect, but it is not well for the penitent to remember that. In moral crises the first demand is for a reality of despair so intense that the audience has vanished and the soul is alone with sin. While any conscious pose remains, and the situation appeals to the penitent as a striking one, the irrevocable past will slip too easily out of mind.

Yet so slight is any such effect that it seems almost an injustice to record it. Granting to the conscious and picturesque elements their full weight, the reality of the man is still abundantly evident underneath, and the theory of acting and pose as an explanation of his general religious life is an absolutely impossible one. The prayers undoubtedly show an unusual finish, and sometimes the premeditation of their style detains the spirit in its attempt to rise to God. Yet a man to whom expression was so severe a conscience and so fine an art, and who had by sheer labour attained such perfection of minute mosaic-work in style, must eventually reach a point at which he cannot express himself otherwise. He is but praying in his own

40

dialect. If we can read these prayers without reverent recognition of a man in real communion with his God, we are no competent critics either of Stevenson or of any other religious man.

In the same way we must judge of many incidents in his career. A story is somewhere told of his carrying an armchair up from Heriot Row to a sick acquaintance in the Old Town. He is said to have carried it on his head, upside down. That was acting. He might conceivably have had it conveyed otherwise. But surely no one will deny that it was also genuine human kindness. Again, the letter quoted on page 17 is no doubt stagey. Yet the postscript shows plainly that he meant it from his heart's depths. In a passage like this : 'You wake every morning, see the gold upon the snow-peaks, become filled with courage, and bless God for your prolonged existence'—in such a passage it is possible to detect in the reference to God a consciousness of artistic and literary effect, and the love of strong language. Yet after all that is granted, it is evident that here is one to whom God is nevertheless a reality and a lifelong presence. He is continually telling us that we must be heroic in all situations. No doubt there were invisible fife-and-drum accompaniments to his thoughts of heroism, but surely it is heroism none the less for these. To deny this would be to judge in the spirit of an age, now happily past, when Christian burial was denied to actors.

Especially must this view be admitted when we recollect how deeply conscious Stevenson was of the danger of posing and of his own temptation to it. He has often impressed upon us the value of truth, to be careless of which 'is the mark of a young ass.' Still more frequently does he expound the difficulty of telling the truth—a somewhat less customary doctrine. In his essay on *Child's Play* there is an eloquent plea for those imaginative children who

41

'walk in a vain show, and among mists and rainbows, who
are passionate after dreams and unconcerned about realities.'
He pleads 'that whatever we are to expect at the hands
of children, it should not be any peddling exactitude about
matters of fact.' The difficulty of saying what we mean in
later life he expounds with great feeling in the fourth of
the *Virginibus Puerisque* essays and in many other places.
It is easy for those who have no imagination to tell the
truth, and when they tell it it is apt to seem intolerably
uninteresting. Stevenson has to watch and pray and strive
for it. He is keenly alive to the danger of a combination
in character of 'outer sensibility and inward toughness,'
which enables a man to appreciate in literature the finest
morality, while he himself remains stolid and unmoved.
Of his own danger he is well aware, and prays, 'Lord defend
me from all idle conformity, to please the face of man; from
all display, to catch applause.' Such a prayer as that is
always answered. To be conscious of the danger, is to be
far on the way to overcome it.

One might go further, and say that the religion of almost
everybody is more or less of this sort. Religion must ever
be expressed in the man's own particular terms and style,
and is seldom quite unconscious of itself. But surely
religion with a romantic air and a dash of scarlet is as
legitimate as religion in dull colours and carrying (as
Stevenson might have put it) a large umbrella. But he
strikes an attitude? My dear reader, so do you and I. The
difference probably is that *his* attitude is picturesque. Do
not let us look askance at the more graceful worshipper.

For indeed in all human life there is acting. When
Shakespeare said that 'all the world's a stage, and all the
men and women merely players,' he spoke neither in jest
nor in bitterness, but uttered the simple fact. In all of us
there are numberless possible attitudes towards good and

42

evil. Among these we choose some and reject others; we think of ourselves in such and such a character, and adopt that as our rôle. At first it may be but a book of words to us which we have to learn painfully. But in time we shall grow accustomed to ourselves in that character—our part will have become reality to us, whether it be that of villain or of hero. Thus to a large extent we must necessarily live from without inwards; from unconnected acts to habits, from words to thoughts, from conduct to character. It is not the acting that is wrong, but the parts we often choose to act; and the highest praise shall go in the end not to those who have simply followed nobler instincts, but to those who have chosen and acted nobler parts.

So it was in Stevenson's experience. Many actions and courses were chosen as his deliberately adopted rôle; and no doubt he was well aware of their picturesqueness and effectiveness. Yet he became identified with the parts he had chosen to play, and was 'transfigured by his work.' The religious part was that which he most deliberately adopted. More and more naturally he fell into it until he was indistinguishable from it, and it became the natural expression of his truest self. In a word, he was so made as to have in him a strong taste for the romantic, a dash of bright colour, and a striking attitude for every part of his life. These elements entered into his religion also. But the religion did not on that account cease to be genuine religion. It was just the religion of Robert Louis Stevenson.

## 2. *Preacher*

It has been frequently remarked that the actor and the preacher have certain qualities in common, and every one must have observed that in the work of many great

preachers there is a strongly histrionic element. Neither
actor nor preacher can live unto himself alone : each is bound
to keep the audience in mind, and each must aim at effectiveness. The actor, indeed, does this as artist, the preacher
as prophet. No doubt the lines of demarcation may often
cross; the actor may be a prophet and the preacher an
artist; but these are not, according to the common estimate,
their immediate and essential vocations. Thus, while the
actor's consciousness of his audience leads him to think
how he shall appear to them, the preacher's consciousness
suggests the question how he shall lead them to act. It is
a radical distinction, and yet it leaves a good deal common
to the two. The combination is obvious in Stevenson.
Even in his most solemn sermon-work he never quite
forgets appearances, and in such writings as the Fables the
pose is so evident as to lend an air of unnaturalness to
the preaching.

Stevenson was a born preacher. It is said that preaching
is in the blood of all Scotsmen, and that they go all over the
world, and in whatsoever place they find themselves, good or
bad, they conceive of it as a pulpit and proceed to deliver a
discourse. With Stevenson there was the additional fact, as
he reminds one of his correspondents when the letter has
become a kind of sermon, that he was 'the grandson of
the manse.' To another he writes, after a few sentences
of sermonising, 'I would rise from the dead to preach!' It
is true that his love of preaching was a somewhat one-sided
affair. Along with some other preachers, he did not like
listening nearly so well as preaching. Like his father
before him he had a particular aversion to all things and
persons 'tutorial,' and the word 'rabbi' stands for him at
the extreme point of disagreeableness. At times he gives
utterance to sweeping statements which would tell against
his own methods if applied to them: 'There is an idea

44

# ACTOR AND PREACHER

abroad among moral people that they should make their neighbours good. One person I have to make good: myself. But my duty to my neighbour is much more nearly expressed by saying that I have to make him happy —if I may.' A curious aversion to the clerical profession is uncompromisingly proclaimed in some of ~his earlier works; but perhaps he was hardly a fair judge of preaching in those bitter days, when his own life was far from peace and needing other sort of help. Even in happier times the only preacher he can tolerate is the cathedral itself, which preaches night and day and sets you preaching to yourself. How any man 'dares to lift up his voice to preach in a cathedral' he cannot fathom. 'What is he to say that will not be an anti-climax?'

Yet the instinct of preaching is in his blood, and in spite of all he has to say against the office he preaches still. Sentences about historical or fictitious characters tail off into allusions to the trespass of Achan or some other biblical theme, in the exact style of the older Scottish pulpit. Every reader has to reckon with this instinct, and, however congenial he may find the general doctrine, may expect some pointed homethrust of unwelcome truth. Little casual touches disclose the preacher everywhere, often with a twinkle of fun in them. His Edinburgh readers are confronted with a picture of themselves which, in the old Scottish phrase, is very faithful dealing; and when Glasgow smiles complacently the preacher turns westward with his threat: 'To the Glasgow people I would say only one word, but that is of gold: *I have not written a book about Glasgow.*' Surely a preacher, in all the glory of cassock, gown, and bands, and one who magnifies his office! Sometimes sermonising is the deliberate and accepted task, and the didactic mood gets free course. The charmingly told conversation with the Plymouth Brother of the Cevennes is

45

a case in point, and that discourse about knowing the Lord ends abruptly with 'I did not know I was so good a preacher.' The Fable is a kind of literature to whose principles he gave special attention, and which he practised with great skill. The sermon to the chiefs in Samoa and the address to the Samoan students at Malua, with its characteristic word 'I am the prophet with the cloth before his face,' are specimens of the pulpit-work of one who entered into his task with gusto. This self-appointed preacher instructs the clergy of the Church of Scotland as to their duty in regard to the ecclesiastical situation, and adds a note, equally authoritative, to the laity. In *Lay Morals* he gives forth the law to teachers and parents, and in *Virginibus Puerisque* to married persons and those looking forward to the married state, with a quite professional confidence, and with a certain old-world and sermonesque air.

The preacher's instinct has much to do with his selection and use of words. His language is generally notable for its compression, the quality he most of all valued and laboured for. So exquisitely did he manipulate his words that the term 'mosaic-work' has been applied to his writings by more than one critic. Even when the style flows most freely there is a certain stateliness that reminds one of the olden times and their grand manner. Such a sentence as 'the comfortable gift of sleep, which comes everywhere and to all men, quenching anxieties and speeding time,' might have rolled forth from the lips of some eloquent divine in the eighteenth century. But more frequently the words are so carefully chosen, and the meaning so compressed, that the flow is checked and the utterance somewhat abrupt. Each word counts for so much that we have to pause and consider it, so that we cannot read as swiftly as if the writing were more careless. This sort of style is not the preacher's. But

46

Stevenson has his own method of reclaiming the effect he loses, and turning even the want of *ore rotundo* in his diction to account. He does this by the introduction of unexpected words, which arrest the attention. Sometimes the words are technical, as when he tells his readers of a building buttressed ' with a great strut of wood like the derrick of a crane,' or of 'the tune of slatting canvas.' To none but builders and seafarers do these words call up any very definitely comprehended images. Yet they are effective, both on account of their interesting sounds, and of the whole apparatus of land and sea machinery which they suggest. He is fond of borrowing technical fragments of various crafts, though he does it only in touches, and never after the wholesale fashion of Kipling. Again, the words are sometimes made to arrest attention by the mere volume or quality of their sound. He was extremely sensitive to sounds, and alive to the fulness and richness of their effect. No author of our time is able, with anything like the same skill, to give their full value to resonant and detonating words. They strike us as with blows from a steel gauntlet. Even where they have no particular significance he can feel them and use them with strong effect. It was a prophecy of this literary ear when in his childhood, as he tells us in the beautiful *Rosa Quo Locorum*, he was fascinated by the Hebrew name which he spells ' Jehovah Tschidkenu.' It was that child, when he became a man, who flung such a weird spell over the tale of the *Merry Men* by the haunting recurrence in the wrecker's soul of the name of the sunken ship *Christ-Anna*.

The artifice of style, however, which he most constantly employs, is that curtailed form of the antithesis in which words are coupled in unexpected combinations. 'The genial dangers of the sea,' 'an agreeable dismay,' 'annoying and attractive, wild, shy, and refined'—such

47

phrases illustrate the figure of speech known to the older rhetoricians as 'the surprise' (παρὰ προσδοκίαν). This wayward use of words is not, as might be imagined by unfriendly critics, simply an affectation. It is a more or less conscious device for forcing the attention, in lieu of those swinging periods which are the customary mode of orators. Walter Pater writes of Flaubert that his search 'was not for the smooth, or winsome, or forcible word . . . but for the word's adjustment to its meaning'; in other terms, for the *exact* word. That is the stylist's instinct, and it would be difficult to find a more perfect canon for style in written work. But the preacher's instinct is different. He has to produce an immediate effect upon his hearer; and while there can be no relaxation of the demand for exactness, it is necessary for him to take account also of forcibleness. His word is a projectile chosen for purposes of attack, and he has to estimate its carrying weight. It was thus that the instinct of preaching did something to mould the style of Stevenson. As we shall see later, it did more than this. It determined the choice of certain unexpected turns of thought as well as of diction. Just as brilliant words flash out and suddenly strike, so realistic descriptions, epigrammatic truths, novel presentations of morals, break on us with surprise. In the play of *Macaire* this kind of work is run into burlesque, but there are many others of his works in which it is to be found in all seriousness.

Much of all this mechanism for producing effect might be classed either as acting or as preaching: even if the word preaching be admitted, we may still be quite outside the province of religion. There is such a thing as a mere instinct of preaching which is entirely destitute of religious quality. In *The Wrong Box* there is a character which well illustrates this fact. Mr. Joseph Finsbury, in the

48

inn-parlour and elsewhere, is prepared to deliver a sermon upon any text, from the relative cost of living in Spitzbergen and Bagdad, to the exact number of letters in the English Bible. As regards the artist—in this case the actor —it is a disputed point whether the quality of the matter should be taken into account at all; whether art is to be allowed to concern itself with anything beyond the style of expression. But with regard to religion, there can be no such question. Whether the instinct of preaching shall produce merely a garrulous kind of egoism, or a prophetic 'burden of the Lord,' depends entirely on the subject-matter of the sermon, and the moral and spiritual purpose of the preacher. The true religion of a literary man is to have a message in his writing, to take his art as a high calling to practical service, and not as a merely decorative art, wholly occupied with style. Like all other prophetic men, he must have been taken possession of by some truth that demands utterance. No conviction is a gospel to a man, nor is any man a prophet, until that conviction has grown so imperative that he feels that 'necessity is laid upon him; yea, woe is unto him if he preach not this gospel.' Judged by this test, Stevenson must certainly be pronounced a prophetic man, a preacher of religion in the true sense. Religion, he tells us, is a practical affair. It is a rule of life; it is an obligation to do well. The preaching of religion, also, is an affair not of style but of matter and of purpose. He has an unbounded contempt for those who 'try to cover their absence of matter by an unwholesome vitality of delivery.' 'It is one of the worst things of sentiment,' he tells us in another book, 'that the voice grows to be more important than the words, and the speaker than that which is spoken.' He thinks but poorly of his own *St. Ives* because it is 'a mere tissue of adventures,' with 'no philosophic pith under the yarn.' Such sayings reveal the

D

preacher's conscience alongside the artist's. In Stevenson's work the instinct of preaching produced no mere phase of artistry or solemn trick of acting. It made him one of the most forceful and effective preachers of religion in modern literature. It was his utterance of the Word of the Lord to his generation.

# CHAPTER IV

## THE CHILD

AT this point we must pause for a little, and turn our attention to the sources from which in early days the life and faith of Stevenson were drawn. In one sense it is true that every personality is a fresh creation, and Carlyle's insistence upon the individual has, at least, reminded all succeeding generations that a man is more than any mere bundle of his ancestors. Yet Carlyle's is a very one-sided truth, and the most original personality can only be understood in the light of influences not controlled by its own will. Ancestry has always to be reckoned with, and the influences which have been brought to bear upon the man in his childhood; and, if he have been a reader, the books which he has read.

The subject of the present chapter is the childhood of Robert Louis Stevenson, and its influence on his later life and work. This has elsewhere been so fully and so charmingly depicted, that little would seem to be left to say. The child 'Smout' is almost as well known and loved as the man Stevenson. Much of what is here noted has been told already, but no account of his religion could possibly be written without some reference to this. It is the period during which the first ideas enter the vacant mind, and occupy its virgin soil; when the wondering baby is receiving his first and strongest impressions of the world. 'A man,' says Richter, 'may be governed through his whole

51

life by one divine image of his spring-time.' Another writer goes the length of asserting that 'a circumnavigator of the world gains less culture from all nations taken together than he did from his nurse.'

It is a rare privilege to get a glimpse into the mind of a child, and to be permitted to watch him thinking. Such glimpses are, in the case of Stevenson, more frequent and more delightful than in that of almost any other man of letters. He has described for us the scenery of early childhood, 'observed as I walked with my nurse, gaping on the universe, and striving vainly to piece together in words my inarticulate but profound impressions.' The same condition is described in the incomparable essay on *Child's Play*: 'They are wheeled in perambulators or dragged about by nurses in a pleasing stupor. A vague, faint, abiding wonderment possesses them. Here and there some specially remarkable circumstance, such as a water-cart or a guardsman, fairly penetrates into the seat of thought and calls them, for half a moment, out of themselves; and you may see them, still towed forward sideways by the inexorable nurse as by a sort of destiny, but still staring at the bright object in their wake.'

Heredity plays as large a part in religion as it does in any department of human life; and in Scotland there are few men or women who cannot trace their religious dispositions to some ancestral source. Mr. Graham Balfour's *Life of Stevenson* and the *Family of Engineers* make it very plain that Robert Louis Stevenson was no exception. The women of the family were, we are told, extremely pious, the men a trifle worldly. Yet the men, too, had religion. They were 'conscious, like all Scots, of the fragility and unreality of that scene in which we play our uncomprehended parts; like all Scots, realising daily and hourly the sense of another will than ours, and a perpetual direction in the affairs of life.' No one who reads the account of the building of the Bell Rock Lighthouse will dispute that statement. The Sunday prayers, the consecration of the tower to 'the Great Architect of the Universe,' and indeed the whole tone of Robert Stevenson's narrative of his work as we read it in *A Family of Engineers*, discloses a rich inheritance of faith and character. Robert Stevenson, like the hero of *Ticonderoga*, was truly 'an ancestor worth disputing,' and Robert Louis Stevenson had a peculiarly strong curiosity about his ancestors. He felt in the study of genealogy 'an expansion of his identity,' and expressed the wish 'to trace my ancestors a thousand years, if I trace them by gallowses!' He made strenuous though futile efforts to run the line of his descent up past the Saxon to the Celtic stock of the clan MacGregor; and there can be no doubt that he felt a bond of honour laid upon him by the religious character which he so plainly descried in the former generations of his family.

We owe much to his biographer for the account he gives us of Thomas Stevenson and his wife. The description of the latter seems strangely familiar to those over whom her son has cast his spell: 'She had in the highest degree that readiness for enjoyment which makes light of discomfort, and turns into a holiday any break of settled routine. Her desire to be pleased, her prompt interest in any experience, however new or unexpected, her resolute refusal to see the unpleasant side of things, all had their counterpart in her son.' The extract from her diary cited in a later page of the biography bears out the estimate: 'We discover that it is a cattle-ship, and that we are going to Havre to take in horses. We agree to look upon it as an adventure and make the best of it. . . . It is very amusing, and like a circus, to see the horses come on board.' Not less valuable is the account of Thomas Stevenson. In it we see the

53

father, and understand with a new intelligence the nature
of the son. The perverse element is there; the many-
sided Celtic temperament, with its 'humour and melancholy,
sternness and softness, attachments and prejudices, chivalry,
generosity, and sensitive conscience.' Above all, practical
engineer though he was, 'yet it was from him that Louis
derived all the romantic and artistic elements that drew
him away from engineering.' The union of so many
qualities gives a very complex character. But all of them,
both in the mother and the father, were rooted and grounded
in faith. It is true that in the Edinburgh days after childhood, the religion which accompanied them appeared to have
dropped away from the son, and that for lack of its controlling peace the other elements struggled in tempestuous
warfare; but in later years it reappeared, and, both in its
brighter and its sterner aspect, gave proof of the greatness
of his religious inheritance.

When we turn to the days of childhood, we enter a
region after the heart of Robert Louis Stevenson. 'I can't
see what any one wants to live for,' he makes Nares say in
*The Wrecker*. 'If I could get into some one else's apple-tree,
and be about twelve years old, and just stick the way I was,
eating stolen apples, I won't say. But there's no sense to
this grown-up business.' That takes us back to the days
of boyhood. 'Children are certainly too good to be true,'
takes us to the nursery in Heriot Row. The story of these
early days is now widely known, and has become classical
in the annals of child-life. We read it in the sketches
entitled *Nurses* and *Nuits Blanches*; in the essay on *Child's
Play* and many other pieces; above all in the *Child's
Garden of Verses*. The long dark nights, the terror of that
galloping horseman the wind, the lights twinkling across
the gardens in Queen Street, the sepulchral quiet broken
at last by the wholesome noises of the morning—these

tell their own tale. It is the tale of a little child whose
nerves, strained to the utmost pitch of intensity, tingle in
response to the faintest light or the most customary sound;
and whose imagination follows close behind, fitting these
sights and sounds to a fine tale of adventure, or with cruel
realism lending them a terrible aspect. This childish
imagination, in its forms both of nightmare and of romance,
does excellent service in *Treasure Island*, and doubtless has
its share in the credit for that book's exceptional popularity
with boys. And then there are the days of sickness, when
the bed becomes now a boat and now a battlefield, until
the dance of evening shadows on the wall ends the day.
All children are poets, and most are dramatists as well, but
in these wonderful descriptions there is the promise of
something quite unusual to follow with the years—a promise
seldom so abundantly fulfilled.

We owe it to Stevenson's peculiar mental constitution
that we know so much of that vivid childhood. Barrie has
defined genius as 'the power to be a boy again at will.'
Certainly Stevenson fulfilled that condition. Writing to
Henry James, at the age of thirty-eight, he tells him: 'I
am one of the few people in the world who do not forget
their own lives.' It is this power that lends its intolerable
pathos to *Ordered South* and its charm to *Rosa Quo Locorum*.
Most of us are so taken up with the business of to-day
and the prospect of to-morrow, that yesterday is seen but
obliquely and in blurred images. Out of the crowded
scenes of the past there may be one or two which retain
through life their sharp edge and outline, and the luscious-
ness of their colouring. But most memories look down
upon us, like the picture in *Olalla*, 'with eyes of paint'—
facts among the other facts of history, which in a logical
conviction we know to have happened to ourselves, but which
in no sense happen to us any longer. They are but pictures,

and most of them are dim. But, as we read Stevenson's account of his past childhood, we feel that his memories are alive. He still hears the sounds and sees the sights just as he did then. The thoughts and feelings, the wonder, fear, and admiration of a little child's life are very different from the blunted and restrained experiences of later years. In an hour of quiet now and then we catch flying glimpses of the old self, only to feel how far away it all is, how hopeless the effort to live at that intensity again. With him it was otherwise. He seems to have had the power literally to be a child again, with all the child's detail and finality in its own experience, and all the stretch and wistfulness of the child's horizons. Many of us, like Mr. Baildon, would give much now to possess that gift. To read the *Child's Garden of Verses*, or any other of the writings in which the early days are still alive, is to receive ourselves back again for a moment from the dead.

Although every book written about him has recorded some of these glimpses, it is impossible to resist the temptation to quote a few of them again. When he describes the welcome country carts passing at last in the morning, you know that he is hearing once more the various sounds that 'creaked, rolled, and pounded past my windows.' When the old gentleman in the Wellington boots assures the little boy that he had been just such another at the same age, and the little boy wonders to himself 'if he had worn at that time little Wellingtons and a little bald head,' we recognise ourselves thinking as we used to think. The *Child's Garden* is full of the same power. Mr. Baildon's selection of the verses on *The Cow* could not perhaps be surpassed. There is *Auntie's Skirts* too:

> 'Whenever Auntie moves around
> Her dresses make a curious sound,
> They trail behind her up the floor,
> And trundle after through the door.'

56

To children upon whom the splendour of an aunt has shone, representing for them their share in the brightly coloured life of some other town, and telling of the kingdoms of the world and the glory of them, these details are irresistible. Equally exact from the child's point of view is *The Gardener*:

> 'The Gardener does not love to talk,
> He makes me keep the gravel walk;
>
> .    .    .    .    .
>
> He digs the flowers, green, red, and blue,
> Nor wishes to be spoken to;
> He digs the flowers and cuts the hay
> And never seems to want to play.'

That is all there is to know about the gardener as the child sees him. One more verse refuses to be passed by. It is the aspect of the day's routine:

> 'Every night my prayers I say
> And get my dinner every day,
> And every day that I've been good
> I get an orange after food.
>
> The child that is not clean and neat,
> With lots of toys and things to eat,
> Must be a naughty child I'm sure,
> Or else his dear papa is poor.'

There is the little land in all its aspects—religion, food, luxury, duty, poverty, and the inevitable moralising on them all.

Nor was this power of recollecting the incidents and reconstructing the thoughts of childhood the only treasure which Stevenson rescued from the past. Childhood was not for him a vision of what lay irrevocably behind, seen wistfully and among irrecoverable things. As we go on through the years, even those whose memory is keenest in imaginative power feel that the great doors of life are closing behind them. Crystal doors they may be, allowing us to see what once we lived in, but doors none the less through which we cannot pass. Stevenson, in his dedication to *Virginibus Puerisque*, confesses that though he clung to the earlier self, time was too much for him, and his work showed signs of advancing age. With characteristic adaptation to the facts of the case he falls back upon the conviction that 'it is good to have been young in youth and, as years go on, to grow older.' For the sturdy aphorism we have good reason to thank him; but we envy him for the extraordinary measure in which for himself it was not true. Doubtless on him too the shades of the prison-house fell, and that heavily. Yet he had greater liberty granted him of escaping from them now and then than is given to almost any. To the end he kept a secret key for the crystal doors, and ran back, almost at pleasure, laughing into his childhood. In one sense he aged before his time; in another and equally true sense he never grew up at all. He never passed that bourne at which the picturesque is laid down in favour of the merely sane, and enthusiasm gives place to common-sense. Every reader of *Vailima Letters* in the old edition must have noted the boyishness of the pictures there, especially that in which he sits on horseback. It reminds one of the ending of Letter xx.—'also please send me a cricket-bat and a cake, and when I come home for the holidays I should like to have a pony. I am, sir, your obedient servant, Jacob Tonson. *P.S.*—I am quite well; I hope you are quite well. The world is too much with us, and my mother bids me bind my hair and lace my bodice blue.'

It is not, however, only in such occasional outbursts of high spirits that the perpetual youthfulness of Stevenson is revealed. He appears to be constantly thinking about toys and games, as children do. The cannibals in *The Isle of Voices* remind him of 'a child when he is all alone and has

58

a wooden sword, and fights, leaping and hewing with the empty air.' The houses in Buritaritari are of all dimensions—'only in the playroom, when the toys are mingled, do we meet such incongruities of scale.' In *The Treasure of Franchard* the Doctor, looking down on Gretz from his hill-top, sees the place dwindle to a toy, a handful of roofs. When, in *The Wrecker*, the searchers are demolishing the stranded *Flying Scud* in search of treasure—'We were now about to taste, in a supreme degree, the double joys of demolishing a toy and playing "Hide the handkerchief"— sports from which we had all perhaps desisted since the days of infancy. And the toy we were to burst in pieces was a deep-sea ship; and the hidden good for which we were to hunt was a prodigious fortune.' The last quotation happily links the work with the play of life, its hard realities with its pleasant and childish fancies. This is no new association; but it is usually not without bitterness that a writer reminds us what babies we all are. 'Ah *vanitas vanitatum*! which of us is happy in this world? Which of us has his desire? or having it is satisfied? Come, children, let us shut up the box and the puppets, for our play is played out.' How different is Thackeray's sad conclusion from the sprightly and deliberate confession of childishness which runs through Stevenson's work.

He not only thought about toys, he played with them. When over thirty years of age we still find him playing and unashamed, playing with tin soldiers, building-bricks, and paint-boxes. At the age of thirty-eight he is composing music for the tin whistle (his favourite instrument of music) and explaining that he has 'always some childishness on hand.' So strong is his passion for games that in Apemama he masters an inconceivably dreary variation of the game of poker, invented by the king, and exults in the distinction of being 'the only white who has fairly grasped its principle.' His favourite pastime was the war-game with tin soldiers. In his house at Vailima, as formerly at Davos, a room was set apart for this amusement, and the campaigns went on for days under elaborate rules of his own invention. He records with interest the curious coincidence that the stepfather of Robert Stevenson of the Bell Rock, fell at the end of his life into the same foible, and 'his family must entertain him with games of tin soldiers, which he took a childish pleasure to array and overset.' As for Robert Louis Stevenson, the delight in toys may be seen in many details of his Vailima life. His relations with the natives, the absorbing attention which he bestows upon the details of his house-building and decoration, besides much else, remind us of child's play. He even went the length of writing for large-sized gilded letters of the alphabet to be designed for the purpose of fixing inscriptions on his inner wall commemorative of the visits of his friends.

There is one small portion of his work, little known indeed, but ranking very high, in which we see the childlikeness of Stevenson at its best. The *Letters from Samoa to Young People* are choice reading. A lady in England wrote him asking for letters about his 'boys,' for the sake of little girls in a home for sick children. The letters are models of child-work—tales and descriptions told by one child to other children. They centre round the personality and adventures of 'the lean man' who writes them. Every figure is alive, and every sentence tells its tale. Along with these are some letters to Austin Strong, as vivid and as fascinating as the rest. There is no laughing at the children. He takes them and their affairs seriously, thinks what would appeal to them, and, by admitting them as it were into partnership of interests with himself, offers them the only kind of flattery that is either decent or helpful.

60

# THE CHILD

It will be apparent to every reader that all this has a religious as well as a psychological significance. Those days of childhood, which he recalled so exactly and in which he lived much to the end, were days in which he was, as he himself says, 'eminently religious.' Out of the many incidents for which we are indebted to Mr. Graham Balfour one only shall be quoted, but it is typical of many more. It is a saying recorded by his mother in the fourth year of his age: 'Lou said, "You can never be good unless you pray." When asked how he knew, he said with great emphasis, "Because I've tried it."' Of course it would be absurd to cite any such incident as evidence for a man's religion, but at least it shows us what was the first atmosphere and climate of his life. No one can tell how much it had to do with the faith and character of later years.

Every child is more or less devout in early childhood. It needs but a touch to awaken the response to God whose heaven lies about us all in our infancy. It would seem that Stevenson's childhood was more than usually religious, and those who appreciate religion must feel that this circumstance sets a special value on his power of recollecting his childhood and continuing to be a child. To revert to such a childhood is to be led constantly in among religious thoughts and ideals. They were to a great extent the thoughts and ideals of his nurse, Alison Cunningham, a Christian believer of the older Scottish school. Yet they were his own also, and long after he had passed out of the influence of her creed he retained much that he had learned from her. The vivid memory of one's former simplicity of faith is to all true men an irresistible appeal for reverence. In the words of Rossetti:

> 'though I loved not holy things,
> To hear them mocked brought pain :
> They were my childhood.'

Still more important to our present study is the fact of his continued childlikeness of spirit. It is by this, most of all, that he has 'made us all children perforce, as a child draws off a reluctant elder to play, and so refreshes and renews his youth.' It would be difficult to overestimate the preciousness of this one service. In the ever-increasing rush and drive of life we grow old all too rapidly. The fever makes us grey before our time. To preserve, in an age like this, the spirit of the child alive to the end, is to be a great benefactor. Even when the darkness oppresses him Stevenson is still the child. At the age of twenty-nine he writes from California: 'But death is no bad friend; a few aches and gasps, and we are done; like the truant child I am beginning to grow weary and timid in this big jostling city, and could run to my nurse, even though she had to whip me before putting me to bed.' Eight months before the end he writes again: 'But as I go on in life, day by day, I become more of a bewildered child; I cannot get used to this world.' That was at the worst, and at the worst it was a good thing for him to be a bewildered child and not a grown-up cynic. But there was a better childhood which remained—a fresh readiness for impressions, an undulled appreciation of whatsoever things were lovely, an unguarded forwardness in entering into new situations and risking new adventures. Beneath all the complex play of thought and feeling upon the varied experience of life, there remained the *naïveté* that is possible only to the childlike.

We need to remind ourselves that this is what Christ claimed to be a characteristic mood of Christianity. To enter that Kingdom a man must be born again, even when he is old, and become a little child. Christian teachers have sometimes misappropriated that 'childhood of the Kingdom.' It does not mean the renunciation of intellect in favour of a church's dogma. It means something far more human and more beautiful. It means wonder, and humility, and responsiveness—the straight gaze of childhood past conventionalities, the simplicity of a mind open to any truth, and a heart with love alive in it.

# CHAPTER V

## THE MAN OF BOOKS

WE have already had glimpses of a very fresh and original manhood evolving itself out of a childhood which may be truly called unique. The natural sequel would be one of those ' eye-minded ' children of Nature, who seem to have no need for the thoughts of others. They live with Nature and hear her message to themselves. They are withdrawn alike from conventionalities and from opinions, aloof from life in the self-dependence of those who live self-poised and

> ' demand not that the things around them
> Yield them love, amusement, sympathy.'

But Stevenson was not one of that company. He was indeed eye-minded, and his keen senses kept him in direct contact with the things around him. Life was more to him than theories of life, and to be vital a higher ambition than to be well informed. Yet he combined with his originality a taste for books and a lifelong habit of hard reading which are rarely found along with it. Indeed, it is in that combination, more perhaps than in any other trait of his, that there lies the secret of his flexible strength and subtle wisdom. He is at once instinctive and educated, and so wields a double-edged sword. In a memorable passage on the morbidness of youth he gives his own experience on the point: ' Books were the proper remedy: books of vivacious human import, forcing upon their

64

minds the issues, pleasures, busyness, importance, and immediacy of that life in which they stand; books of smiling or heroic temper to excite or to console; books of a large design, shadowing the complexity of that game of consequences to which we all sit down, the hanger-back not least.'

Thus did books help him, and yet he never was a student in the severe and technical sense. It was the vital spirit of the books that appealed to him rather than any exact system of knowledge which they might have built up. Some books, indeed, he read mainly for their literary value, in the days when he was training himself by vigorous discipline to the achievement of style. But there was always a deeper quest in his reading—a quest for truth and life. Never could it be said, like the reading of the Master of Ballantrae, to 'pass high above his head like summer thunder,' nor to be to him 'a source of entertainment only, like the scraping of a fiddle in a change-house.' It was one of the main sources from which his personality drew its richness and variety. 'I have only to read books, to think,' he tells us, . . . 'the mass of people are merely speaking in their sleep.'

The paternal library would seem to have been of the austere order, with a few bright and surprising islands such as *Rob Roy* and *Robinson Crusoe* in its grey sea of information. These were soon mastered, and then came the time when he went forth to discover his own reading in the wide world of literature. From first to last he must have read an amazing variety of books. The lists of volumes he sends for in letters from the South Seas show a catholic appetite and a power of digestion equal to the most miscellaneous intellectual provender. Of American literature there are fewer traces than might have been expected, and it is curious to note that the Americanisms in diction,

E

which most Britons who cross the Atlantic find so infectious, are with one or two exceptions conspicuous by their absence in his work. Thoreau and Whitman were congenial, and his essays on these authors show how deeply they had influenced him. Emerson also has had his effect —who that has ever opened his books has remained unaffected? It may very likely be a chance coincidence, but if so it is a striking one, that Stevenson's *House Beautiful* is to a large extent but an exquisite expansion of Emerson's words: 'Crossing a bare common, in snow puddles, at twilight under a clouded sky, without having in my thoughts any occurrence of special good fortune, I have enjoyed a perfect exhilaration. I am glad to the brink of fear.'

The influence of French literature is far more evident. He had felt the mighty power of Hugo, and even his criticisms of that great novelist bear witness to his admiration. Dumas is the counterpart influence to that of Hugo, the aggressively living and human force of D'Artagnan appealing to one side of his nature as strongly as the cosmic tragedy of Hugo's great trilogy appeals to another side. In Sainte-Beuve's work, with its wealth of psychological criticism, he found much that was congenial. In Montaigne—that unblushing, erudite, common-sense pagan—he found perhaps even more. In regard to contemporary British authors, one is not surprised to find him abandoning Carlyle. It was to save his style that he did this, but in truth there is much difference of a deeper sort between their points of view. Meredith he knew and loved as a friend; and though there is a somewhat extraordinary lack of reference to his novels, their influence, both as regards mannerism and thought, is frequently in evidence. Browning was not so well known in the seventies as he is to-day. Yet in 1871 Stevenson quotes a verse of *A Grammarian's Funeral* in one of his *College Papers*; and there are a good many traces of *Paracelsus, Christmas Eve,* and other poems. In their general tone and attitude the two are closely and deeply allied, and he quotes the famous lines on temptation in the last volume of *The Ring and the Book* as 'the noblest passage in one of the noblest books of this century.'

It is, however, among the older English and Scottish writers that we must look in order to find the literature to which he owed most. For the English literature of the eighteenth century he had a strong admiration, although he never felt the spell of Addison. Doubtless its opulent and placid worldliness attracted him on one side of his nature, but it was perhaps more an attraction of style than of matter. To this attraction we owe a certain occasional smooth eloquence and careful balance in his construction of sentences which at times makes his work sound antiquated.

In the Scottish life and literature of the past we have a mine from which he dug far richer treasure. The passionate loyalty with which his heart always warmed to Scotland is familiar to every reader. Frail health, which forced him to leave and stay away from his native land, added to his patriotism all the intensity of exile. Even the climate, which when near at hand he had pronounced 'one of the vilest climates under heaven,' becomes glorified to 'winds austere and pure' when remembered in Samoa. Among the books of his father's collection which we find him reading as a boy is Billings's *Antiquities of Scotland.* But the stones of Edinburgh were his great Scottish book. Among them he wandered, identifying the houses which romantic history had marked for its own. He repeopled the changed streets with their ancient dead, until the modern life of the city seemed utterly irrelevant. Of all

67

books written about Edinburgh since Sir Walter Scott's
there are none that come anywhere within sight of what
he has written for vividness and feeling. 'That dear city
of Zeus,' which casts so strong a spell over those who know
it as their home, seems to open new depths of its heart and
to unroll new aspects of its beauty every time we turn
these living and loving pages.

There was a side of old Edinburgh life—the side of
which Scott has given the world a glimpse in *Guy Man-
nering*, of which Creech and Jupiter Carlyle knew and
told,—whose significance is usually overestimated by our
critics. This aspect of the past has been taken in connection with Robert Louis Stevenson as typical of his Scottish
heritage. That it is a real side of old Edinburgh life, no
one denies. But a Scotsman's heritage is, like a well-known
personage's acquaintance with London, extensive as well as
peculiar. While the period is typical of one side of ancient
Scottish life, it is but just to remember that behind it lie
the events which have peculiarly marked Scotland for their
own — the Covenants, the Reformation, and the Wars.
No doubt the kennel flowed on alongside them all, but
what land can claim that it is otherwise with any chapter
of its past?

When Stevenson wandered through the ancient life of
Edinburgh in search of history and romance, he found that
as well as other matters, and recorded it. In his picture of
New Year's Day drunkenness he has noted one of the most
obvious instances in which its tradition remains; and in
Mother Clarke's room in *Deacon Brodie* he has pictured its
lower side very faithfully. Among the 'numbered houses
of romance' there still runs a curious, dark, and ancient
alley bearing the name of 'Brodie's Wynd.' Its tradition is
of a leading eighteenth-century citizen, a master-craftsman,
an ornament of the secular and religious life of his time,

68

who lived a double life—leader of respectability by day, burglar and debauchee by night. The subject was irresistible to a romantic genius like Stevenson's, who himself had made acquaintance with the strange under-world of Edinburgh society; and he gave us, in collaboration with Mr. Henley, his play of *Deacon Brodie, or The Double Life.* Apart from its merits or demerits as a play, the piece is noteworthy as a living picture of the times it represents. By countless minutest touches it wakens response in a Scottish reader. Even its use of the title 'Deacon' ('lie there, deacon,' etc. etc.) is true to the life; for the old-time Scotsman rejoiced in all that was in the nature of a title. He named himself from his work, and was to his neighbours 'the smith,' 'the minister,' and so on, as by a conscious claim of right. In this characteristic trifle and many other touches besides, the native reader sees to what purpose Stevenson loved and studied Scotland. Yet beyond all that there is the grim psychology of the closing scenes of the play, to say nothing of their melodrama. Very different this from Sir Walter's amused acceptance of the situation. He who would know the real meaning of Stevenson's visit to Brodie's Wynd must read *Dr. Jekyll and Mr. Hyde,* which is its ultimate product, and which appeared six years afterwards. For the sake of its romance it interested him, but not for that alone. It took him in among the tragic facts of Scottish Calvinism, and formed a stepping-stone in his journey back to the earlier times of the Covenanters.

The influence which the covenanting history of Scotland exercised over him was profound, and there is hardly a book of his that does not bear some trace of it. Part of its interest is romantic, as any one may see who reads Patrick Walker's account of Richard Peden, or indeed any other covenanting book; and that romantic spell is over the whole of *Weir of Hermiston.* Yet there is far more that connects Stevenson with the Covenanters than the cry of the whaups about the graves of the martyrs, or the 'grey recumbent tombs of the dead in desert places.' He had a covenanting ancestry. On the mother's side are James Balfour of St. Giles, connected by marriage with Andrew Melville the Reformer; and possibly John Balfour of Burley, the Balfour of *Old Mortality*. In tracing his father's ancestry in *A Family of Engineers* he dwells, with evident pride in the connection, on one John Stevenson, land-labourer in the parish of Daily in Carrick,—'that eminently pious man,' whose remarkable experiences, bodily and spiritual, he relates at length. In a letter written from Samoa he speaks of 'his old Presbyterian spirit,' and reminds his correspondent that he is 'a child of the Covenanters.'

His childhood, as we have already noticed, was spent under the gentle domination of 'Cummy,' the nurse. Her religion was of that pronounced and impressive type which is sure to leave a very deep mark upon a child. It was not indeed forced upon him, for he adopted it with a child's whole-hearted *abandon*, and literally 'had a covenanting childhood,' as he tells us. Cummy's private library was, like Stevenson's childhood, 'eminently religious.' Her favourite books were the *Bible*, the *Shorter Catechism*, the *Life of Robert Murray M'Cheyne*, *The Cameronian's Dream*, *The Cloud of Witnesses*, and the writings of Wodrow and Peden. To these must be added Patrick Walker's *Biographia Presbyteriana* borrowed from his father's library. The result is obvious in his books. No reader of *Edinburgh Picturesque Notes* is likely to forget that long and grim quotation from the last-named author, in which are described the gruesome adventures of the dishevelled and decayed fragments of five martyrs; the table in Mr. Schaw's summer-house; the 'doubled linen,' and the 'coffin stufft with shavings.' For ghastly realism, mingled with human tenderness and reverence, the passage stands alone. Had Stevenson been able to finish the tale of *Heathercat*, we should have had a noteworthy addition to our Covenanting literature. The fragment which we possess is one of the most striking of his conceptions. Here is part of the description of a conventicle :—

'On the far side the ground swelled into a bare heath, black with junipers, and spotted with the presence of the standing stones for which the place was famous. They were many in that part, shapeless, white with lichen—you would have said with age : and had made their abode there for untold centuries, since first the heathens shouted for their installation. The ancients had hallowed them to some ill religion, and their neighbourhood had long been avoided by the prudent before the fall of day ; but of late, on the upspringing of new requirements, these lonely stones on the moor had again become a place of assembly. . . . The minister spoke from a knowe close to the edge of the ring, and poured out the words God gave him on the very threshold of the devils of yore. . . . And the congregation sat partly clustered on the slope below, and partly among the idolatrous monoliths and on the turfy soil of the ring itself. In truth the situation was well qualified to give a zest to Christian doctrines, had there been any wanted. But these congregations assembled under conditions at once so formidable and romantic as made a zealot of the most cold. They were the last of the faithful ; God, who had averted his face from all other countries of the world, still leaned from heaven to observe, with swelling sympathy, the doings of his moorland remnant ; Christ was by them with his eternal wounds, with dropping tears ; the Holy Ghost (never perfectly realised nor firmly adopted by Protestant imaginations) was dimly supposed to be in the heart of each and on the lips of the minister. And over against them was the army of the hierarchies, from the men Charles and James Stuart, on to King Lewie and the Emperor ; and the scarlet Pope and the muckle black devil himself, peering out the red mouth of hell in an ecstasy of hate and hope. "One pull more !" he seemed to cry ; "one pull more, and it's done. There's only Clydesdale

71

and the Stewartry and the three Bailiaries of Ayr, left for God." And with such an august assistance of powers and principalities looking on at the last conflict of good and evil, it was scarce possible to spare a thought to those old, infirm, debile, *ab agendo* devils whose holy place they were now violating.'

It is difficult to read that passage without an almost rebellious bitterness, as we remember for the thousandth time that the hand that wrote it will write no more. The subtle borrowing of magic power from ancient paganism for the new religion which had already much glamour of its own; the cloud of witnesses so daringly yet so exactly revealed; the depth of artistic and religious sympathy with the scene and its personages—these are indeed the effect of covenanting blood. This was among the latest of his works. The first of them relates to the same subject. *The Pentland Rising*, published in his sixteenth year, is an essay in covenanting history. It is a carefully executed piece of work, showing but little trace of the literary skill he was afterwards to learn, but it gives abundant proof of the thoroughness with which he was even then acquainting himself with history. Though it is a pamphlet of but few pages, it contains references to a dozen old books on its subject. Stevenson is not blind to the faults either of the martyrs or of their historians. Some of Patrick Walker's controversial matter he frankly calls insane, and the word is hardly too strong for such wild invective. He quotes, in *Heathercat*, one of Walker's coarsest passages, adding that no doubt it was written to excuse his slaughter of Gordon, 'and I have never heard it claimed for Walker that he was either a just witness or an indulgent judge.' As for the Covenanters themselves, he plainly sees that something of what they took to be their duty was a misapprehension. Yet no one has more justly appreciated their heroism, their historic value to Scotland, and the vast debt which Scotland owes to them for her religion.

Stevenson's books are literally strewn with more or less conscious quotations and imitations of this literature. In his *Thrawn Janet*—one of the most powerful of his essays in the ghastly—Mr. Crockett has recognised Walker's 'old singular Christian woman in the Cummerhead, named Jean Brown.' In the same sketch we have Mr. Soulis the minister, 'fu' o' booklearnin', but wi' nae leevin' experience in religion.' Like other ministers of his time Mr. Soulis had been at the college; but he 'would have learned more sitting in a peat-bog, like their forebears o' the persecution, wi' a Bible under their oxter an' a speerit o' prayer in their heart.' All this is to the manner born, and there is much more of the same sort. The sermon in *Heathercat* is almost a transcription of such preaching as Patrick Walker reports : 'In that day ye may go thirty mile and not hear a crawing cock; and fifty mile and not get a light to your pipe; and an hundred mile and not see a smoking house. For there 'll be naething in all Scotland but deid men's banes and blackness, and the living anger of the Lord. O, where to find a bield —O sirs, where to find a bield from the wind of the Lord's anger ?' The two phrases for whose recurrence one watches in reading Patrick Walker are 'left-hand defections and right-hand extremes,' and 'to get cleanly off the stage' (the metaphor for death), a curious unexpected allusion to things theatrical. These two are quoted many times by Stevenson—or misquoted, for he sometimes reverses the right and left hands of the former quotation, and the latter passes through several variations. He rejoices in the epithet 'rank conformity' as a name for his pet aversion, respectability; he speaks of 'concerned and serious old folk'—a combination of words bearing on it the peculiar stamp of covenanting days. On its lurid and ghastly side the old literature especially attracted him. Where else, for instance, could he have found the suggestion for those 'deils in the deep sea that would yoke on a communicant'; or for that other idea in the *Merry Men*, of the sea as 'a muckle yett to hell' for the unprepared souls of mariners; or for the prayer in the *Master of Ballantrae*: 'O Lord, I thank Thee, and my son thanks Thee, for thy manifold great mercies. Let us have peace for a little; defend us from the evil man. Smite him, O Lord, upon the lying mouth'? Such words, and the wild talk of the lady of Montroymont, might strike the uninitiated as savage to the point of blasphemy. Yet they are modelled with the most detailed fidelity on many passages of the *Biographia*.

So deeply was he versed in the books of those grim Scottish days that they affected his style, even in writings entirely remote from them. Most of the peculiarities in the use of English, which are apt to strike the reader as affectations, are to be traced to this source. In the last year of his life we find him reverting to the reading of covenanting books, and making the curious discovery that his style comes from them. Nothing could be more evident to those who read him with some of the said books at their elbow. 'Scarce' and 'exceeding' do duty for 'scarcely' and 'exceedingly'; 'discomfortable' for 'uncomfortable'; 'in' for 'into' ('burst in a flame,' etc. etc.). Antique words and constructions are of constant recurrence: 'the story leaves to tell of his voyaging,' 'there befell a strange coincidence,' 'to prepare his angle for fishing,' and so on. The word 'brisk' is one of many that strike the ear, as you read his work, with an unusual aptness and vivacity. Here it is, in old Patrick Walker's not very ingenuous account of the killing of a certain trooper: 'ont of a pocket-pistol, rather fit for diverting a boy than killing such a furious, mad, brisk man.'

74

# THE MAN OF BOOKS

As it was to Patrick Walker that Stevenson owed by far the largest of his debts among writers of the covenanting times, we may devote a little further space to him before we let him 'go cleanly off the stage.' An uneducated man so far as college or the higher learning go, he is an example of that native wit for which Scotland is justly famous. He identified himself with the covenanting cause in those dark times of persecution in the seventeenth century which have proved at once the costliest and the most enriching of all periods of Scottish history. Under examination eighteen times, he was once at least tortured by boot and thumbikins. In later days he kept 'a small shop for the sale of religious tracts, etc., at Bristo Port, opposite the Society Gate' of Edinburgh. His house, at one time, was near at hand—one of those eerie little houses in the Candlemaker Row whose lower walls, on the west side, buttress the Greyfriars Churchyard. Its grass grows high above the level of their ground-floor rooms; and its graves are overlooked, with an altogether indecent familiarity, by back windows, and overhung by many-coloured garments on washing-days. At a later time he employed himself in wandering about the country to gather up the old stories which are printed in his book, *Biographia Presbyteriana.* It is a curious collection of the lives of six of the leading Covenanters by Walker, with a life of Mr. Renwick added by the Rev. Alexander Shields. Its contempt for grammar and for the ordinary canons of style, its mixed metaphors and long strings of adjectives unconnected by any conjunction, only serve to throw out in more impressive relief its extraordinary qualities of clear vision and of rugged power.[1]   The untrained style is wonderfully ex-

---

[1] Walker's part of it has been re-edited of late by Mr. Hay Fleming, under the title of *Six Saints of the Covenant,* with a foreword by Mr. Crockett.

pressive, and there is a refreshing quaintness about the whole book. In later pages, as we trace the characteristics of Stevenson's genius, we shall have to note many a point which he has in common with this strange volume. Especially is this the case as regards the gifts of vision and vivacity. In respect of both these gifts, it is well to separate Mr. Shields's *Life of Renwick* from Walker's *Lives*. To pass from the latter to the former is to feel a sore decline. In itself, Shields's work might not seem so bad; but after Walker it is dull and pedestrian in the extreme.

The *Biographia* is redolent of its times. Its variety of language and expression is surprising, yet there are phrases upon which it comes back incessantly, and they are what might be called the covenanting vernacular. We read of the 'singular gift of prefacing,' of the 'heights, lengths,' etc. with which the faithful were taunted; the ministers' business is that of 'preaching up all duties and down all sins,' their ideal character is that of 'godly, zealous, painful ministers of Christ.' The church, for want of 'exercised' and 'self-denied' members, is a 'back-slidden and upsitten church,' which God will visit with 'Moth-judgements and Lion-judgements.' Scripture is constantly quoted, and is so deeply involved in the writer's thought, that without its key much of the book would be only very partially intelligible. Subtle allusions to Old and New Testament texts are everywhere embedded in the sentences and epithets. In depicting the injustice and cruelty of the persecutions the author breaks out often in terror-striking eloquence, that knows not the meaning of restraint. Violence and death stalk like demons through many pages, in a succession of pictures whose ghastly realism haunts and terrifies the imagination. 'The broth was hell-hot in those days,' he tells us; and he scornfully speculates about the unfaithful, 'how they would tremble and sweat, if they were in the

76

Grassmarket, and other such places, going up the Ladder, with the Rope before them, and the Lad with the Pyoted Coat at their Tail.' There is no uncertainty about Walker; he knows exactly where he is. His path is narrow, but it runs straight forward. He has as hard words for extremists like Gibb as he has for compliers like Wodrow. He has an unconcealed aversion to the 'Englishes.' When hard words are desired, he has them at command, and floods of personalities that Billingsgate would pause to listen to pour themselves out upon his enemies. Even in his milder vein he protests against the 'gasping and gollering of preachers' and their 'wisned, warsh, coldrife, formal sermons.' Nor is there lack of sardonic humour—the native thistle in the language of Scotland. Samson is 'a rackle-handed saint,' and there are some like him still. Their enemies demanded prayer for the king, and he concedes the prayer 'that the Lord would make him what he should be, or take him away and give them better.' Most sardonic of all is his account of the death of the soldier he is supposed to have shot: 'Thus he was 4 miles from Lanark and near a mile from his Comrade, seeking his own death, and got it.'

His relations with the unseen world give the impression of much uncanny intercourse with the Devil, and a stern familiarity with God. There is a firm belief in magic of both kinds, white and black. We read of men praying all night long upon the moors with a light shining round about them, and of not a little second-sight and witchcraft. Field conventicles are 'the Devil's eyesore.' But God is near also; there are men who in their childhood 'fell in love with the ways of God,' and 'it is praying folk that will win through the storm.' Yet the man and his book are human, with a charming freshness that appeals to us in many ways. That well-worn stage metaphor, for instance—how fresh it

77

is! 'To get off the stage,' as a metaphor for death, tells of a time when weary actors watched for the end of heavy parts. Yet the figure becomes quite lightsome when it has thoroughly established itself. Not only is the death of martyrs so described, but even the Apostles have 'gone off the stage' in their day. It actually ceases to be a figure, as the mixed metaphors show when we read of 'worthy gleanings' which are 'for the most part off the stage'; and Peden breaks out 'into a Rapture about our Martyrs saying they were going off the Stage with fresh Gales and full Sails, and now they are all glancing with Glory.' The nautical allusion is frequent. Mr. M'Ward prays 'with more than ordinary Gale upon his Spirit'—a phrase, by the way, which reappears unchanged in Stevenson's *The Scotsman's Return from Abroad.* Another obvious link with Stevenson is Walker's oft-repeated aspiration to 'steir a steddy course.' Like Stevenson, too, his senses are strong within him, especially the sense of vision. We are told of 'a merciful Cast of Free Grace,' at the Kirk of Shotts, which 'perfumed and gave a scent to Clydesdale.' Again we find Compliance 'painted with the Vermilion of Prudence and Peace'; and yet again we catch glints of 'the Light of sun-blink days.' The human nature of the book appears plainly in those deeper and more affecting passages which thrill with an infinite pity for the 'precious dear blood,' and the lads cold upon the hills; and for those who, like Richard Cameron's father, are kissing the bloody head and severed hands of their dearest. It is perhaps this, more than all else about it, that explains Mr. Crockett's confession 'that to-day certain cadences of honest Patrick's speech touch my heart like nothing else in the world save the memory of a mother's voice heard praying at a child's bedside in the night.' In all this of Patrick Walker's there is a wonderful affinity with the genius of Stevenson. If he has occupied

78

a large portion of this chapter, it is because it would seem
that he, more than any other writer, has influenced both
the style and the thought of the other 'child of the
Covenant.'

Behind all a Scotsman's memories of the Covenanters there
stands, large and masterful, the older image of John Knox.
As a living influence upon Stevenson's thought, it may be
questioned whether Knox can be said to have counted for
very much; yet we everywhere come upon indications of
the profound impression which the great statesman and
churchman had made upon his imagination. With the
audacity of youth he essayed the task of humanising his
memory in *John Knox and his Relations to Women.* Knox,
from Stevenson's point of view, lay 'dead and buried in the
works of the learned and unreadable M'Crie.' His effort to
'break the tomb, and bring him forth, alive again and
breathing, in a human book,' was not altogether successful,
nor was it even a pleasant failure. 'With the best inten-
tions in the world,' he himself confesses, 'I have only added
two more flagstones.' He never again attempted the subject,
but the reformer often looks down on us, through a window
as it were, in passing allusions which show him unforgotten
by the writer. The happiest of his allusions to Knox is
in *Edinburgh Picturesque Notes*: 'In the Parliament Close,
trodden daily underfoot by advocates, two letters and a date
mark the resting-place of the man who made Scotland over
again in his own image, the indefatigable, undissuadable
John Knox. He sleeps within call of the church that so
often echoed to his preaching. Hard by the reformer, a
bandy-legged and garlanded Charles Second, made of lead,
bestrides a tun-bellied charger. The King has his back
turned, and, as you look, seems to be trotting clumsily
away from such a dangerous neighbour. Often, for hours
together, these two will be alone in the Close, for it lies out

of the way of all but legal traffic.' The man who wrote these words had surely 'sat under' the great preacher, as an occasional hearer at least.

Two other religious writers of the early times must be included among the master-influences of Stevenson's life. William Penn was a late acquaintance. Stevenson found a copy of the *Fruits of Solitude*[1] on a San Francisco bookstall when, in his thirtieth year, he was passing through a crisis. The book moved him to the depths. It was 'carried in my pocket all about the San Francisco streets, read in street-cars, and ferry-boats, when I was sick unto death, and found in all times and places a peaceful and sweet companion. . . . there is not the man living— no, nor recently dead—that could put, with so lovely a spirit, so much honest, kind wisdom into words.'

Penn's note is one of brisk and yet quiet optimism. His letters to his wife and family are full of the alert repose of the man who knows his work and has found his place in life. He is 'well, diligent, and successful.' 'Keep thy place,' he advises, 'I am in mine.' He warns them against letting their usefulness be scattered by 'the snare of doing good to everybody,' and counsels them to 'see with their own eyes, not another's.' The *Fruits of Solitude* is a collection, in two parts, of eight hundred and fifty-five reflections and maxims upon all sorts of practical subjects. The point of view is a bright and healthy one, calm in its outlook, energetic in its purpose. The maxims are natural and un-laboured. They often light up their subjects with a sudden flame that seems to crackle as you read. There are endless points of contact with Stevenson in the book, but a few of the maxims, selected almost at random, must suffice for

[1] The *Fruits of Solitude* has been re-edited, and published in a charming little volume, by Mr. Edmund Gosse, with an introduction and a portrait.

illustration: 'If we would amend the World, we should mend *Our selves.*' 'As *Puppets* are to Men, and *Babies* to Children, so is Man's Workmanship to God's. We are the *Picture*, he the *Reality.*' 'Where *Right* or *Religion* gives a *Call*, a Neuter must be a *Coward* or an *Hypocrite.*' 'It is a Preposterous thing, that Men can venture their Souls where they will not venture their Money: For they will take their Religion upon trust, but not trust a *Synod* about the Goodness of Half a Crown.' 'No religion is better than an *Unnatural One.*' '*Hardly* any Thing is given us for our *Selves*, but the Publick may claim a *Share* with us. But of all we call ours, we are *most accountable* to God and the Publick for our Estates: In this we are but *Stewards* and to *Hord* up all to ourselves is great *Injustice* as well as Ingratitude.' . . . 'those Higher Ranks of Men are but the *Trustees* of Heaven for the Benefit of lesser Mortals. . . . And 'tis certain, where that *Use* is not made of the Bounties of Providence, they are *Imbezzll'd* and Wasted.' Lovers of Stevenson will recognise familiar sentiments and turns of phrase in all of these; and many more could be quoted.

'Lastly,' he tells us in his list of books which had influenced him, 'I must name the *Pilgrim's Progress*, a book that breathes of every beautiful and valuable emotion.' It was the book in all English literature which he knew best, and to which he oftenest alluded. This is probably rather the rule than the exception in Christian homes in Scotland. One remembers the inimitable scene in Mr. Barrie's *Margaret Ogilvy*, where the child has presumed to take liberties with the quasi-sacred volume, to the extent of constructing a Slough of Despond in the garden; the seriousness of the affair in the mother's eyes; and the adventurous infant regarding himself for some days as a 'dark character' in consequence. Into Stevenson's childhood also it entered, for this was one of the nurse's-favourites; and his mother, unlike Barrie's, went so far as to allow him to retain his playthings of a Sunday, 'when a pack was sewn on to the back of one of the wooden figures, and I had then duly promised to play at nothing but "Pilgrim's Progress."' One of the sweetest impressions in *Rosa Quo Locorum* is that of the building up of his childish picture of the Twenty-Third Psalm, where the 'foes,' in whose presence the table is furnished, are supplied by the imps—surely the neatest little demons in art—in the pictures of his copy of the allegory, drawn by Miss Eunice Bagster.

But it is not only the accidental circumstance of a book which had come early into his hands that explains his love for Bunyan. The two had much in common. In each there was the strain of Puritanism, tempered by a very pagan element indeed; though the proportions of the blend and the particular form of its elements are widely different. Both delighted in the spirit of chivalry, and the masculine and heroic verses of *Our Lady of the Snows* might have been sung by Greatheart himself. Both were dreamers, and men of constructive and vivid imagination. Both had, above all else that was common to them, the instinct of travel and the delight in allegory and symbolic double meaning.

The instinct of travel falls to be considered more fully in a later chapter. All that concerns us here is the connection which it establishes between the two writers. In their treatment of natural scenery, the two are far apart. John Bunyan has no sense of scenery properly so called. He will tell you of a meadow 'curiously diversified with lilies'—a pre-Raphælite touch that points back to the romances of an older day—but in the main his scenery is estimated, like Dante's, solely by its ease or difficulty for the foot. Stevenson's view of Nature is of course entirely different. Thomson, and Gray, and Wordsworth had lived between Bunyan's time and his. He delights in nature—in the trees of the forest and the large open spaces of the plain, in the grass at his feet and in the mountains blue in the distance. But in regard to the human life of the road, they are brothers. Bunyan's road is crowded with moving figures—indeed, it exists solely for their procession and adventure. Stevenson's eye for Nature does not debar him from the love and desire for fellow-travellers: 'As I felt myself on the road at last,' he tells us in his *Essay on Roads*, 'I was so pleased at my own happiness that I could let none past me till I had taken them into my confidence. I asked my way from every one, and took good care to let them all know, before they left me, what my object was, and how many years since my last visit.' This fact, that their delights are with the sons of men, links the two together. Yet in how different a fashion do they journey! Bunyan's road is the solemn path of duty; the interest of its fellow-occupants is the tragic interest of tempters, or helpers, or persons needing help for their souls that may be saved or lost. Stevenson is at times wholly irresponsible. He journeys in 'the most enviable of all humours,' that in which a person 'may gratify his every whim and fancy without a pang of reproving conscience or the least jostle to his self-respect.' So, at least, it would appear. But there is another side to this, which we shall consider by and by, and which brings the two travellers into a still deeper sympathy of solemn responsibility and passionate helpfulness for fellow-wayfarers.

Stevenson's works are full of references to and quotations from the great allegory with which his mind had been familiarised in childhood. In relating a South-Sea graveyard story of the Paumotus—a story whose savage realism touches the very bottom limit of the *macabre*—he at once recalls what Christian saw in the Valley of the Shadow. The forest of Fontainebleau is described in terms of the Land of Beulah,

with 'that subtle something, that quality of the air, that
emanation from the old trees, that so wonderfully changes
and renews a weary spirit.' In estimating the character of
Burns, 'to call him bad, with a self-righteous chuckle, is to
be talking in one's sleep with Heedless and Too-bold in the
arbour.' When his own life has taken him into the thirties,
and its great work is not yet done or even conceived, 'as one
goes on the wood seems to thicken, the footpath to narrow,
and the House Beautiful on the hill's summit to draw
further and further away.'

These are but specimens to which many more might be
added. Another curious reminiscence of Bunyan is to be
seen in the imitations which here and there he gives us.
Sometimes this is but exuberant nonsense, as in that notable
signature to a letter: 'I am, yours,

Mr. Muddler.
Mr. Addlehead.
Mr. Wandering Butterwits.
Mr. Shiftless Inconsistency.
Sir Indecision Contentment.'

Again, in a letter to his parents, he talks of resignation
under the similitude of a garden—'John, do you see that
bed of resignation?' etc. etc., and signs at the foot 'John
Bunyan.' That is in a more serious vein, and when we
come to the third example we find him in no mood for
anything but dead earnest—'The mean man doubted
Greatheart was deceived. "Very well," said Greatheart.'
A longer and even more clever imitation may be found in
*An Apology for Idlers.*

Two more allusions are necessary to complete our study of
his connection with Bunyan. First, there is the very clever
frontispiece to *Travels with a Donkey*, etched by Walter
Crane, surely with Stevenson's suggestion. It is entirely in
the manner of those old-fashioned perspective views of the

84

*Pilgrim's Progress*, half picture and half map, in which the distances are foreshortened, and in the course of an upward zig-zagging track, we are presented with small pictures of the main events of the tale, while the 'ingenious dreamer' lies large and conspicuous across the foot of the page. Here, in exactly that manner, is the ingenious dreamer, in the form of Robert Louis Stevenson, awake and smoking, though still enveloped for the most part in his sleeping-bag. Modestine, the donkey, is at hand, and above stretches the zig-zag with the pictured events. In the distance, the knapsack has become indistinguishable from Christian's burden as it is seen in old prints. The final goal and meaning of the journey is signified by the silhouette at the extreme summit, of the Pilgrim clear against a rising sun.

The etching shows how congenial to his imagination had been the picturesque aspect of the famous allegory, and this is borne out by the second matter to which we must refer —the paper on *Bagster's Pilgrim's Progress*. That curious edition, many of whose woodcuts are familiar in various modern reprints, was to an older generation of Scottish boys, inseparable in imagination from the thought of the book. Those of us who were fortunate enough to possess a copy of it in childhood, can never be satisfied with any other pictures. David Scott's illustrations are no doubt wonderful works of art; Bennett's are drawn from the life of London Streets. But they are not 'The Pilgrim' in the same way that these quaint little wood-cuts of an inch square were and will be to the end. So, at least, this reader felt. The pictures fascinated him, and in the course of his appreciative discussion of them he was led to write about the book also—a very living and admirable piece of criticism. As might be expected of one who was himself fond of using similitudes, the interest centres in a discussion of Bunyan's management of

85

allegory. But appreciation of the deeper qualities of the book breaks through in many passages of the most vital and sympathetic sort. The pictures lead him back to his favourite characters—Mr. Valiant-for-Truth giving 'my sword to him that shall succeed me in my pilgrimage, *and my courage and skill to him that can get it*'; Greatheart, 'a stout, honest, big-busted ancient, adjusting his shoulder-belts, twirling his long moustaches as he speaks.' His estimate of Bunyan is well worth recording :—'he feared nothing, and said anything ; and he was greatly served in this by a certain rustic privilege of his style, which, like the talk of strong, uneducated men, when it does not impress by its force, still charms by its simplicity. The mere story and the allegorical design enjoyed perhaps his equal favour. He believed in both with an energy of faith that was capable of moving mountains.' 'In every page the book is stamped with the same energy of vision and the same energy of belief. . . . Trivial talk over a meal, the dying words of heroes . . . all have been imagined with the same clearness, all written of with equal gusto and precision, all created in that same mixed element, of simplicity that is almost comical, and art that, for its purpose, is faultless.'

The one point in which he adversely criticises the pictures is that of their religious significance, in which the text outstrips its illustrations. The 'human-hearted piety of Bunyan touches and ennobles, convinces, accuses the reader' . . . 'to feel the contact of essential goodness, to be made in love with piety, the book must be read, and not the prints examined.' Yet he closes with a last word of gratitude for the pictures, which since his childhood have shown him 'every turn and town along the road to the Celestial City, and that bright place itself, seen as to a stave of music, shining afar off upon the hill-top, the candle of the world.'

86

There are several other religious books which more or less influenced his childhood, and of which traces appear throughout his later work. His earliest memories were of 'nursery rhymes, the Bible, and Mr. M'Cheyne.' The last of these, a name honoured among many of the religious people of Scotland with a veneration accorded only to one or two writers outside the sacred volume, was a favourite of Alison Cunningham's. Some of M'Cheyne's verses, and still more of his ardent spirit, remained with Stevenson through life. Of other writers of a similar school, traces are to be found. Among the last words of *Admiral Guinea* are 'But for the grace of God, there lies John Gaunt'—a famous saying of John Bradford's, adopted with only the change of name, and the substitution of 'lies' for 'goes.' Bradford is said to have used the words on seeing a criminal passing to the gallows.

But it is his close acquaintance with the language of the Bible which has most significance for us. He was literally steeped in its thought and sentiment, for his nurse read it through to him several times, and must have read some parts of it until he knew them by heart. The matchless power and beauty of its language in the Authorised Version have so permeated our literature, that it would be precarious to judge, by collected references, as to its direct effect on any author. Yet Stevenson quotes and alludes to it with a frequency, an aptness, and a sympathy, that bear witness to much first-hand knowledge. Nothing could surpass the appositeness and power with which the gambling quarrel at Mother Clarke's in *Deacon Brodie* is interrupted by the Psalm without:

> 'Lord, who shall stand, if Thou, O Lord,
> Should'st mark iniquity?
> But yet with thee forgiveness is,
> That feared thou mayest be.'

—it needs a covenanting childhood, and the lilt of a certain old tune in the minor key, to feel the full force of that. The strongest praise he can find for Walt Whitman is that 'he has sayings that come home to one like the Bible.' It would be an endless task to gather together the borrowings from the Old and New Testaments, which are to be found in Stevenson's books. Caleb and Joshua, John the Baptist and Peter the Apostle are there, and countless others, each in character and drawn from the life. Miss Simpson has told us that Isaiah lviii. was his especial chapter, with its repudiation of cant and its demand for self-denying beneficence. Many of the words of Christ, which carry out to fuller completeness the teaching of the Prophet, might be quoted from his works.

It is true that his dealing with the Scriptures was unscientific, and that that fact led to misconceptions. With the exception of a few playful allusions in his verses, Stevenson makes hardly any reference to the contemporary struggle between the newer and the more traditional forms of Christian thought. Not only in regard to the Bible, but all along the line of faith, there has been of late years a change in form of expression and in point of view. Fundamentally the two are at one, and their differences are but differences in the aspects of the same essential truth. The new phase is not less spiritual than the old, though it is less mystical; it is as loyal to Christ and His work, although it does not profess the same competence to define these. It is in closer touch with human nature and the general life of man, and it prefers the psychological and ethical standpoint to that of metaphysical theology. It is no disparagement or want of reverence for the past, to hold that the present may have other needs. The fact is patent that many earnest people are finding it impossible to-day to ignore certain difficulties from which the traditional presentation of Christianity affords them no relief. To many of these, the newer presentation appears the truer one. For some it is the only way; and it is keeping open the door of faith to-day, for a large and growing number of thoughtful men and women, who but for this would be absolutely shut out from Christian belief.

The case of Stevenson illustrates, as aptly as could be imagined, the need for such help as these newer methods seek to give. On the one hand, he was unprotected against the destructive tendencies of sceptical criticism, and unable to distinguish between accredited results and fanciful guesses. Not only was he prepared to question the Old Testament account of picturesque historical figures like Ahab and Jezebel; he found the New Testament also 'an unsettling book.' In one of the *Vailima Letters*, he discusses Renan's 'L'Antéchrist.'[1] With characteristic instinct for fact, he perceives it to be ' so little like history, that one almost blames oneself for wasting time.' Yet, a few lines further on, we find 'the Apostle John rather discredited,' and the impossible and exploded anti-Pauline theory of the Apocalypse accepted as entirely obvious.

With unbounded hospitality for picturesque theories, he combines, in other directions, an equally extreme insistence upon the letter of the text. To this he seems to have been driven by some time-serving interpreters. He is never more scornful than when, in *Lay Morals*, he describes the toning down of apparently hard scriptures by 'the tender Greatheart of the parish'—'All was plain. The Bible as usual meant nothing in particular; it was merely an obscure and figurative copy-book.' It was in rebellion against the patent insincerity of such preaching and the type of religion which it fostered, that Stevenson

---

[1] ' L'Antéchrist ' is the fourth division of Renan's *Histoire des Origines du Christianisme.*

adopted a severe literalism in his interpretation of Christ's words. This is but 'the right-hand extreme' in exchange for 'the left-hand defection.' Pressing the demands of the Sermon on the Mount and other sayings of Jesus, into their crudest and most untempered absoluteness, he confronts himself and the world with a conception of Christ like that of Tolstoï. Severe and inhuman, the Christ of *Lay Morals* undoubtedly is 'too hard on man.' Judged by such a standard, ordinary Christianity truly 'disagrees with Christ,' and calls by His name a system He would not have owned. That system Stevenson for the time rejects in favour of the sterner view. Little is gained by the exchange, for the precepts are confessedly so sweeping as to make obedience a sheer impossibility for human nature. Yet in some of his other writings a totally different aspect is presented. Thus, in the kindness, generosity, readiness to give and to forgive, which are seen in some of the South Sea Islanders, he finds 'a mind far liker Christ's than any of the races of Europe.' If we were to be so foolish as to attempt the piecing of these fragmentary aspects together, the result would be an incoherent conception of the Divine Man, at once more hard and more soft than that of Christendom.

It is necessary here again to remind the reader that in the case of a man like Stevenson his formal account of his beliefs will ever be an under-statement of the actual faith from which he is working. It would seem as if for such men, Christ is best seen in glimpses—'by a receding light,' as Browning used to say. Following Him thus, they are very sure of Him; but when they seek to look upon Him with the plain, direct gaze that they are accustomed to bend on men and things, they lose the wonder and the fascination, and their attempt at description gives you but a harsh or disproportioned figure. Such a figure does not accurately represent the Christ either of history or of experience. The great and difficult necessity here is obviously to understand Christ, and all who 'disagree with Him' must first have misunderstood. But Christ was a poet, and no man can understand Him whose method is that of mere logical prose. At every point Christ's inexpressibleness in formulæ is manifest. His words elude the literalist, and strike home with a far subtler and more penetrating stroke than anything he can understand. It is this direct and instinctive spiritual appeal, this fact that Christ's words are charged with so convincing and yet indefinable a quality, that makes men still confess that 'never man spake like this man.' It is this matchless spiritual power that has constrained the world to recognise in Him the Word become flesh. The literalist presents us in Christ with a man speaking extreme and irreconcilable things, impossible to obey in their totality—a man withdrawn and severely remote. The wiser listener hears the voice of the Divine Interpreter of life, offering him indeed no treatise upon the art of living, but flashing upon his soul a light which searches its depths, interprets its mystery, and guides its course.

It is greatly to be regretted that Stevenson, in his earlier work at least, adopted the rôle of literalist. It was not a rôle which in any way suited his genius. In the prosaic and conventional, one expects to find it; it is the only way of regarding things they know. But he was a poet— none more sensitive to subtle and instinctive interpretations of spiritual facts than he. It must be supposed that by some means or other the thought of Christ had for him become identified with a prosaic attempt to define the indefinable, and had acquired a certain flatness and rigidness in consequence. Had he brought to the task of understanding Christ the same spiritual receptivity as

91

that with which he approached, say, John Bunyan, we should have been spared some of his most inadequate religious work. But of such work, after all, there is very little. Christ is spiritually discerned by the writer of many of the letters and of the prayers; and indeed in all the writings except a few of those in which he sets himself the task of discussing Him.

# CHAPTER VI

## REVOLT AND ORIGINALITY

A NATURALLY strong personality, nurtured in such a childhood and fed by vital and non-conforming books, was sure to assert itself sooner or later in some violent form. On one side of his nature confident, wayward, and fearlessly sure of himself, yet on another side he was self-conscious, sensitive, and apt to distrust his moods. These are explosive elements when combined in the person of a vigorous youth. Revolt is as inevitable as life itself for such a man. Had he been physically more robust, it might have been averted. Field-sports are the safety-valve for much of the wildness of young days, and happy families owe more to them than to any other agency for their fresh breeze and pleasant healthfulness. But Stevenson was no sportsman nor lover of outdoor games, and the pent-up vitality found other means of escape.

This period and its painful experiences are usually associated with his father. Mr. Graham Balfour has described the situation admirably—'one period of misunderstanding they had, but it was brief, and might have been avoided had either of the pair been less sincere or less in earnest. Afterwards, and perhaps as a consequence, their comprehension and appreciation of each other grew complete, and their attachment was even deeper than that usually subsisting between father and only son.' The misunderstanding was unavoidable and it ran deep. Thomas

93

# THE FAITH OF R. L. STEVENSON

Stevenson's nature was rich and many-sided, with much in it from which Robert derived his most distinguishing qualities. Yet it was inevitable that the son should perplex the father, who was strongly attached to the proprieties and set forms of the society in which he moved, and whose habits of thought did not permit him suddenly to accommodate himself to new views of life or new scales of proportion. The breach may be said to have begun regarding Robert's choice of a profession. The father had, apparently, taken it for granted that every generation of Stevensons would accept its destiny in engineering and the Northern Lights. The son had other views, and cared for nothing but literature. After some vain attempts to foster an engineering enthusiasm, the uncongenial compromise of the Law was adopted, and the would-be author found himself chafing against the dulness of an office, and playing at the law-student business in the university. He succeeded, somehow or other, in passing his examinations, and entered the Parliament House[1] as an advocate. But the only joy he had there was that which its picturesque and romantic aspects afforded. Some historic portraits, the statue of Forbes of Culloden, and a certain room full of 'grim lumber' where the *productions* from criminal cases are preserved—these gave its meaning to Parliament House for him. The evident half-heartedness of his interest in Law naturally disappointed the uncomprehending father. The breach deepened, and they found themselves on opposite sides in politics, in social tastes, in moral principles, and in religious convictions.

Nothing could more clearly show the mark which this breach had made upon him than his treatment in fiction of the relations of father and son. Remembering *The Story*

[1] The old Parliament House of Scotland is now occupied by the Law Courts.

*of a Lie*, and *John Nicholson*, and several other such instances, one feels that he has been less than just to fathers. The iron has entered into his soul, and some of the domestic scenes are little better than caricatures. The Poems, however, might reassure us; the *Letters* and the *Life* are absolutely reassuring, for the reconciliation manifest in them could not be more perfect. Still more do those other passages remove the memory of old estrangements, in which he regards the relation from the father's point of view:—
'The love of parents for their children is, of all natural affections, the most ill-starred. . . . A good son, who can fulfil what is expected of him, has done his work in life. He has to redeem the sins of many, and restore the world's confidence in children.'

The revolt, once begun, had to run its course. Everything conspired to send him forth into its wild freedom. His romantic figure stood out, in his own imagination, against the background of conventional Edinburgh,—type for him of conventionality in general. It must be surprising to those who know the life of Edinburgh in a different aspect, to remember that from Stevenson's point of view it was a place chiefly notable for conscious rectitude—eminently respectable, and formal to the point of freezing. Its parties he abominated. Its proprieties he violated with an enthusiasm worthy of a better cause. There is something infinitely comical in the remembrance of that weird apparition, of strange raiment and uncut hair, which now and then amazed the Princes Street of the early seventies. The revolt was heightened by his own romantic conception of the city—'this dream in masonry and living rock'—a conception due partly to historical associations, partly to the splendid thrust of the skylines of the old town, and their matchless *chiaroscuro* of opalescent grey. 'By all the canons of romance' he tells us, 'the place demands to be

95

half-deserted and leaning towards decay; birds we might admit in profusion, the play of the sun and winds, and a few gipsies encamped in the chief thoroughfare; but these citizens, with their cabs and tramways, their trains and posters, are altogether out of key. . . . To see them thronging by, in their neat clothes and conscious moral rectitude, and with a little air of possession that verges on the absurd, is not the least striking feature of the place.' For himself, he consistently adopted the part he had assigned to the ideal inhabitant, and was a veritable 'gipsy, encamped in the thoroughfare.'

His student life fell upon days congenial to his spirit. There was no Students' Representative Council then, nor had the instincts of the noble savage yielded to modern civilisation in respect of women-students, or snow-balling, or the conduct of torch-light processions. It was the time when, as in the days of Israel's judges, every man did that which was right in his own eyes. The fact that in 1870 he was arrested for snow-balling and bound over to keep the peace, need cause no vexation to his admirers. It is said that he did not deserve arrest; certainly there were many others who deserved it better. The serious business of the classes was to him a rather irritating detail. He was an irregular and inattentive undergraduate—in his own words, 'a certain lean, ugly, idle, unpopular student, full of changing humours, fine occasional purposes of good, unflinching acceptance of evil, shiverings on wet east-windy mornings, journeys up to class, infinite yawnings during lectures, and unquestionable gusto in the delights of truancy.'

It was not long until the revolt became a revolution, which marked everything belonging to the accepted order for destruction, or at least for hatred. 'Respectability' became a byword with him for 'the deadliest gag and wet-blanket that can be laid on man.' It was for its dul-

ness that he most despised it, its stupid acceptance of meaningless and unnecessary restrictions. 'I cannot bear idiots,'
he tells us, and the bondage of respectability appeared
to him the commonest type of idiocy. 'There is something stupefying in the recurrence of unimportant things,'
he announces; and respectability stands as the proof of
that. 'A man's view of the universe is mostly a view of the
civilised society in which he lives. Other men and women
are so much more grossly and so much more intimately
palpable to his perceptions, that they stand between him
and all the rest. . . . And hence the laws that affect his
intercourse with his fellow-men, although merely customary,
and the creatures of a generation, are more clearly and
continually before his mind than those which bind him into
the eternal system of things.' He protests against this in
*Men and Books* and *Lay Morals*, after the manner of the
following—'I can think of no more melancholy disgrace for
a creature who professes either reason or pleasure for his
guide, than to spend the smallest fraction of his income
upon that which he does not desire; and to keep a carriage
in which you do not wish to drive, or a butler of whom you
are afraid, is a pathetic kind of folly.' In a word, 'to
do anything because others do it, and not because the thing
is good or kind or honest in its own right, is to resign all
moral control and captaincy upon yourself, and go post
haste to the devil with the greater number.'

For much of this we may all be profoundly grateful to
him. But the revolt expresses itself in superlatives and
sweeping invectives along the whole line of modern life.
The essence of our education he declares to be the incul-
cation of three bad things—the terror of public opinion, and
the desire of wealth and applause—to which may be added
'some dim notions of divinity, perhaps, and book-keeping,
and how to walk through a quadrille.' Commerce fares no

better at his hands. He endorses Thoreau's contempt for 'so-called *business*,' and believes that he lives ' in an age where the spirit of honesty is so sparingly cultivated that all business is conducted upon lies.' Even to its detail he follows the life of the day with sword and fire. Such harmless, necessary adjuncts of civilisation as the marriage gift and the umbrella have to bear the out-pouring of the vials of his wrath.

The last-mentioned adjunct he has made, in a sense, classical, by adopting it for the very emblem and oriflamme of respectability. This curious innovation in heraldry is expounded with extreme facetiousness in *The Philosophy of Umbrellas*, a college paper which might serve as a footnote to *Sartor Resartus*. Again, and again, as we read his works, we are poked at by this objectionable article. It recurs oftener than the cathedral,[1] playing the ridiculous to the cathedral's sublime. Always when it appears one suspects a subtle symbolic reference to respectability, and the suspicion is usually confirmed. Who, for example, can forget the sally against those who give one the impression that 'never to forget your umbrella through a long life would seem a higher and wiser flight of achievement than to go smiling to the stake'?—a company to which the author evidently did not belong, for we read on his return to Swanston from a month's yachting tour, 'I left my pipe on board the yacht, my umbrella in the dog-cart, and my portmanteau by the way.'

When a being like Robert Louis Stevenson breaks loose from conventionalities, we may expect him to break loose with a vengeance. Nor do the facts in any way belie the expectation. He had in him a strain of the Bohemian, which guaranteed that. He distinguishes between the imaginary Bohemian,—that mere adventurer who drinks and

[1] Cf. page 20.

wears strange clothes,—and the true Bohemian, who 'lives wholly to himself, does what he wishes, and not what is thought proper.' No doubt he had a touch of both sorts of Bohemia, and the simple passion of being different from other people became a kind of new virtue with him at times. Yet there was in him also a native and essential tendency to revert to the elementary and the savage. The same delight with which in the South Sea voyages he hails his escape from the shadow of the Roman Empire, is the explanation of his having found the submerged part of the society of Edinburgh so congenial long before. 'I was the companion of seamen, chimney-sweeps, and thieves,' he tells us; 'my circle was being continually changed by the action of the police magistrate.' Again, that acquaintance with the closes and dens of lowest Edinburgh is but another phase of the delight in the unconventional which made him prefer the open-air ablution in a stream of the Cevennes to 'dabbling among dishes in a bedroom'; and which inspired the happy sentiment written from the schooner *Equator*, 'Life is far better fun than people dream who fall asleep among the chimney-stacks and telegraph wires.'

The time of revolt was a time of Bohemianism turned to bitterness. In all ways, during that time, the accepted principle of his life was to be against the Government. Nor did his rebellion extend only to the province of the earthly magistrate. He appears as the self-appointed critic of a world in which man delights him not nor woman neither. In the preface to *An Inland Voyage* he remarks that though the book runs to more than two hundred pages 'it contains not a single reference to the imbecility of God's universe, nor so much as a single hint that I could have made a better one myself.' The genial confession was made after the waters of his deluge were subsiding: there had been a time when his friends had many broad hints that he could have made a vastly better universe himself. Of the college days, then eight or ten years past, he tells us that 'he began to perceive that life was a handicap upon strange wrong-sided principles, and not, as he had been told, a fair and equal race'; and that he was 'unsettled and discouraged, and filled full with that trumpeting anger with which young men regard injustices in the first blush of youth.' So, when he was not declaiming, he would sit back and laugh at it all. It was hardly a great laughter and not at all a wholesome one. Above all, it was very young.

As was to be expected, the province of morality did not escape the revolt. Of all conventions, conventional morality appeared to him the most irritating. In this connection, the umbrella metaphor reminds one of a tale (or legend) regarding Kant. Looking out from his window after finishing his *Critique of Pure Reason*, he saw old Ludwig his gardener, laboriously digging in the rain. 'Ah,' said the philosopher, 'this Critique is all very well for me, but what is there left to protect *him* from the rain? I must provide an umbrella for poor old Ludwig.' So he sat down to write his *Metaphysic of Ethics*. It was very much as another such umbrella that Stevenson regarded the popular notions of morality. At the best, they only serve to keep men from thinking for themselves. The Jews compiled their six hundred and fifty precepts 'to make a pocket-book of reference on morals, which should stand to life in some such relation, say, as Hoyle stands in to the scientific game of whist.' Such morality is but playing by rule, and results in what he designated 'clockwork virtues'; when it is perfectly achieved it produces nothing better than the pattern woman with her 'irritating deliberation and correctness.' 'If she would only write bad grammar, or forget to finish a sentence, or do something or other that looks fallible, it would be a relief.' Still more irritating to him than even

100

the complacency of the respectable, was the hypocrisy he detected in them. In the rhyme of *The Pirate and the Apothecary* we see this brought to its plainest issue, and that is but his extreme delineation of those safe and petty vices of respectability which he most of all abhorred. The bourgeois dislike to capital punishment, combined with the bourgeois way of treating domestic servants, was to him a flaunting emblem of the same kind of hypocrisy. It is, he considers, like much else that society approves, the inevitable result of a want of directness and immediacy in dealing with life's problems. The cautious regulation of life, with a politic eye on the future, and an unceasing regard to the opinions of those round about us, may produce 'a docile citizen, but never a man.' For in such instances respectability becomes the rival and the antagonist of virtue.

As is the habit with those who take it as their first duty to run full tilt against conventionalities, Stevenson selected certain matters in the accepted code, which appeared to him especially conventional, and ostentatiously paraded his defiance of them. In the respect of strong language he is entirely indifferent to ordinary usage. His views and practice with regard to the observance of Sunday were not only far removed from Scottish traditions; they were apparently adopted without any consideration of the social and economic aspects of the question. These are matters whose significance is by no means so slight as it is sometimes supposed to be. Such conventions are more intimately connected with public and social well-being than they appear to those who count them merely conventional. Yet these were by no means the limits of the revolt. In his youthful rage against conventionality, Stevenson seems for a time to have lost the sense of any real distinction between the conventional and the moral, and the whole field of ethics to have lost its landmarks. The mood is well described in *Forest Notes*: 'You may see from afar what it will come to in the end. . . . And yet it will seem well to break all the network bound about your feet by birth and old companionship and loyal love, and bear your shovelful of phosphates to and fro, in town and country, until the hour of the great dissolvent.' Of that time of wandering, a reckless free-lance all round, there are many hints in his own writings and in those of others. With its details we need not concern ourselves. It was a phase of life, characteristic but essentially abnormal. It did not represent the true manhood and permanent self of Stevenson; it represented only these in the crude stages of their development, exaggerated and embittered by the circumstances of his life at the time.

In very much the same way the revolt affected his religion. Many things may have conspired to this result. He may have rebelled against M'Cheyne in the days of boyhood. In youth, the traditional doctrines of orthodox Calvinism did certainly provoke him to an angry contradiction. We have already noted his statement that he had found the New Testament 'an unsettling book.' He may possibly have met in real life some caricature of godliness such as he depicts for us in *Admiral Guinea*. There may be a personal touch in that strongly drawn episode in *John Nicholson's Misadventure*, where the somewhat inhuman friend insists on John's falling at once upon his knees and begging God's forgiveness—'And the great baby plumped upon his knees and did as he was bid; and none the worse for that! But while he was heartily enough requesting forgiveness on general principles, the rational side of him distinguished, and wondered if, perhaps, the apology were not due upon the other part.' With these and similar experiences of the

102

'coiled perplexities of youth,' most readers must sympathise, as they remember how they too have seen faith distorted and rendered for the time impossible in hours of like bitterness.

But apart from all such personal and minor causes, the spirit of revolt itself seems to be the real explanation; and since religion is the most commanding of all elements in life, it is obvious that a serious revolution must reach its climax there. Accordingly we observe how everything connected even with the externals of the religious life, came within the sphere of his denunciations. 'The average sermon' we read, 'flees the point, disporting itself in that Eternity of which we know, and need to know, so little, avoiding the bright, crowded, and momentous fields of life where destiny awaits us.' Even the music of church bells is 'a hideous clangour, not many uproars in the world more dismal.' So, with the comprehensiveness of a Satanic rebellion against everything in general, he abjured religion and pronounced himself an atheist. There were scenes with his parents which deeply wounded all the three concerned. His metaphor for these scenes is that of a cross, studded with rusty nails to tear the fingers that carry it, of which the heavy end falls with lacerating weight upon the parents. In such scenes, we find him stubbornly convinced that honesty demands the part he takes. He repudiates the accusation of being a 'light-hearted scoffer' or a 'careless infidel,' and takes himself throughout with the most extreme seriousness.

This latter fact should give pause to those who, whether on the side of religion or against it, are inclined to pass sweeping judgments on his memory. Life, at such times of crisis, is a very complicated affair, and it generally shows the most incongruous elements in close proximity. Even at the height of his revolt, there seem to have been seasons

103

of moral earnestness and religious enthusiasm, though these were but occasional and apparently ineffective. Through all, the preaching instinct was strong in him; at the worst he was rather a Puritan backslidden into a revel than a reveller masquerading as a Puritan; and there was a certain upright stock in his manhood wherein lay the deepest truth of his character and thought even at the worst times. Afterwards, when his father came to recognise and admit his honesty in regard to the religious difference his trust in him was fully restored.

One thing is quite obvious, and the change in the spirit of the age between 1873 and 1903 has made it already familiar. That is the distinction between essential religion and the forms in which it may be embodied for the time being. To a large extent the bitterness of this difference between father and son lay in the fact that, as Mr. Graham Balfour has expressed it, 'the one was questioning dogmas and observances which the other regarded as impious to examine.' The father's conception of religion was strong and clear, but it was utterly inelastic, allowing for none of those differences in matters of faith which the complexity of human life and the difficulties that beset all intellectual adventure demand. The son, unable honestly to adopt his father's point of view, imagined himself driven to the opposite extreme of 'youthful atheism.' Neither father nor son at that time knew of the existence of a middle space in religious thought. Their intellectual world had but two poles, and both of them were arctic; while the sunny and fruitful lands between were as yet an undiscovered continent to them. In this phase of his revolt, Stevenson is representative of a very large number of the young men and women of our time. It is daily becoming more obvious that while religion may appeal to ourselves only in certain stated forms of doctrine and observance, we must all allow

104

that there are some to whom it will appeal only when expressed in other forms. To wholly identify the Christian religion with even the most venerable of the forms in which it has expressed itself, is to throw it into immediate contrast with the breadth of our intellectual life, to give it an inhuman aspect, and to exclude many from its acceptance.

As to essential morality, it would be as untrue as it would be dangerous to say that a revolt is inevitable for all strong natures. The facts of a thousand lives give to such a view point-blank denial—lives hard pressed with temptation, forsaken for the time by their former faith, and yet carrying through all 'the white flower of a blameless life.' Theirs is the most brilliant victory over the world; and, if one may read between the lines, Stevenson would be the first to admit this. It cannot be too strongly impressed upon each new generation, that such revolt is not a perquisite of genius, but a stain upon its memory. But apart from the great loyalties of conscience, the general spirit of revolt was an inevitable phase of his experience. 'If a man' says King- lake in *Eothen* 'be not born of his mother with a chiffney- bit in his mouth, there comes to him a time for loathing the wearisome ways of society—a time for not liking tamed people—a time for not sitting in pews—a time for impugn- ing the foregone opinions of men, and haughtily dividing truth from falsehood—a time, in short, for questioning, scoffing, and railing.' That time came fiercely upon Stevenson and he did not repent of it. 'Because I have reached Paris,' he informs us, 'I am not ashamed of having passed through Newhaven and Dieppe.' 'Shelley was a young fool . . . for God's sake give me the young man who has brains enough to make a fool of himself.'

No sensible person thinks worse of a lad because he has

105

passed through such a phase, yet it is easy to take the matter too seriously. It is but a stage, in itself irrational, valuable only in the light of those goals in later life to which it leads. But on the one hand the respectable Mrs. Grundy is apt to be shocked by it: it so impresses her that she can see nothing else about the man beyond it. On the other hand there are sure to be some who like it so well that they refuse to recognise any later aspect, and insist on retaining the youthful revolutionist for the final picture of the man. Each of these kinds of critic manifests either a want of intelligence or a want of the will to understand. In reply to all of them it must be repeated that that period is only intelligible when seen in its place in the development of life and character. In it we see Stevenson coming to himself, but not yet arrived. By deliberate acts of will he chose the better part. All that remained of the bitter and turbulent days was an occasional struggle with old temptations, a large and generous allowance for the failings of others, and an unconcealed contempt for such moral weaklings as make no fight for the flag, but settle down at their worst and talk cynically about the duty they have neglected and the ideals on which they have turned their back.

Meanwhile we may look upon this distressful period as the time when he was clearing the ground for the free action of his personality among the many facts of life. Breaking away, somewhat violently it must be confessed, from what seemed to him unwarrantable restraints, he would face the future with a mind flexible and untrammelled. The only meaning of such an experience that has any real or permanent value lies in the clearing of the ground that a man may be his true self.

This leads us to the consideration of Stevenson's *origin-*

*ality.* It was not by any means an unattached and irresponsible reception of thoughts which seemed to come to him out of nowhere, for he rooted his thought deeply in books and in a careful study of men and things. But he insisted on judging all such materials for himself and using them in his own way. At first there are signs of a certain wilfulness and freakishness, in which we detect the conscious rebel against the accepted order. Later, and in growing fulness, we perceive that naturalness which is a quality only of the mature.

Nor must his originality be confounded with the mere thirst for change. Many of the views he had once adopted remained with him to the end. He was in politics a conservative, and the socialism of early days was hardly a break in the conservatism. The two extremes, as recent political history clearly shows, are not so wide apart as might be thought. The middle course of liberalism was wholly uncongenial to his taste, appearing to him pedestrian at its best. He had little sympathy with bourgeoisie either in theory or in the persons of those who represent it. His repeated statement that in Polynesia 'the higher the family the better the man' had really a wider application. His conservatism is a far-reaching and important element in his nature. New light he always welcomed, but it fell upon a mind which had schooled itself to a sense of history, and whose convictions were not easily altered. Every one must remember the scenes in the *Travels with a Donkey* whose vivid account of the Catholics and Protestants of the Cevennes has for its often-repeated moral, 'It is not good to change.' The same sentiment reaches its climax in *St. Ives,* when Mr. Anne's servant expresses his willingness to become a Catholic like his master, and is answered: 'I wish to take my chances with my own people, and so should you. If it is a question of

107

going to hell, go to hell like a gentleman with your ancestors.' The greatest of his fables, that *House of Eld* which strikes home so far and pitilessly, is a protest against theological reform. The other fable of *The Four Reformers* is a sarcasm upon reform of any kind.

Not that he altogether disbelieved in change. 'All our attributes are modified or changed; and it will be a poor account of us if our views do not modify and change in a proportion. To hold the same views at forty as we held at twenty is to have been stupefied for a score of years, and take rank, not as a prophet, but as an unteachable brat, well birched and none the wiser.' In all his moralising upon Travel we find the amplification of the same views. But he insisted on naturalness in any changes he might undergo; for there is such a thing as a stereotyped process of change, a formal system of development. Under such a system progress turns out to mean only the exchange of one set of formulæ for another. Stevenson would never commit himself to any policy of forward movement, political or religious. The wind must blow upon him as it listed, and not out of a quarter prescribed even by himself. Such detachment is involved in the meaning of the word originality as he understands it, and from this we see how words like 'progress,' 'orthodoxy,' 'heterodoxy' are meaningless as applied to him. He has shaken himself clear of them, and to estimate his position we are forced to work with quite another set of categories.

We have seen him down at the bed-rock of things, far beneath the conventionalities of the world's surface. There is 'something elemental, something rude, violent, and savage' in the mood, and we feel that life there is dangerously near the brute levels. Yet all this turns out to be not a nihilistic but a constructive criticism of life. It is but the consistent action of that interest in himself, that sense of the value of his own soul, which we found to be a fundamental factor in his character. He thinks too much of himself to be content with half-measures. He will not build his house of life on foundations chosen for him by society. From the very bottom he will be a law unto himself—'I, too, have a soul of my own, arrogantly upright, and to that I will listen and conform.' This is the great principle of *Lay Morals*, Be thyself—and for that end first find out what it is in thee to be. The great function of all teaching is to remind the pupil of his soul; to make him feel in the most literal sense the truth of the supreme question What shall it profit a man if he gain the whole world and *lose himself*? In occasional moods he appears momentarily to tire of this unchartered freedom, as when he praises the disciplined routine of the monastery in the Cevennes—'We speak of hardships, but the true hardship is to be a dull fool, and permitted to mismanage life in our own dull and foolish manner.' But then Stevenson was no dull fool, as he was very well aware. Like Thoreau, he cannot understand why a man should ask his neighbour's advice, when there is a nearer and a more loquacious neighbour within. In a word, 'To know what you prefer, instead of humbly saying Amen to what the world tells you you ought to prefer, is to have kept your soul alive. . . . Such a man may be a man, acting on his own instincts, keeping in his own shape that God made him in; and not a mere crank in the social engine-house, welded on principles that he does not understand, and for purposes that he does not care for.'

The forms in which his originality showed itself, and some of the views to which it led, will be noted in later chapters. Meanwhile, we are prepared to find that it will offer fresh standards and scales of proportion which may sometimes lead to startling views, both on moral and

109

religious questions. With these in their detail we may
agree, or we may differ from them; in either case we
shall find them stimulating and suggestive. There may
even be some to whom it will do no harm to be reminded
that a man whose strong language shocks them, may yet
have reached heights of self-sacrifice which they have never
attempted; or that their stricter views upon Sabbath
observance can hardly turn the scale against his more
severe interpretation of commercial honesty. Our present
point is to note the principle on which he arrived at all
his views, viz., that 'what is right is that for which
a man's central self is ever ready to sacrifice immediate or
distant interests; what is wrong, is what the central self
discards or rejects as incompatible with the fixed design of
righteousness.' The moral outcome of this principle may
be summed up in his oft-repeated adherence to Christ's substitution of a spirit for a set of rules. The moral man,
according to Stevenson, is he who, acquainting himself with
the inner spirit of righteousness, works out his own salvation, rather than adopts the regulations laid down for him by
another. As to religion, having swept the ground clear of
preconceptions, he lives by what vision of God and what
glimpses of spiritual light he can have directly for himself.
It will no doubt appear to many readers to be a dangerous
policy, this disowning of accepted formulæ of morality, and
laughing at current systems of religious belief—dangerous
especially in a young conservative, whose laughter may be
expected to show a tendency towards cynicism. Yet it would
seem that for Stevenson it was a necessity. Without such
revolt there could have been no real reconstruction either
of character or of faith such as his mind demanded. This
at least may be said of him with assurance, that once the
ground was cleared, he committed himself to his new
principles. There was no timid reaction, no cautious

retreat, such as soon changes the course of many youthful adventurers into homeward - bound thoughts and conforming conduct. He took the lifelong risk, and consistently followed the light that was granted him to the end.

# CHAPTER VII

## THE GIFT OF VISION

AFTER so thorough and so costly a clearing of the ground for the play of a man's originality, we are entitled to expect something remarkable when we continue our study on its more positive side. Here, especially, we must remember that in Stevenson there is always a close connection between the physical and the spiritual; so that all spiritual faculties which are peculiarly well developed are founded upon physical bases equally conspicuous.

His sense of hearing, as well as that of sight, was keen beyond the average. The two are at times combined in metaphors which reveal him in a double intensity, as when he gives a list of the names of British poets and exclaims, 'what a constellation of lordly words!' As to the sense of sound, that was developed in him to so fine a pitch of sensitiveness, that it might have almost been chosen instead of vision for our typical instance. So far as technical mastery of the art of music goes, he seems to deserve credit rather for appreciation than for performance, in spite of various learned and technical discussions of 'a dominant eleventh' or 'a seventh on the D,' and so on. The penny whistle, which retained his fidelity to the end, is hardly an instrument likely to hold captive the soul of a heaven-born musician. Yet his hearing was delicate in the extreme. Only one whose ear was sensitive could have made the bugles from the Castle touch the heart as he has done, with

their 'unspeakable appeal,' ' as if something yearningly cried
to me out of the darkness overhead to come thither and find
rest.' Nor could a dull ear have contrasted the silence of a
deserted house with ' that low stir (perhaps audible rather
to the ear of the spirit than to the ear of the flesh) by which
a house announces and betrays its human lodgers.' This
faculty not only gave him an exquisite ear for style; it
infected him unconsciously with the mannerism and the
rhythm of the time in which his stories moved. Beau
Austin speaks the language of his day with hardly a slip.
*Heathercat* might have been written by a Covenanter.

Yet there can be no doubt that the gift of vision was
his particular and supreme endowment. Perhaps the most
surprising of all his personal notes and comments, is the
statement that in his young days he never had any real
pictorial vision. He had a decided talent for drawing, and
a passion for working with colours. But he had discovered
that he drew from fancy, and not an actual picture of
things that were before him. In Arnold's phrase, his eye was
not on the object. One can understand this better in the light
of his subjectiveness. He was constantly aware of himself,
and what he saw was not the crude fact of the object,
but that fact as part of his own experience, interpreted
by many private feelings and associations. To some extent
this continued to be true of him throughout; and there
are few who would wish it otherwise. One thing at least
is certain, that he saw, and made his readers see, with a
power of vision that has been rarely matched. His eyes,
as we know them from pictures and descriptions, were
eminently seeing eyes. 'They were the most striking
feature of the face,' says his biographer; 'they were of the
deepest brown in colour, set extraordinarily wide apart.
At most times they had only a shy, quick glance that was
most attractive; but when he was moved to anger or any

H                                                    113

fierce emotion, they seemed literally to blaze and glow with a fiery light.' Even those who have seen them only in pictures, have perceived how busy and effective they must have been in their work of seeing, and have felt an almost sinister power in them, as if they had seen too much.

From his *Letters* we perceive a gradual change from vision to hearing, and indeed from the youthful sensitiveness and intensity of physical life, to the subtler and more spiritual power of psychological perception and analysis. He confessed, in a remarkable passage written in his last year, that his visual sense was being starved, and that one of his two aims in writing was 'death to the optic nerve.' When we remember *Weir of Hermiston* we are relieved to find that in this aim he signally failed. Take any of his descriptions—especially those of women—and judge them by this test. Of Mrs. Weir he says, that 'her view of history was wholly artless, a design in snow and ink.' The picture of the younger Kirstie in church is perhaps as good an example as could be selected: 'About her face clustered a disorder of dark ringlets, a little garland of yellow French roses surmounted her brow, and the whole was crowned by a village hat of chipped straw. Amongst all the rosy and all the weathered faces that surrounded her in church, she glowed like an opening flower—girl and raiment, and the cairngorm that caught the daylight and returned it in a fiery flash, and the threads of bronze and gold that played in her hair.' In these and innumerable other passages there is a quite reassuring vitality of optic nerve.

The lifelong gift of vision affords him now and then the luxury of that purely spectacular mood which he has so well described in his essays on *Idlers*, *Walking Tours*, and *Roads*. He blames, indeed, the readers of his generation for not living *in* a book or character, but standing afar off, spectators at a puppet-show. Yet in the mood referred to, that

114

is precisely what he himself did. He is the man at the window, the wayfaring man at the inn, and the world is but a spectacle to him. Men and women who go by 'are not people in any living and kindly sense.' 'To sit still and contemplate . . . to be everything and everywhere in sympathy, and yet content to remain where and what you are—is not this to know both wisdom and virtue, and to dwell with happiness? After all, it is not they who carry flags, but they who look upon it from a private chamber, who have the fun of the procession.' Thus is Stevenson at times—especially in the days of youth— merely 'interested in the phases of life and human character,' 'insatiably curious in the aspects of life.'

Sometimes such vision culminates in moments of magnificent colour and brightness, the spectacle appearing as 'a splendid nightmare of light and heat.' Yet it is in quieter tints that the procession passes oftenest. Incapable of being bored—except, of course, by 'idiots'—he is like Walt Whitman in his fondness for the dioramic view of everyday things. An idler, and prince of idlers, he can sit all day by a burnside, or beside the stream of human life, and 'no think lang.' In *Roads* he gives us minute directions for that luxurious and systematic dilettantism which is requisite before a man can enjoy, to its quintessence, the delight of scenery. The essay on *Unpleasant Places* completes the education of the epicure in vision, telling us that 'any place is good enough to live a life in, while it is only in a few, and those highly-favoured, that we can pass a few hours agreeably.'

This mood represents, in its extreme and isolated form, one half of the character of Stevenson, the other half being that of strenuousness and exertion. To be more precise, in his own words three-fifths of him is artist and two-fifths adventurer. These two elements, traced from their physical

115

beginnings up to their highest moral and spiritual developments, form the burden of our chapters on vision and travel,
and are of central importance to the study of his character.
They represent life as he viewed it, on its two sides of
theory and practice; the spectacle and the business of
living.   In the present chapter and the next, we shall
consider the former of these, the gift of vision, first in the
sense of visual perception, then in the wider sense of
imagination in general, and particularly imagination in the
moral and spiritual region.

Power of vision may be judged by many criteria, two
of which mainly concern us here—its exactness and its
intensity.   The distinguishing quality of Stevenson's vision
is the degree in which it has achieved the combination
of these two, each at an unusually high power.  Its *exactness* is everywhere apparent, in spite of his confession that
it was from fancy rather than from fact that he drew in
early days.   Visitors in any house may be divided into
the two classes of those who see the patterns on wall-papers
and floor carpets, and those to whom such unimportant
items of daily life are but a pleasing or displeasing blur of
colours.  Stevenson was of those who saw.  Every detail
in the visible world was for him a matter of minute observation, and it is this eye for detail which lends their
vividness to many of his descriptions and metaphors.   In
no book is this more striking than in his volume on the
*South Seas*, a collection of curious facts for many of which
posterity will thank him.   What could be more vivid, for
example, than this—'On a sudden, the trade-wind, coming
in a gust over the isthmus, struck and scattered the fans of
the palms above the den; and behold! in two of the tops
there sat a native, motionless as an idol and watching us,
you would have said, without a wink.  The next moment
the tree closed and the glimpse was gone.'   The same eyes

116

which saw that, saw also what the 'charming lad' bought
in the store—'five ship-biscuits, a bottle of scent, and two
balls of washing blue.' One king he creates for us as we
read 'a puppet and a trembler, the unwieldy shuttlecock of
orators'; another, wearing a European woman's calico
gown, a pith helmet, and blue spectacles, and armed with a
Winchester rifle, is introduced as 'this chimæra waiting
with his deadly engine.' Similar detail-work may be
observed in the account of John Nicholson's return to the
house in Randolph Crescent. There is the clothes-brush,
and the hat-stand with its coats and hats, and the bust
near the stair railings—reading which we know that
lobby as we know our own. He has learned from Virgil
and from Dante their habit of comparing great things with
small, and making an abstract or poetic conception spring
to sudden reality by a metaphor drawn from the workaday
world. Thus in the *Feast of Famine*, the spirit of evil
moving the savages to wicked designs in the dark heat of
a tropical night, is compared to the sweltering baker, working alone amidst the sleeping city in his kneading trough.
Sometimes this unexpected introduction of homely and
familiar things comes upon us with what is little less than
a brutal assault on the imagination. Duncan Jopp stands
his trial before Weir of Hermiston, and afterwards goes to
the gallows, with a soiled rag of flannel round his sore throat
—and we instinctively resent the shock that flannel gives
us. In this, from *Island Nights Entertainments*, it is even
harsher—'With that I gave him the cold steel for all I
was worth. His body kicked under me *like a spring sofa*,
he gave a dreadful kind of a long moan, and lay still.' It
is, perhaps, difficult to forgive him for these and the like;
it is at least impossible to forget them. They are the work
of that vision in detail which, with or against our will,
enslaves the memory. The same vividness appears in

117

many pleasanter metaphors, such as that curious and intricate imagination in *Lay Morals*, of a man attempting with cords and pegs to mark out the boundary of the shadow of a great oak, lying abroad upon the ground at noon, perfect, clear, and apparently stable like the earth, but really fleeing with all its multiplicity of leaves before the travelling sun. That also, in all its detail, he has seen. In such a line as this, from *The House Beautiful*—

'A shivering pool before the door'

we feel the wind of the naked moors, and again note the power of exact observation that has revealed to us a thing at once so familiar and so unremarked.

A faculty of observation like this seldom goes with large and unified grasp of the whole situation. The man of facts and isolated impressions is usually incapable of taking 'conjunct views.' He knows the wall-paper, but has missed the landscape. Stevenson's greatest achievement as mere man of letters is that he has combined the two faculties in so remarkable a degree. In *Weir of Hermiston* this reaches its greatest perfection. The most marvellous thing in that great novel is its combination of exquisiteness of detail, with a continuous and proportioned grasp of the main purpose and large design. It is an achievement which, had it not been actually accomplished, might well have been pronounced impossible. It is the wedding of pre-Raphaelite with impressionist art, each at its highest point of excellence.

The *intensity* of his vision may be illustrated best by his delight in colour, and his skill in its literary manipulation. That delight in vividness which is so often gratified in his unbridled use of language, finds its visual counterpart in the passionate colour-work illuminating every book of his. There was once a corner shop in Leith Walk, which has

118

given us that essay in *Memories and Portraits*—ever the favourite with Edinburgh boys—the inimitable 1*d. plain and* 2*d. coloured.* Its successor is no longer dark, nor does it 'smell of Bibles' like Mr. Smith's old shop. But what glory of improvement will ever thrill the heart again as did those small-paned windows of long ago? 'One Penny Plain and Twopence Coloured'—it was not only an advertisement of certain pasteboard properties of a toy theatre; it was life itself in a nutshell. So it was, at least, to Robert Louis Stevenson; and whoso would understand this riddle must go to the essay named, and read it with as much as may be of the fervour with which we used to read its title in that shop-window. Postage stamps there were too in that window, and postage stamps then were but beginning to come to their kingdom. The soul-satisfying colours of them (for the early stamps were more aggressive than later issues), the quaint devices of foreign birds and American engines, the triangular Cape of Good Hopes, the dainty little Victorian halfpenny stamps—these were side by side with the now classical advertisement, as if to prove its scale of values just.

But enough of this. Suffice it that from those days to the end of his life Stevenson gladly paid his extra penny for the colour. All through his manhood he amused himself with the colouring of prints. His soul leapt to the splendour of crimson lake and shrank in superstitious dread from a certain shade of brown. When he desires a silencing epithet for finest action he can say no more than that it is better than purple. Whether it was the luscious depth of colour in jewels, or 'the trivial brightness of white paint' on lighthouse buildings, his heart loved it. In a youthful essay he appreciates the peacock as affording the most satisfying colour in nature to the lust of a man's eyes, and he heightens the effect by a masterly background of 'stone-

119

coloured heavens and russet woods, and grey-brown plough-
lands and white roads.' Towards the end, his ideal of style
grew more chastened and severe. 'I like more and more
naked writing,' he tells us in 1893 ; 'and yet sometimes one
has a longing for full colour.' Fortunately for us, the longing was generally gratified. We see him illuminating the
South Seas with a red sash worn round his waist, and
describing the shells and fish of the lagoons until they seem
to flash out in rainbows. At need he can use colour with
fearsome power, as when he introduces the old man of Aros,
the whites of whose eyes were 'yellow, like old stained
ivory, or the bones of the dead'; or Mountain, with his
'eyeball swimming clear of the lids upon a field of blood-
shot white !'

But we might go on for many pages illustrating from his
colour-work the intensity of his powers of vision. One
more note must suffice for this preliminary part of our
study. We have already noticed how it is his custom to
introduce surprising collocations of words apparently incongruous. It is his most characteristic figure of speech, and
it illustrates perfectly the combination of exactness with
intensity of vision. In such phrases as 'looking upon the
bright face of danger,' and many others of the same kind,
we have exactness in the choice of individual words,
intensity in the general effect of brilliance given by the
combination. In the remaining part of the present chapter
we shall have abundant opportunity for observing these
characteristics as we further illustrate the gift of vision
along its most apparent lines.

Most obvious of all is his physical love of light. There
is, in the old garden at Swanston, a tree now moribund and
clamped up with bands of iron, on which are to be seen the
carved letters T.S., his father's initials. Above them is
the emblem of 'The Rising Son.' The little

engraving is not without some touch of that cleverness
which is manifest in the work executed later at Davos. Its
emblem is for him the most appropriate in the world. The
love of light was hereditary with him, for the ancestral
Smiths had illuminated the city, while the Stevensons had
illuminated the sea. In his camp in the Cevennes we have
a clear picture of the small lamp lit amidst the wide darkness, 'The light was both livid and shifting; but it cut
me off from the universe, and doubled the darkness of the
surrounding night.' It is in thoughts connected with the
play of light and darkness that the physical sensitiveness
and intensity of Stevenson are found at their utmost. His
fondness for brilliance, his physical necessity for brightness,
is everywhere unmistakable. No better proof of this could
be cited than the strong effect produced on him by darkness. At night in Silverado he goes out to the platform
for 'a bath of darkness'—a phrase whose sensuous fulness
of meaning is seen by contrast with the great splash of
candle-light falling through the window upon the thicket
and the overhanging rock. Darkness usually produces a
kind of physical horror in him. The bitterest depths of
the Master of Ballantrae and Deacon Brodie, are expressed
in the thought of 'the old familiar faces gone into darkness.'
There is nothing in all his work more significant than the
reappearance in *Admiral Guinea* of the blind man Pew
from *Treasure Island*. As we hear his approaching footsteps, with the stick beating the ground, and expect another
exhibition of his keen and sinister character, we perceive
the mingled pity and horror with which the man of vision
is attracted to the blind.

The surprising possibilities of lamp-light and candle-light
are explored with a wealth of imagination which would
yield material for a very fascinating monograph. Sometimes it is the mere brightness of the light that forms the

121

attraction. One is startled by the vividness of metaphor
when the limbs of a sufferer are said to be 'lighted up'
with torturing pain. The drive through a city delights him
by its flashing street lamps, and especially by those more
gorgeous luminaries that send their shafts of overpowering
colour from chemists' windows. He would have his house
at Vailima lighted up full blaze in his absence, that he
might enjoy the luxury of its brightness as he returned
through the dark. He loves the phantasmagoria of lamp-
light—'the lurching sphere of light' divided by the shadow
of the man who bears the lantern across the field. He
thus describes a night-scene on the verandah at Vailima:
'The faces of the company, the spars of the trellis, stood
out suddenly bright on a ground of blue and silver, faintly
designed with palm-tops and the peaked roofs of houses.
Here and there the gloss upon a leaf, or the fracture of
a stone, returned an isolated sparkle. All else had vanished.
We hung there, illuminated like a galaxy of stars *in vacuo* ;
we sat, manifest and blind, amid the general ambush of the
darkness.' The fragment entitled *The Great North Road*
abounds in such Rembrandt impressions. In it the ostler's
lantern lets up 'spouts of candle-light through the holes
with which its conical roof was peppered.' The mail-coach
arrives from the south, and 'its lamps were very large and
bright, and threw their radiance forward in overlapping
cones. . . . the body of the coach followed like a great
shadow; and this lit picture slid with a sort of ineffectual
swiftness over the black field of night.' The fantastic play
of lights may even lend itself to the weird and gruesome
so as to produce strong effects. The evil spirits that haunt
the woods of Samoa seem quite indisputable when you
walk 'by the moving light of a lantern, with nothing about
you but a curious whirl of shadows, and the black night
above and beyond.' All the world knows now of the duel

by candle-light in the grounds of the house of Durrisdeer ; the idea seems to have appealed strongly to Stevenson's imagination, for a candle stands burning also on the gravel walk of a second house, in Murrayfield, within which a dead man lies in his blood.   In another mood, he turns for sentiment to lamps again—the street lamps of Edinburgh, not seen directly, but reflected in her wet streets—though the pathos is even keener when he remembers the fainter 'sheen of the rainy streets towards afternoon.'  Lights of candles and of lamps supply him with some of his most vivid metaphors, and not a few of the innermost secret places of his thought and emotion are illuminated by them.   The sight of Olalla extinguishes in her lover his romantic fancy for the portrait, which 'had fallen dead, like a candle after sunrise.'  Nance, in *The Great North Road*, draws her finest moral from the tale of a strange land where they used to run races with lighted candles—'that was like life : a man's good conscience is the flame he gets to carry, and if he comes to the winning post with that still burning, why, take it how you will, the man's a hero.'  The finest example is in *The Lantern-Bearers*, but of that we shall judge later on.

As was to be expected, there is much reference to light-houses, and the passages which mention them seldom fail to show an exaltation of spirit that draws the writing to its own high level.   The location of the lighthouse inspirits him, set up in the air among heather over which sea-birds fly.  *Underwoods* has some memorable descriptions, among which the following is perhaps the finest :

'Eternal granite hewn from the living isle
And dowelled with brute iron, rears a tower
That from its wet foundation to its crown
Of glittering glass, stands, in the sweep of winds,
Immovable, immortal, eminent.'

123

In another poem, published only in *The Edinburgh Edition*, *The Light-Keeper* thus describes his station:

> 'The brilliant kernel of the night,
>   The flaming light-room circles me :
> I sit within a blaze of light
>   Held high above the dusky sea. . . .'

Passing from artificial lights to natural, we find him, like the lone seaman of the rhyme, sailing astonished among stars. If it be the case that many of his most vivid impressions are shown by the light of lanterns, it is equally true that much of his most moving work is done by starlight. The green islands and the bright sea would not be to him what they are if it were not for those 'forty million stars' that shine upon so many of his scenes 'with an imperial brightness.' And the stars, like the street lamps, acquire a new beauty when we see them reflected in water. Now it is a lagoon, bright with ten thousand of them, now a star-reflecting harbour, that is shown. The hero of one tale stoops and drinks, putting his mouth to the level of a starry pool; or, descending the rope in his escape from the castle, he sees 'the stars overhead, and the reflected stars below him in the moat, whirling like dead leaves before the tempest.'

Moonlight does not affect him so strongly. Once indeed, he speaks of the 'exhilarating lustre' of the moon in winter but even that is not strong enough to satisfy him, and moonlight generally serves as a background of indistinct beauty for some more vivid sight. 'The burning valley by moonlight' he delights in, and the clean-edged tracery visible when 'the moon drew shadows of trees on the naked bodies of men.' Daylight and the sun are more to his mind, and the day's flash and colour that 'flames, dazzles and puts to sleep.' Every phase of it is known to him, from dawn yellow as sulphur in the Pacific; on through the

124

Spanish morning hour, when the whole face of nature is 'austerely smiling, the heavens of a cold blue, and sown with great cloud islands, and the mountain-sides mapped forth into provinces of light and shadow'; down to the sunset embers and the 'indigo twilight, starred with street-lamps,' of the Edinburgh evening.

In his descriptions of landscape and natural scenery, we note the same combination of exactness and intensity which is characteristic of all his vision. Mr. Cornford, in his *Robert Louis Stevenson,* has a chapter entitled ' The Limner of Landscape,' in which he brings together as remarkable a collection of such descriptions as could well be compiled. Some of Stevenson's pictures are marked by that pure and simple sense for Nature—that love of Nature for her own sake—which, since Wordsworth, has been so great and beautiful an element in our literature. These again and again remind us of the classical contrast in the *Family of Engineers* between his father's point of view and his own :— 'The river was to me a pretty and various spectacle; I could not see—I could not be made to see—it otherwise. To my father it was a chequer-board of lively forces, which he traced from pool to shallow with minute appreciation and enduring interest.' Certainly the loss to engineering has been abundantly compensated by the gain to letters.

Yet it is but seldom that his descriptions of Nature have either the detachment or the repose of Wordsworth. They come in passionate flashes, often with an effect of startling brilliance and poignancy. To illustrate this by quotations would tempt us farther afield than our limits permit, but almost any of the Nature-work in *Silverado Squatters* or *Prince Otto*—and in these it is at its best—will furnish examples. From the latter volume, the night scene in the forest, to which Cornford justly gives the palm, offers us the clue. 'This slow transfiguration [the dawn] reached her heart and played upon it, and transpierced it with a serious thrill. She looked all about, the whole face of Nature looked back, brimful of meaning, finger on lip, leaking its glad secret.' That is not Nature in herself, but Nature as she is in the experience of a human soul. It is the subjective element that gives its peculiar value to Stevenson's vision of Nature. Not only do the natural settings adapt themselves to the human interest and follow the change of incident—that is but a necessity of fiction common to all novelists, whose privilege it is to arrange their own weather. In a far more intimate sense is Stevenson's Nature-work subjective. In *The Woodman* we have the whole forest of Vailima quickened into semi-human life and consciousness, with a result as sinister and uncanny as could well be conceived. The toothless and killing sensitive-plant, plucked by the green hair, shrinks back—

> 'And straining by his anchor-strand
> Captured and scratched the rooting hand.
> I saw him crouch, I felt him bite.'

Straightway the woodman's eyes are opened, and he knows the life of the wood from within—half-human, half-demoniac. *The House Beautiful* is the finest example on the pleasant side. In itself bare and bleak, Nature is there seen by the poetic eye, so as to attain with no other help than that of the days' and seasons' change, to incomparable pomp and splendour, the wizardry of moonlight, and the enchanted beauty of frost.

In his descriptions of the city which he loved best, he is peculiarly happy. Princes Street lies under our eye, in 'mild sunshine, and the little thrill of easterly wind that tossed the flags along that terrace of palaces.' Leith Walk is the stone gully up which the north wind rushes upon the city. The old town builds itself up, on a misty day,

126

house above house, fitting its architecture to the contour of the rock until the whole seems to be of a piece. In such work the subjective element has been supplied already by the art of man. Again, in his delineation of storms at sea, Stevenson is at his very best. It is probably no exaggeration to say that nothing ever written has excelled the 'Hurricane' chapter in *A Footnote to History* or the race of the *Norah Creina* in the *Wrecker*. The secret of these is easy to discover, for it is the experience of the storm rather than the mere commotion of the elements, that is described :—'The squall itself, the catch at the heart, the opened sluices of the sky; and the relief, the renewed loveliness of life, when all is over, the sun forth again, and our out-fought enemy only a blot upon the leeward sea.' 'The frightened leaps of the poor *Norah Creina*, spanking like a stag for bare existence . . . Overhead the wild huntsman of the storm passed continuously in one blare of mingled noises; screaming wind, straining timber, lashing rope's-end, pounding block, and bursting sea.' When the scene to be described is of a quieter character, he often introduces some very strongly outlined piece of foreground, to give distinction and human interest to his picture. A stranded ship in the strong sun under a cloud of sea-birds, or 'a huge truncheon of wreck half-buried in the sands,' are but specimens of many similar expedients for sharpening the picture to exactness and intensity. The finest example, and one of the best pieces of description he ever wrote, is the first glimpse of the *Flying Scud* caught by the searchers in *The Wrecker*. For a moment, among high waves, a vista opens, and they see 'the masts and rigging of a brig pencilled on heaven, with an ensign streaming at the main, and the ragged ribbons of a topsail thrashing from the yard.'

127

# CHAPTER VIII

### THE GIFT OF VISION (*continued*)

HAVING seen the splendid beginning of the Gift of Vision in the physical, we have now to see its spiritual development in imagination and insight. Imagination was, in Stevenson's own account of himself, an intoxicating pleasure, so intense as sometimes to weaken or even to destroy the sense of reality. 'It is quite possible,' he affirms, 'and even comparatively easy, so to enfold oneself in pleasant fancies that the realities of life may seem but as the white snow-shower in the street, that only gives a relish to the swept hearth and lively fire within.' . . ..This power of imagination affected his inner life in many directions. It 'painted images brightly on the darkness'; it 'put an edge on almost everything'; and on it he counted in many trying times for heartening and refreshment. Sometimes it forsook him, and then he was left desolate, with the taste for all other things than its lost splendours blunted and enfeebled; but in the main it abode faithful. A scientific paper on *The Thermal Influence of Forests*, written for a Royal Society, might seem to promise little but statistics. Yet we have hardly begun to read it when we find ourselves in 'the crypt of the forest,' and the whole treatise illustrates the value of poetry to science.

The simplest exercise which involves the play of imagination is memory—the recalling of images received in the past. The further exercise of constructing images of facts that lie

128

beyond our actual experience, is closely connected with memory, for it is out of fragments of images once actually received that we are able to construct new wholes. Imagination, exercised in either of these two ways, may be called perception *in absentia*—perception of what is there only as idea and not in outward material fact—and the faculty of such perception was in Stevenson developed to an exceptional degree. One example of simple imagination of the past we have already noted in his vivid recollection of the inmost feelings and the minutest details of life as seen through the eyes of a little child. Another is the accuracy and the graphic force of his thoughts of home from abroad. Nothing could surpass the quality of

'Grey recumbent tombs of the dead in desert places,
    Standing stones on the vacant wine-red moor,
Hills of sheep, and homes of the silent vanished races
    And winds, austere and pure.'

Yet these lines are dated from Vailima. From Vailima *Weir of Hermiston* also comes to us, and it is safe to say that there is no novel in the language which has more perfectly expressed the colours and the forms of Scottish moorland. The great field of the hills is there, with plover and curlew and lark crying down the wind, and hill-tops that 'huddle one behind another, like a herd of cattle, into the sunset.' Where else shall we go in books to find just such 'a great rooty sweetness of bogs in the air, and at all seasons such an infinite melancholy piping of hill birds'? As to constructive imagination, all his novels are a proof of that, and almost everything else which he has written. One example must suffice, and that a quite casual and unlaboured one. Writing to Austin Strong, and having nothing in particular to say, he fills his letter with a description of those profoundest depths of the ocean in which life begins to reappear again below the zone of death. He describes 'our flimsy fellow-creatures,' the fish that live in these lowest places, held together by the great weight of water, but bursting into tatters long before they can be brought to the surface. 'But I dare say,' he adds, 'a cannon sometimes comes careering solemnly down, and circling like a dead leaf.' There we have a specimen of visual imagination than which it would be difficult to find any more interesting or characteristic.

The wealth and variety of a writer's imagination lie very largely in the development of his mind's faculty for the so-called 'association of ideas.' All of us have immense reserves of impressions stored somewhere in the brain; but they are stored as it were in separate compartments, and do not come forth readily at the command of new impressions. Genius has been defined as the power of seeing likenesses and relations among things. If that be a sound definition it must be admitted that Stevenson was a genius of the first rank. It seemed as if he had but to open the doors of his mind, and cognate impressions would press and throng in to the side of the one idea already in possession, crowding the stage of thought from every quarter of experience and knowledge. Each new idea seems to have 'thrown down a barrier which concealed significance and beauty,' and to have revealed a new world of relations.

One of the most interesting examples of this is his treatment of the subject of Treasure. Every reader must have remarked how often it occurs. In *Treasure Island, The Wrecker, The Merry Men, The Master of Ballantrae, The Treasure of Franchard*, and many other stories, either the interest centres on this, or it forms the most conspicuous feature after the plot. Its emphasis is as remarkable as is the absence of the customary love plot. Stevenson has been blamed for this, and indeed it is utterly unlike his character. Generous and lavish to a fault, miserliness is assuredly the vice for which he needs least of all to blush. The explanation is that Treasure has recondite secrets of attractiveness. When we read of the man who 'by the blaze of a great fire of wreckwood measures ingots by the bucketful on the uproarious beach,' we can see plainly that the writer's interest in the treasure-hunting was a more picturesque one than that of avarice. It was obviously the ancient Saxon's delight in his buried hoard of rings and cups of gold; delight in the glitter and sparkling beauty of what is rich and rare and bright, and not in its commercial value. But *The Treasure of Franchard* gives the real clue. The value of treasure is a spending and not a hoarding value; it signifies the delightful things which it will buy. 'You have no imagination,' cried the doctor. 'Picture to yourself the scene. Dwell on the idea—a great treasure lying in the earth for centuries: the material for a giddy, copious, opulent existence not employed,' and so on—dresses, pictures, horses, castles, parks, ships, 'all lying unborn in a coffin—and the stupid trees growing overhead in the sunlight, year after year.'

A further step leads us to Personification, which here must be understood in its widest sense, viz. the endowing of an object with the life or nature proper to another class of objects. By this means a new spirit may transform the old idea, as if new blood went tingling down its veins. It is a trick of imagination closely akin to that collocation of apparently incongruous ideas which we have already noticed, and it has an extraordinary power of heightening the value of an impression. In *Child's Play* he recalls the miracle by which cold mutton suddenly became appetising when the child had agreed with himself to call it venison. Mutton is at best but dead sheep; venison implies a live huntsman. One of the quaintest and most beautiful passages in *An Inland Voyage* likens Noyon Cathedral to an old battleship,

131

point for point; and the church gains immense interest from the comparison. So does that coral reef of which we read that it is 'sunk *to the gunwale* in the ocean.' The wind, with Stevenson, is always a kind of Erlking or mystic horseman; the shadows are species of ineffective domestic genii. Destiny, when we read of her 'hand of brass,' gains much the same fearsomeness which belongs to Fenimore Cooper's *Water Witch*, and the brazen leaves of her book of fate. Further instances innumerable might be quoted, but we add only one, in which the italicised words give a personification worthy of Homer. It is from the *Feast of Famine*:

' All day long from the high place, the drums and the singing came,
And the even fell and the sun went down, a wheel of flame ;
And night came *gleaning the shadows* and hushing the sounds of the wood.'

In this connection the most interesting fact of all is that of 'the Brownies'—the help which Stevenson acknowledges that he received in dreams. For the details of this, we must refer the reader to one of his most charming essays, the *Chapter on Dreams*. Suffice it to say that to this source he traces two of his most brilliant pieces of imaginative work, *Dr. Jekyll and Mr. Hyde*, and *Olalla*. The subject is an extremely curious one, and it has been discussed by most of those who have written about him. The one point which appears to be significant for our present purpose is that this phenomenon shows us the author as a recipient rather than a creator. Dreams may be regarded as the complex of our thoughts and feelings released from the directing and controlling power of will, undistracted by casual impressions of the external world, and so left absolutely subject to the play of involuntary physical processes which may awaken them to consciousness and direct their sequence. There was a time when all dreams were regarded as revelations, and men lay down to sleep in sacred places, that they might be able to secure such gifts of revelation from the gods. Psychology has changed all that, apparently; and yet perhaps the change is not so great after all. The religious man owns, in theory at least, that all his powers are gifts from above. Yet, when the exercise of a faculty involves strong and sustained effort of will, the consciousness of his own exertion gives the man an apparent claim to the faculty; the slighter the action of will, the more obviously does he perceive the faculty to be indeed a gift; in dreams the apparent claim is gone, and the fact that our powers are not our own is manifest. This in itself looks toward a religious meaning, and keeps a man from forgetting that he can boast of nothing which he has not received.

It would, indeed, be vain to look for any very definite ethical or religious message which his dreams revealed to Stevenson. 'I do most of the morality, worse luck!' he tells us, 'and my Brownies have not a rudiment of what we call a conscience.' The nearest approach to religious revelation is in the parable which he sometimes finds in a dream. 'Sometimes I cannot but suppose my Brownies have been aping Bunyan, and yet in no case with what would possibly be called a moral in a tract; never with the ethical narrowness; conveying hints, instead, of life's larger limitations, and that sort of sense which we seem to perceive in the arabesque of time and space.' The psychologist will have no difficulty in explaining the part which Bunyan played in the dreams of so faithful a student of the *Pilgrim's Progress*. Yet that in no way alters the fact that the effect of such dreams upon a man like Stevenson must be a more or less definite consciousness of a Giver to whom he owes all his best. At times this evidently amounts to a sense of sacredness in his hours of literary inspiration. It is a principle always very definitely realised and proclaimed: 'The true ignorance is when a man does not know that he has received

a good gift, or begins to imagine that he has got it for himself. The self-made man is the funniest windbag after all!
There is a marked difference between decreeing light in
chaos, and lighting the gas in a metropolitan back parlour
with a box of patent matches; and do what we will, there is
always something made to our hand, if it were only our
fingers.' Thus, along the whole range of vision, this true
seer confesses that he can rightly lay claim to none of all
the powers that are within him.

Perceiving his power of vision to be a gift, he set no
bounds to the freedom with which he looked and saw
around him. In strangely opposite directions the gift of
vision intensified his life. The most obvious and perhaps
the most familiar of these is his imagination of the *ghastly
and horrible*. In his tales and in some of his other work
there is a surprising, and often quite an unnecessary
amount of murder and of bloodshed. Cold steel flashes
and then grows warm in groaning flesh; the spine cracks,
and the body falls slack in the grasp of strong hands;
blood flows and clots, wounds gape and the livid flesh
changes colour, with that shameless nakedness which
England first learned from the songs of pagan Saxons. In
such a tale as *The Black Arrow* no chapter is complete till
it has added to the pile of corpses. In the fights, men go
down like ninepins, and the Wrecker is not the only hero
of his who learns to 'entertain and welcome the grim
thought of bloodshed.' Sometimes the horror is drawn out
in a leisurely paragraph of the *South Seas* which becomes
almost unreadable; again it flashes forth in a single lurid
sentence like that uttered by the murderer in *A Lodging for
the Night*: 'What right has a man to have red hair when
he is dead?'

Death itself, in all its crude realism, is much in evidence;
and the morbid interest in its paraphernalia which is

characteristic of a certain type of Scottish folklore, is unsparingly introduced. From the bloody winding-sheet of the Covenanter, and the grim loquacity of Scottish grave-diggers, to the long baskets at the feasts of cannibals and their drums in whose tramp you hear 'the beat of the heart of death,' the sinister interest is passed on. Even as a child, playing beside a churchyard, he discovers a light in a cranny of the retaining wall, and wonders 'whether the hole pierced right through into a grave, and it was some dead man who was sitting up in his coffin and watching us with that strange fixed eye.'

Nor does death end all. He deals freely in the horrors which inhabit the region beyond the grave. Spectral presences that haunt the imagination are familiar in the greater part of his work; but especially in the Scottish and the South Sea writings, between which they form an uncanny link of connection. As in so many families of Scotland, this element was hereditary with him. In *A Family of Engineers* two stories are told of apparitions of the dead seen *in articulo mortis* by ancestors of his own. Old covenanting superstitions of flames rising from certain graves, gruesome legends of haunted houses, particular forms of demons like the brown dog described in the *Chapter on Dreams*, are introduced with unmistakable zest. In the *South Seas*, we find ourselves again in islands 'beleaguered by the dead,' in ghost-haunted and devil-haunted woods, in the midst of a people who live in fear of magicians, and who look upon their recently buried dead as new 'ogres loosed upon the isle.' Few passages, even of his Samoan work, are written with a more sympathetic touch, than that which describes the struggle with the mad Paatalise, who had met his dead brother in the bush. 'And remember!' he says, 'we are fighting the dead, and they [the black boys of the household] had to go out again in the

135

black night, which is the dead man's empire,' though they believed the man's ravings, and 'knew that his dead family, thirty strong, crowded the front verandah and called on him to come to the other world.' The palm goes, however, without doubt to the Scottish work of this kind. Tod Lapraik and Thrawn Janet are immortal spectres. Of them he says that if he had never written anything else, 'still I'd have been a writer.' Of that there can be no question. Tod Lapraik dances on the Bass Rock still for all readers of *Catriona.* Who has ever forgotten the scene in *Thrawn Janet,* where Mr. Soulis is standing beside his candle at the stairfoot ? 'A foot gaed to an' fro in the chalmer whaur the corp was hingin'; syne the door was opened,—though he minded weel that he had lockit it ; an' syne there was a step upon the landin', and it seemed to him as if the corp was lookin' ower the rail an' doon upon him whaur he stood.'

His skill and freedom in the manipulation of supernatural machinery are very great. The sustained horror of *Dr. Jekyll and Mr. Hyde* alone is proof of this. No conceivable imagination could be more precarious than that story, so close does it keep to the edge over which the sublime falls suddenly to the ridiculous. A slip at any point might have made the situation not only grotesque but fatuous. Yet the story retains its power unbroken to the end. At times—so masterful is his handling of supernatural terrors—he intentionally relieves the strain ; as when the Master of Ballantrae, apparently chiming in with Mackellar's fears, asks him if he knows what the sudden dash of rain forebodes, and answers his own question—'that there'll be a man Mackellar unco' sick at sea.'

Yet it may be questioned whether he ever attains perfection in his management of the ghastly. The most powerful effect can only be reached by way of reticence and suggestion, and Stevenson saw too clearly to be quite master of that art. He can make you see a horrible image with a vividness which few writers can match. The subtler power of making you tremble at what you cannot see, is not usually at his command. To this extent his gift of vision overreaches itself, and fails because of its extraordinary success.

On the other hand, he has an eye for beauty as keen as his perception of its opposite. Many passages quoted elsewhere show not only how vivid but how full of beauty the world appeared to Stevenson. It was his favourite task to explore and point out the wayside beauty that lies all around us. His essay on *Walt Whitman* exhibits him in the company of a most congenial spirit. In many ways the thought and purpose of the two are one; yet nothing in that essay is more significant than the criticism in its latter part. Every reader of Whitman knows the large and reckless manner in which he tumbles great things and small together in huge heaps, that he may appreciate and delight in the whole contents of the universe. Nothing could be more to Stevenson's taste than this, and he blames Whitman, not for his intention, but for the unconvincing way in which it is carried out. It is not enough to praise the hill-tops and the factory in one breath, the stately ships in the harbour and the contents of the hatter's shop. To Stevenson as to Whitman all these and all other such facts are capable of revealing beauty, and it is the duty of the writer to make that beauty plain. But to do this more is required than a rollicking catalogue of miscellaneous articles. 'To show beauty in common things is the work of the rarest tact. It is not to be done by the wishing.' The critic knew this as only one could know who had himself laboured hard at such work of the rarest tact. He proves this beyond dispute in *The House Beautiful*, which is a well-nigh perfect expression of beauty in common things.

# THE FAITH OF R. L. STEVENSON

It is true that looking back long afterward upon his life he describes his chase of the ideal thus:

> 'Still
> Somewhere on the sunny hill,
> Or along the winding stream
> Through the willows, flits a dream;
> Flits but shows a smiling face,
> Flees but with so quaint a grace,
> None can choose to stay at home,
> All must follow, all must roam.
> This is unborn beauty.'

The chase is vain, though it is worth while. As 'with grey hair we stumble on,' the vision fades away at last, never to be plainly seen. The fading of the sense of beauty in times of ill-health is described with unusual wealth of metaphor in *Ordered South*. The most pathetic part of the invalid's experience is that he inhabits a disenchanted world, which he knows intellectually to be beautiful, but whose beauty he no longer feels. But such confessions of failure are proof of extraordinary success. The eye is not satisfied with seeing because it knows what seeing has sometimes meant. Nothing is more characteristic of Stevenson than his exacting fastidiousness in the search for beauty and for words in which to express it. It is the fastidiousness of the high priest, who feels a certain claim and proprietory right in the shrine. If we may quote one figure as peculiarly typical of his vision of the beautiful, it shall be the image of the Garden, which occurs in his books almost as frequently as any except such as are drawn from the battlefield. Most of his tales have one garden-scene at least. *The Ideal House* has a passage on gardens quite in the style of Bacon's famous essay. Spiritualised, the garden stands for all that is sweetest and gentlest in the inner life. The tortured and dying Du Chayla declares that his soul is 'like a garden full of shelter and of

138

fountains.' 'It is a shaggy world' we read in *Pan's Pipes*, 'and yet studded with gardens; where the salt and tumbling sea receives clear rivers running from among reeds and lilies.'

The ghastly and the beautiful are combined in one of his favourite and most characteristic ideas. We have already noted how subjective his treatment of Nature is. He openly confesses that the work he expects his imagination to do upon natural scenery is to let him 'see satyrs in the thicket, or picture a highwayman riding down the lane.' The highwayman is often in evidence, but it is the satyr that lends to Nature her peculiar meaning for him, and the etching of a satyr among reeds prefixed to *An Inland Voyage* is the work of rare insight. *Pan's Pipes* gives the key to this almost pagan aspect of the world. The whole of that wonderful little essay is concentrated in one phrase of his *Inland Voyage*, in which the music of the river-side reeds is interpreted as the sound that tells of 'the beauty and the terror of the world.' Of the terror he is acutely conscious. The clearing of ground from tropical weeds appears as a battle with inhuman, spiteful, snakelike things, and fills him with a superstitious horror. In *Weir of Hermiston*, Kirstie describes how the dead body of the would-be assassin is taken charge of all night by the river, which 'dunts' the dead thing on the stones, and 'grunds' it on the shallows, and flings it head over heels at the waterfall. And yet this cruel, lewd, and treacherous Nature is full of the most tender beauty all the time. An overhanging branch had caught him, and he was left clinging to it while his canoe went down the Oise. He felt 'what a dead pull a river makes against a man. Death himself had me by the heels. . . . The devouring element in the universe had leaped out against me in this green valley quickened by a running stream.' Then he realised the mystery of Nature that could be at once so cruel

139

and so beautiful. This combination of terror and beauty is very frequently introduced, and it is evidently one of the conceptions which most deeply impressed his imagination.

All that concerns us at the present stage is that Stevenson's vision both of the ghastly and the beautiful was intense and clear. In a certain sense he is a realist, though not even such vague terms as realist and idealist can define him. He is a realist in so far as he records the facts of life as they appear to him, impartially, and without selection of those which suit the purposes of some particular view. There is another sense in which the term realism is sometimes understood. Under the pretext of an impartial record, this realism tacitly selects the ugly and the evil facts, and, with great ostentation of courage and sincerity, offers these for its picture of life as it actually is. The fallacy is obvious, and such realism is but the inverted form of that so-called idealism which selects the pretty and the innocent facts for its whole picture. There are times when one trembles to think what the work of Stevenson might have been, had he chosen to be a realist of this latter sort. In some rare instances, such as *The Wrong Box*, with its very ugly story of the travels of a dead body in a packing-case, he makes us feel against our will the attraction which the ugly might have had for him. In a letter to a friend he declares that if that story is not funny, he does not know what is. But this is in no way representative. He pours his scorn upon that kind of literature in which the ugly is *de rigueur*. He is true to himself when, in approaching the leper island, he describes his feelings: ' My horror of the horrible is about my weakest point; but the moral loveliness at my elbow blotted all else out.' The truth is that though he unquestionably delights in the horrible, it is not because of its horror but because of its conspicuousness. Vision is

140

his great delight and strong desire. What there is to see in this mingled world, he will see, and what is most vivid will first catch his eye. Obviously the terror and the beauty of the world are its most conspicuous points, and accordingly he sees and shows them. But the special merit of his writing is that it has insisted on the conspicuousness of beauty. It is a cheap and easy way of enlisting interest which the horrible affords; and without strenuous effort, descriptions of the beautiful are apt to be dull. He has put forth his strength to show that beauty may be made as conspicuous as ugliness, as brilliant as horror. To have succeeded in this is to have rendered a great service to literature.

When we pass on to the sphere of psychology and of moral and spiritual vision, we take but a short step, and the change is hardly perceptible. The points of similarity between the two regions are so many, that the word insight is hardly a metaphor as regards Stevenson's highest life, and the same powers and effects which we have already noted are still observable. Indeed he has a way of linking together natural colouring and emotional experience with peculiarly subtle skill, and often with great effect. The ancient singers of Wales were wont to alternate a line about the wind-blown reeds, the river, or the trees, with the patriotic or moral sentiments of their poems, in a fashion which Professor Masson has called 'the flag and feeling device.' This we may sometimes find in Stevenson, as when he gives his memorable account of the student reading night and day for his examination. On the morning of the examination day he rose from his books and pulled up his blind in a jocund humour. 'Day was breaking, the east was tinging with strange fires'—a nameless terror seized upon him, and when he came to the examination

141

hall he had forgotten his name. In like manner 'strange fires' many a time illuminate Stevenson's mental pictures, and blend with them in the reader's memory.

The characters of his tales are notable for their firmness and clear outline. 'There was nothing oblique or vague about him. What he saw he saw, and what he saw he could describe.' Not only are his men and women clearly visible, they are alive. In one of his books 'they became detached from the flat paper, they turned their backs on me, and walked off bodily.' In another, certain questions as to the development of the plot must answer themselves 'when I get near enough to see.' Nor was this vision of men and women merely artistic. 'I am at bottom a psychologist,' he tells us. The insight shown in his psychological analysis is as penetrating as his artistic work is brilliant and harmonious. His delight is in 'looking through a window into other people's lives,' and 'lifting up their roofs' that he may see what is going on in their house of life. So great is this power, and so constantly is it exercised, that it is unnecessary to offer illustrations. Open any page of his work at random, and whatever may be absent it may be safely prophesied that you shall find some evidence of this. It was in *Weir of Hermiston* that it reached its greatest, and Professor Sidney Colvin writes of that book, 'If in the literature of romance there is to be found work more masterly, of more piercing human insight or more concentrated imaginative vision and beauty, I do not know it.' We know, for example, the heart of the elder Kirstie—and what a heart it is!—and we know its play of concealed and half-conscious motives, and the irrationalities, and the secret fears, and the passion suppressed within iron bands; we know these things as we read, with a certainty which surprises us at every page, and yet which never fails to convince us in any detail.

142

The moral insight is even more extraordinary. The danger of the artist is that, finding the actual facts of the moral world inharmonious, he should change their emphasis and grouping to suit his taste. 'A man of imagination,' says Dr. Desprez, 'is never moral; he outsoars literal demarcations, and reviews life under too many shifting lights to rest content with the invidious distinctions of the law.' But Stevenson can write on morals under a plain white light. His descriptions are often given in words carefully weighed and chosen not for effect but for accuracy. In no part of his work is he less the actor than in this. The result for the reader is a succession of surprising revelations, in which he constantly recognises himself or some other, though he has never had them expressed before. We know what Stevenson means when he divides men into the two classes of those who incline 'to think all things *rather wrong*,' and those who suppose them '*right enough for all practical purposes*.' We have met the man of whom he says, 'Convictions existed in him by divine right; they were virgin, unwrought, the brute metal of decision.' Who can forget the Master of Ballantrae 'worming himself with singular dexterity' into the family troubles, 'as the hand of a bone-setter artfully divides and interrogates the muscles, and settles strongly on the injured place'? or Frank Innes, whose practice it was 'to approach any one person at the expense of some one else'? 'He offered you an alliance against the some one else; he flattered you by slighting him; you were drawn into a small intrigue against him before you knew how.' The casual notes on character are often startling, revealing men to themselves abruptly as with a sudden challenge. One man, in whom we had been watching the progress of what we took to be insanity, turns out not to have gone out of his mind, 'but to have drifted from character.' The irritation which is 'too frequently the uppermost feeling on the sickness of those dear to us,' and the anger which is kindled within us 'against those who make themselves the spokesmen of plain obligations,' are other cases in point.

His best work is done when he finds himself face to face with complex moral situations in which ordinary judgments fail us, and we need a subtler and a clearer insight than that of most men to let us see the case exactly. The supreme instance of this is that passage in his *Essay on Burns*, which is at once one of the most courageous and one of the truest things he ever wrote. It is the passage in which he describes the man (if we may paraphrase another of his sayings) as playing sedulous ape to two consciences. 'It is the punishment of Don Juanism to create continually false positions—relations in life which are wrong in themselves and which it is equally wrong to break or to perpetuate. . . . It was true he could not do as he did without brutally wounding Clarinda; that was the punishment of his bygone fault; he was, as he truly says, "damned with a choice only of different species of error and misconduct." . . . If he had been strong enough to refrain, or bad enough to persevere in evil; if he had only not been Don Juan at all, or been Don Juan altogether, there had been some possible road for him throughout this troublesome world; but a man, alas! who is equally at the call of his worse and better instincts, stands among changing events without foundation or resource.'

In the moral sphere we see the same characteristics as have been already noted under the general subject of imagination. The delight in brilliance for its own sake runs through all his work, and here, as elsewhere, it gives the strongest possible effects both in the ghastly and the beautiful. He is artist as well as moralist, and though it is true, as we said on the preceding page, that in many

144

cases he works at the moral situations with the enthusiasm
of a purely ethical interest, yet he does not ever quite sink
the artist in the man of conscience. He is artist still, and
artist in the manner of Rembrandt, dealing in high lights,
and even darkening his shadows to create them.

Of the ghastly side of morals he treats with freedom
and mastery. Sometimes the horror is conveyed in suggestions, as in the *Merry Men*, but usually it is of the broadest
kind. Nothing could be more loudly proclaimed than the
terrific moral tragedy in *The Bottle Imp* or *Dr. Jekyll and
Mr. Hyde*. And this introduces a further point, of much
interest in itself, and closely parallel to that delight in
the truculent and sanguinary which is so frequent in his
novels, viz. the two or three wholly unrelieved pictures he
has given us of ugly and disgusting sin. Deacon Brodie is
hardly a case in point, though he comes very near it.
Much as the Deacon interested Stevenson, he resisted the
temptation to make him a hero, in any sense 'magnificent
in sin.' *The Master of Ballantrae* 'is all I know of a devil,'
he tells us. Mackellar's gorge sometimes 'rose against him
as though he were deformed, and sometimes I would draw
away as though from something partly spectral.' *The
Ebb Tide* is the darkest example, and it has been much
criticised for its portrayal of unrelieved moral ugliness.
He himself regarded it with increasing disgust as it went
on. He heaps upon it such adjectives as 'devilish,' 'grimy,'
and 'rancid,' and says, 'There are only four characters, to be
sure, but they are such a troop of swine!' In Huish he
has probably touched bottom in the possibilities of describing an unmitigated cad. In this connection a curious fact
may be noted, viz. the recurring allusions to certain wholly
bad men he had met in real life. He persuaded Fleeming
Jenkin against his will that such a man existed. Another
character in the same class is he who is described in

the lurid sketch *A Character*. By 1887 he seems to have met two such men. In the Gilbert Islands he met another, whom he describes as an incarnation of baseness. These were to him hatefully impressive, with 'a depravity beyond measure depraved, a thirst after wickedness, the pure, disinterested love of Hell for its own sake.'

This lingering over the sheer nastiness of sin has been commented upon, and indeed we are all thankful that there is so little of it in his work. Yet whatever Art may have to say, the moralist must be grateful for it. Fra Angelico is an eternally lovely soul, but the moral condition of the world demands a man who *can* paint a devil. The devil-pictures of some of the greatest geniuses in literature have been failures when judged by the moralist's standard. Milton's Satan is only too 'magnificent in sin'; Goethe's Mephistopheles is so clever and interesting as almost to justify his existence. Stevenson's devils are loathsome; and their sin is not only exceeding sinful, but utterly unpleasant. We have the right to claim such work as showing genuine moral purpose, though he may not have stated this to himself as a definite aim. His own conscience of evil is never obtruded, but the rare confessions which we have are eloquent of its depth. Once, by an error of memory, he had broken faith with one of his publishers, and it cut him to the quick. He felt himself involved in dishonour, and he could not sleep for the misery of the thought. 'You remember my lectures on Ajax, or the Unintentional Sin?' he writes. 'Well, I know all about that now. Nothing seems so unjust to the sufferer; or is more just in essence.' Again there is this, from one of the prayers: 'Help us to look back on the long way that Thou hast brought us, on the long days in which we have been served not according to our deserts but our desires; on the pit and the miry clay, the blackness of despair, the horror of misconduct, from

146

which our feet have been plucked out. For our sins forgiven or prevented, for our shame unpublished, we bless and thank Thee, O God.' These extracts throw some light on his delineation of badness unrelieved by anything that makes it attractive, and the following fragment of a fine passage taken from his preface to *Men and Books* states his attitude definitely : 'And when we find a man persevering indeed, in his fault, as all of us do, and openly overtaken, as not all of us are, by its consequences, to gloss the matter over, with too polite biographers, is to do the work of the wrecker, disfiguring beacons on a perilous seaboard.'

Not less noteworthy is his delight in moral beauty and his power in depicting it. He took to heart Fleeming Jenkin's reply to his proof that one man was irredeemably bad : 'Yes, I'm afraid that *is* a bad man. I wonder if it isn't a very unfortunate thing for you to have met him . . . this badness is such an easy, lazy explanation. Won't you be tempted to use it instead of trying to understand people ?' One of the two men he could not forgive 'was he who first taught me, in my twenty-seventh year, to believe that it was possible for a man to be evil with premeditation.' In morals, the kind of realism which selects the unclean and ugly for attention, is a most leprous spirit. Yet it is always sure of an audience, for vice has a strong interest of its own, and virtue has for some no beauty that they should desire it. There is no diviner task than that of making goodness appear fascinating, and changing from a pious phrase to a vivid reality 'The Beauty of Holiness.' That Stevenson himself felt this, there can be no question. 'Love is so startlingly real' in his view 'that it takes rank upon an equal footing of reality with the consciousness of personal existence. We are as heartily persuaded of the identity of those we love as of our own identity.' And again: 'Such things as honour and love are not only nobler

147

than food and drink, but indeed I think we desire them more, and suffer more sharply for their absence.' The artist in him came to his aid in enforcing this, as well as the converse doctrine. As many later extracts will show, he succeeded in adding brilliance to the thought of goodness. He did this by the air of chivalry with which he invested it. He found his examples among knights and admirals; and in making himself the champion of righteousness he seems to have sworn, like William the Conqueror, by the splendour of God. Such a poem as *Our Lady of the Snows* gives this impression at its full brilliance. His good men and women are veritable saints in light, winsome and heroic both. This in itself is no small matter; indeed it would be difficult to exaggerate the value of this one service to morals. It is not difficult to decry sin and to extol goodness, but too often the result is but to make sin appear interesting and goodness deadly dull. He who can succeed in making sin distasteful and virtue not merely proper but fascinating has done much for that healthful belief in life which lies at the roots not only of morality but of faith.

Following up the gift of vision, we come finally to faith itself, *i.e.* faith in the theoretical sense as distinguished from the practical, in which it appears as faithfulness. Faith in the former sense has been variously defined, but there is no definition which comes so near exactness as that of 'seeing the invisible'—a new and higher range for the faculty of vision. The controversy between faith and reason is an unmeaning one. Faith is a kind of perception, the perception of a certain class of phenomena called the spiritual. It neither contradicts reason nor transcends it, for the objects of faith are actually there, and perception of what is really there is part of reason. Thus faith is but the highest exercise of the gift of vision. Such a view of faith has important consequences, for if this be true it follows that a

148

man who has cultivated his powers of vision with success along all the lower lines, has at least the capacity for the higher vision also. No man gifted with keen powers of vision can justly complain that faith is a faculty in which he is impotent. Thus it has seemed truest to Stevenson to review in detail the gift of vision as exercised in regions apparently remote from religion. A man's faith is but one phase of his insight. He sees God with the same faculty which reveals to him the other facts of life. Before we concern ourselves with the details of what a man has seen in the religious region, it is well to ascertain the way in which he looks at things in general, and the power of seeing them which he possesses. The blossoms of the tree of life are curious and beautiful, but the roots are the essential tree.

It may be boldly asserted that every unprejudiced man who looks searchingly and steadily at life shall sooner or later see God. God is no phantasm; He is there, and those who fail to see Him, fail because they have not looked fairly, or with sufficiently intense and patient gaze. Stevenson, at least, had the reward of his search. Quotations might be multiplied at great length, but those given in Chapter I. are quite conclusive evidence that he saw God in Nature and in his own life's experiences. True, it was in the aspects of the world that the vision was revealed, rather than apart from and beyond them; yet it was enough to persuade him that 'there is a manifest God for those who care to look for Him.' At times the spectacle of the world is all that is visible, and he cries:

'God, if this were enough,
That I see things bare to the buff . . .
God, if this were faith!'

Again, the conflicting aspects of the natural world appear to deaden for a time the vision of God:

149

'And methought that beauty and terror are only one, not two ;
And the world has room for love, and death, and thunder, and dew ;
And all the sinews of hell slumber in summer air ;
And the face of God is a rock, but the face of the rock is fair.'

At all times the sense of mystery kept his vision from over-familiarity, and even deprived it of some clearness of outline which it might have had without sacrifice either of truth or of reverence. Yet the vision was direct and instinctive. He ridicules the man who counts it 'a credit to believe in God on the evidence of some crack-jaw philosopher, although it is a decided slur to believe in Him on His own authority.' His definition of Faith is explicit: 'Faith is not to believe in the Bible, but to believe in God; if you believe in God, where is there any more room for terror? . . . If you are sure that God, in the long run, means kindness by you, you should be happy; and, if happy, surely you should be kind.' He speaks, through the mouth of the hero of his *Merry Men*, some words concerning prayer which have an unusual wealth of significance: 'A generous prayer is never presented in vain; the petition may be refused, but the petitioner is always, I believe, rewarded by some gracious visitation. The horror, at least, was lifted from my mind; I could look with calm of spirit on that great bright creature, God's ocean.' In these words two things are plain. There is the belief in a direct and personal contact with the Divine; and there is the vision of God through Nature. It is but one of countless instances in which the eyes that knew so well their task of seeing the bright spectacle of the world, had caught a glimpse beyond the world of the King in His beauty.

# CHAPTER IX

### THE INSTINCT OF TRAVEL

THE Instinct of Travel, like the Gift of Vision, is an element in human nature which may be traced up from the physical to the moral and spiritual regions of life. At first the moods of Vision and Travel might seem to be opposed. The one is passive, regarding life as a spectacle, the other active, thinking of it as a campaign. It is undeniable that Stevenson not only had sympathies with both moods, but that he indulged both freely. Now he is artist, now labourer; now French ideals claim him by their mere picturesqueness, again he is the Scottish Puritan and Calvinist, with nothing to be seen about him but the conscience of work.

It would be easy to say simply that there were two Stevensons, after the manner of Jekyll and Hyde, and the question demanding answer would be which was the real one. There are always the two classes of men, one of whom writes the noun and adjective with capitals, the other the verb—men exclusively of thought or feeling, and men exclusively of action. To which of these classes did he belong? But a broad and hard division like this, while it has great value for practical purposes, is useless in any attempt at the exact analysis of a man's character. Human nature is far subtler than any such imaginary pairs or groups existing separately within one single personality. However different a man's characteristics may be from one another, they all intermingle as they grow together, and each affects the others. It is this fact that gives its fascination to the analysis of character. If it were not for the blending and interaction of the various elements, character-study would not be worth beginning. In Stevenson the two sides—the seeing and the travelling—are both constantly present, and they blend and modify each other in the most intimate ways. The spectacular is seldom a mere background for the practical, nor is the practical often quite forgotten in the spectacular. So that the main criterion for judging which of the two is the dominant spirit of his work and thought must be the fall of emphasis, now on the one and again on the other side.

Sometimes we have a mood in which *the practical is subordinated to the spectacular*. In this mood, travel becomes for him simply a means of gratifying the lust of the eyes, concerned not with reality but with imagination, in which the whole actual working and suffering of the world is but so much stage furniture. For himself, he is, so far as practical ends are concerned, in 'a pleasing stupor,' like those drivers he has described, 'who pass much of their time in a great vacancy of the intellect, and threading the sights of a familiar country.' He is without responsibilities, living for the moment only, unfettered even by those unimportant projects (such as the resolution to go a given distance in a given time, or to halt at a certain inn) which become duties for the moment and are apt to grow into painful bonds of obligation to all but the few who can entirely detach themselves. In this mood 'you forget the narrow lane where all men jostle together in unchivalrous contention, and the kennel, deep and unclean, that gapes on either hand for the defeated. Life is simple enough, it seems, and the very idea of sacrifice becomes like a mad fancy out of a last night's dream. Your ideal is not perhaps high, but it is

152

plain and possible. You become enamoured of a life of change and movement and the open air, where the muscles shall be more exercised than the affections.' At another time travel quickens imagination to romance, but still without awakening any conscience of action. 'Clear vision goes with the quick foot,' he tells us, and this clear vision of the quick-footed not only shows us things in sane and natural proportions; it adds to them a positive charm by its suggestions of hidden interesting qualities, and it quickens the imagination by the very exercise of motion. In all such moods we see him subordinating the practical to the spectacular. Morals retain a picturesque interest only, and spiritual things are valued only by their brilliance or dulness as parts of the spectacle of the world. He himself is, like his own Prince Florizel, 'the skilled expert in life . . . the man who seemed, like a god, to know all things and to have suffered nothing.'

This, however, is but an exceptional mood—a relapse from that higher one which evidently represents his real and deepest self. In this latter, *the spectacular is subordinated to the practical*; he no longer travels in order to see, but sees in order to travel. 'It is to this wandering and uneasy spirit of anticipation that roads minister. Every little vista, every little glimpse that we have of what lies before us, gives the impatient imagination rein, so that it can outstrip the body and already plunge into the shadow of the woods, and overlook from the hill-top the plain beyond it, and wander in the windings of the valley that are still far in front. The road is already there—we shall not be long behind.' Thus may vision be brought into the direct service of travel, even on the material plane. When we come to morals, this is even more profoundly true. A German theologian has told us, in one of those pregnant sentences whose meaning seems to grow continually fuller,

153

that the first thing requisite for gaining the victory over the world is that we shall understand the lie of the world. So, in the serious business of life, all clear vision is for the sake of the quick foot. This is true along the whole line, in Stevenson's judgment, and in the highest matter of faith it is supremely true. Morality springs directly from faith. There is no use of a belief in God, or almost none, except to take that belief for a foundation on which to build your sense of what is right, and your attempt to do it. In a word, it was in its practical form, as faithfulness, that faith chiefly interested Robert Louis Stevenson.

In the most literal sense, the instinct of travel was strong in Stevenson. There is no need for our enlarging on this obvious fact, but it is so far-reaching and influential that a few notes can hardly be omitted. To begin with, he had the geographical sense and instinct, which manifested itself in many different ways. As a child this was constantly with him, adding a new interest to all his employments. The favourite Saturday walk in his boyhood was to the docks at Leith, for he loved a ship 'as a man loves Burgundy or daybreak.' In earlier years, the invalid child had lain in bed, interpreting the hills and hollows of the white sheets as mountains and valleys in a broad land; or had looked upon his favourite garden as a continent 'cut into provinces' by its beech hedge. *Rosa quo Locorum* shows this geographical instinct in a religious light in childhood. The Scottish metrical version of the twenty-third psalm was for him a scripture of very tender private interpretations. '"The pastures green" were represented by a certain suburban stubble-field, where I had once walked with my nurse, under an autumnal sunset, on the banks of the Water of Leith.' '"Death's dark vale" was a certain archway in the Warriston Cemetery; a formidable yet beloved spot.'

154

# THE INSTINCT OF TRAVEL

His love of maps was strong from first to last. 'The author,' he tells us, 'must know his countryside, whether real or imaginary, like his hand.' Accordingly, before he wrote *Treasure Island*, he made an elaborate and coloured map of an island, and as he paused over that map the characters seemed to peep out and pass to and fro until the tale was made. Among the furniture of *The Ideal House*, maps have an unusual prominence, and charts with 'the reefs, soundings, anchors, sailing marks and little pilot-pictures,' and there are even to be tables for modelling imaginary or actual countries in putty and plaster. The war game was played at Davos, in an attic room upon whose floor 'a map was roughly drawn in chalks of different colours, with mountains, rivers, towns, bridges, and roads of two classes.' Not less than in maps he delights in stringing together the names of far-off places, especially when the names are sonorous, or suggestive of curious and interesting things that have been brought from far. In *Will o' the Mill* the miller tries to tell Will where the river goes to, and opens his heart up for new longings by the account of its way by cities and bridges, through marshes and sands to the sea 'where the ships are that bring parrots and tobacco from the Indies.' 'Dollars of mine,' says *The Wrecker*, 'were tacking off the shores of Mexico, in peril of the deep and the guardacostas; they rang on saloon counters in the city of Tombstone, Arizona; they shone in faro-tents among the mountain diggings.' The 'industrious pirate' of the *Moral Emblems* daily sweeps his telescope round the horizon 'from Hatteras or Matapan.' The *Child's Garden* is full of allusions to distant lands. Japan and Babylon, Tartary and California, all the width of the world is there, and the whole book is a sort of children's hymn of praise for the wide world. Indeed George Mac-Donald's lines come to mind often as we read Stevenson's books:

# THE FAITH OF R. L. STEVENSON

' O all wide spaces, far from feverous towns !
    Great shining seas ! pine forests ] mountains wild !
  Rock-bosomed shores ! rough heaths ! and sheep-cropt downs !
    Vast pallid clouds ! blue spaces undefiled !
  Room ! give me room ! give loneliness and air !
  Free things and plenteous in your regions fair.'

In other ways, very delicately and often with extraordinarily powerful suggestion of the unexplored, he impresses us
with his sense of the width of the world. The present spot
whereon he stands is always seen in relation with other
places held apart from it by vast breadths of sea or land.
The quaintest of all instances that come to memory is that
verse from *The Child's Garden*:

> ' The rain is raining all around,
>   It rains on field and tree,
>   It rains on the umbrellas here,
>   And on the ships at sea.'

Nothing could surpass that coupling of the umbrellas and
the ships, in which we see the comfort and the adventure of
the world brought together under the dark but homely roof of
the clouds. Again he can detach himself from the spot, and
view Scotland from the outside, seeing it for the time
being purely with the eye of the geographer—' this neck of
barren hills between two inclement seaways.' To him there
is no foreign land, ' every place is a centre to the earth,
whence highways radiate or ships set sail.' The Marquesan
cemetery impresses him with the thought ' how far these
sleepers had all travelled, and from what diverse ports they
had set forth, to lie here in the end together.' On Pagopago
a bell rings for service, and he reminds us how various its
associations are—to the natives a new, strange, outlandish
thing; to the priests calling up memories of French and
Flemish cities, to himself ' talking of the grey metropolis of
the north, of a village on a stream, of vanished faces and
silent tongues.'

156

# THE INSTINCT OF TRAVEL

He was from first to last a great traveller. The nomadic habit he declared to be part of himself, and regarded it as the natural state to which mankind reverts on the slightest provocation. By sea and land, with a canoe, with a donkey, or tramping the roads with a knapsack, he is ever at his best when journeying. The passion for exploring takes him masterfully by the hand; friendly voices call him further and further into the unknown regions. The safe comfort of the untravelled he mocks with delicious raillery:

> 'The frozen peaks he once explored
> But now he's dead and by the board;
> How better far at home to have stayed,
> Attended by the parlour maid.'

In more serious mood is *Will o' the Mill*, which many critics have placed among his best achievements. It is the study of a man who, living in a secluded spot, far from the great activities of the world although on the highway that leads to them, is often tempted to the adventure of travel, yet always hangs back, hesitates, and stays in his place. The increasing formality, the sense of unnatural and even inhuman aloofness in the man, alienates the reader more and more as the tale proceeds. In Stevenson's hands it could not have been otherwise. The travelling life is for him the only normal type. His delight in seafaring was inherited. His grandfather, we are told, so loved his annual cruise among the Northern Lights that, when told that his death was fast approaching, he seemed to feel more keenly the loss of the voyage than the coming of the last enemy. The chief delight of Stevenson's own early days was that same cruise in the *Pharos*. Many years later we still find him enjoying above all things the excitement of a landfall among the islands of the South Seas; and declaring that even literary fame is ' no good compared to a yacht.'

Walking is, however, the ultimate test for the instinct of

157

travel. Your steamer or Pullman car have many adventitious elements of interest—the plain road is the joy of none but the heaven-born traveller. Here again Stevenson is not wanting. His essay on *Walking Tours* is proof of this, and there is the inimitable conversation with the Commissary at Châtillon: *C.* 'Why, then, do you travel?' *R. L. S.* 'I travel for pleasure.' *C.* (pointing to the knapsack, and with sublime incredulity) 'With that? Look here, I am a person of intelligence!' Yet, in spite of the Commissary, that word 'I travel for pleasure' counts for much. It is significant that to this delight in walking we owe the *Essay on Roads*, which was one of his own chief favourites among his writings, and which certainly exhibits some of his most perfect work. In it he has caught the nomadic spirit and has described it, giving literary expression to the meaning of the road in a manner which is altogether beyond praise. The following extracts are but a fragment of one of the completest pieces of picturesque analysis in the language :

'Conspicuous among these sources of quiet pleasure (is) the character and variety of the road itself, along which he takes his way. Not only near at hand, in the lithe contortions with which it adapts itself to the interchanges of level and slope, but far away also, when he sees a few hundred feet of it upheaved against a hill, and shining in the afternoon sun, he will find it an object so changeful and enlivening that he can always pleasurably busy his mind about it. He may leave the riverside, or fall out of the way of villages, but the road he has always with him; and in the true humour of observation, will find in that sufficient company. From its subtle windings and changes of level there arises a keen and continuous interest, that keeps the attention ever alert and cheerful. Every sensitive adjustment to the contour of the ground, every little dip and swerve, seems instinct with life and an exquisite sense of balance and beauty. The road rolls upon the easy slopes of the country, like a long ship in the hollows of the sea. . . . The

158

traveller is also aware of a sympathy of mood between himself and the road he travels. We have all seen ways that have wandered into heavy sand near the sea-coast, and trail wearily over the dunes like a trodden serpent : here we too must plod forward at a dull, laborious pace ; and so a sympathy is preserved between our frame of mind and the expression of the relaxed, heavy curves of the roadway. . . . Something that we have seen from miles back upon an eminence, is so long hid from us, as we wander through folded valleys or among woods, that our expectation of seeing it again is quickened into a violent appetite, and as we draw nearer we impatiently quicken our steps and turn every corner with a beating heart. It is through these prolongations of expectancy, this succession of one hope to another, that we live out long seasons of pleasure in a few hours' walk. It is in following these capricious sinuosities that we learn, only bit by bit, and through one coquettish reticence after another, much as we learn the heart of a friend, the whole loveliness of the country.'

The place which Travel has in his books is one of their most constant and essential features. Wherever he is, his thoughts are in some other place. At home, he wistfully dreams of the Antipodes ; in the Antipodes his heart is full of the exile's longing for home. All his romances are famous for their long sweeps of journey across Scotland or England, or over seas. The titles of many poems—*Songs of Travel, The Song of the Road, The Vagabond*, etc.—bear witness to this ; and one of the finest of his unfinished stories is entitled *The Great North Road*. Roadside inns are often introduced, and always with a peculiar gusto. It is true that the excessive indulgence in the delights of travel lends sometimes to his tales a globe-trotting and restless air, and threatens their artistic unity. He utilises the distances of the world almost unfairly. When the adventures slacken and the pace threatens to slow down he whisks you away to New York, or Fontainebleau, or Sydney. The change acts like a new stimulus upon the book, and the

159

tale at once leaps. In Prince Florizel we have travel gone
crazy. *The Wrecker* has scenes in San Francisco, Paris,
Midway Island, Honolulu, Edinburgh, Tai-o-hae, and
Fontainebleau; and no novel has nerves that can stand
that amount of change in five-and-twenty chapters. *The
Master of Ballantrae*, with all its power and its magnificent
insight, and its sustained and even growing interest, still is
broken-backed: the Scottish and American parts, from
the point of view of literary art, fall asunder. Yet any
such defects are amply compensated by the magnificent
stride—the sense of distance and movement—which the
constant travelling imparts to his work. *The Vagabond*
gives the note of this in swinging lines:

'Give to me the life I love,
  Let the lave go by me;
Give the jolly heaven above,
  And the byway nigh me. . . .
Let the blow fall soon or late,
  Let what will be o'er me;
Give the face of earth around,
  And the road before me.'

That note is sustained, and to read his books is to feel
an exhilaration like that of a swift walk through breezy
morning air. 'The valleys are but a stride to you; you
cast your shoe over the hill-tops; your ears and your heart
sing; in the words of an unverified quotation from the
Scotch psalms, you feel yourself fit "on the wings of all the
winds" to "come flying all abroad." Europe and your
mind are too narrow for that flood of energy.'

# CHAPTER X

### THE INSTINCT OF TRAVEL (*continued*)

JUST as the physical gift of vision passes over naturally and unconsciously into mental and spiritual insight, so does the physical urgency of travel pass into the inner life. There it appears as a courageous doctrine which he took with him throughout, and which largely determined his energetic dealing with all problems, the doctrine of *travel for travel's sake*. 'For my part, I travel not to go anywhere, but to go. I travel for travel's sake. The great affair is to move.' He moves accordingly—travels in the matter, as the suggestive old ecclesiastical phrase has it—under the prompting of 'that divine unrest, that old stinging trouble of humanity that makes all high achievements and all miserable failure.' One of his subtlest essays in analysis is *Will o' the Mill*, which, as we have seen, describes with marvellous insight the inner life of one who hesitates ever upon the brink of action, and who never steps forward either into travel or love. For his own part, he is otherwise minded. Love he regards as a voyage to the unknown and lovely country of a woman's soul, and afterwards a journey there (for there is the keeping in love as well as the falling in love) through the years towards the still unattained ideal. Similarly in all the other business of life, travel is the law: 'The artist who says *It will do* is on the downward path.' The true El Dorado is not ahead, but on the road—'to have many aspirations is to be spiritually rich.' In fine, 'to

L                                           161

travel hopefully is a better thing than to arrive, and the true success is to labour.'

In this doctrine there is involved a curious combination of 'an instinctive fascination by the future, and a rational distrust of it. He hears continually the call of the time to come, the *Song of the Morrow*; yet the mysterious fable to which he has given that title is heavy with sinister anticipation. Compare it with Montaigne's lightsome essay on *To-morrow's a New Day*—an essay with which Stevenson was doubtless familiar,—and you feel an ominous sense of the inevitable tragedy of life. In plain words, he asks, in the person of Florizel, 'Is there anything in life so disenchanting as attainment?' and declares success to be impossible for man upon this earth; we are not intended to succeed. Nothing is commoner in his letters than those touches for which every earnest worker loves him, in which he describes himself as pursuing an ideal which he can never quite reach; and with him the result is not the usual wailing confession of failure, but the acceptance of failure only to glorify it with a new and altogether healthful meaning. 'Our business in this world,' he tells us, 'is not to succeed, but to continue to fail, in good spirits.' When the end shall come he is content with this for his epitaph, 'Here lies one who meant well, tried a little, failed much,' and 'there goes another Faithful Failure!'

It is bold teaching, and in truth the doctrine is only a safe one for the strenuous. There are plenty of us who would willingly believe it, and in the strength of that belief accept the situation and consent to fail. For all such, a hopeless lapse to pessimism is the inevitable result, and they will find words of his to confirm it:

> 'On every hand the roads begin,
> And people walk with zeal therein;
> But wheresoe'er the highways tend,
> Be sure there's nothing at the end.'

162

Yet those who find pessimism in *A Christmas Sermon*, the essay which most carefully expounds the doctrine of failure, have read it to little purpose. For the strenuous there is no defeat, and Stevenson, with all his theory of failure, *never consents to fail.* He knows, like St. Paul, that at no future time shall he be able to boast that he has already attained, or is already perfect. Yet he turns back with undeadened enthusiasm to the gallant task of life in the present hour, and accepts the 'glory of going on,' for his never-failing and sufficient reward. 'God forbid it should be man that wearies in well-doing, that despairs of unrewarded effort, or utters the language of complaint. Let it be enough for faith, that the whole creation groans in mortal frailty, strives with unconquerable constancy: surely not all in vain.'

This view of life throws light upon Stevenson's sayings about immortality. His doctrine of travel for travel's sake, with its accompanying disparagement of success, goes with an extreme objection to the hope of reward as an incentive to labour. 'The soul of piety was killed long ago by that idea of reward' he affirms. 'Nor is happiness, whether eternal or temporal, the reward that mankind seeks. Happinesses are but his wayside campings; his soul is in the journey.' He hates working for money, he holds all racing 'as a creature of the devil,' and discounts even the desire for fame as the ruling motive of heroic deeds. Indeed even 'To ask to see some fruit of our endeavour is but a transcendental way of serving for reward.'

It would not be difficult to show that there is another side to this question. Life is a very complicated engagement, and among the many motives to noble deeds, that of reward plays no mean part. Since good conduct, and still more good character, is so very difficult to achieve, we cannot afford to discard any of its incentives; and it were

163

wiser to take our stand on the simple human ground of
Shakspeare's *Cymbeline* :

> 'Fear no more the heat of the sun,
>   Nor the furious winter's rages ;
> Thou thy worldly task hast done,
>   Home art gone, and ta'en thy wages.'

Yet those who are least inclined to agree with Stevenson
in his view of reward may still appreciate and admire the
spirit of which it is the outcome. It can do none of us
any harm to have our attention recalled at times from the
future to the present, and to be told emphatically that
energetic living is good enough in itself without a bribe.
As for immortality, while there are passages in which his
objection to serving for hire leads him to discount it, there
are many other passages in which it is presupposed and
accepted as that to which life leads on its travellers. His
general attitude to the whole question is summed up in
one memorable sentence of his *Memories and Portraits*, 'To
believe in immortality is one thing, but it is first needful
to believe in life.'

The first result of the Instinct of Travel with Stevenson
is seen in that demand for *immediacy* which was always so
imperative with him. In his novels the lapse of time is
hardly noticed. Few of his characters change very materially,
nor does age, in any one instance, really overtake the people
of his creation. The times given for the action in his four
plays are 48 hours; 10 hours; part of a day and night;
12 to 14 hours. This swiftness of thought and action is
unconsciously expressed in his insistence on compression
as the essential thing in writing, 'the note of a really
sovereign style.' He is always at his best when he feels
the jog of travel, not pausing long in passages of descriptive
information, but giving scenery and impressions in flashes,
as they appear to one moving swiftly. *Will o' the Mill* has

164

been several times alluded to. It is a great piece of work, such as is possible only to high genius. It is his deliberate attempt to live from within a character in which life runs slow. Its want of spontaneity shows how impossible the task was for him.

Immediacy is the word which perhaps better than any other summarises the practical side of Stevenson's character. The eagerness and forcefulness of his attack upon whatever thing it is that confronts him, is of the very essence of the man. He refused to deaden his vitality by a cautious calculation of consequences, remote or near. It was the moment that called him to its duty or its pleasure, and he rose at once to its summons. Of himself, as of St. Ives, it could be said that he had never chosen the cheap and easy—only that he had staked his life upon the most immediate. Nothing strikes fire from the flint more frequently in his books than this. When duty presents an immediate challenge, the situation flashes out into brilliance, and the very words seem to blaze. The captain in the Fable despises the man who would omit to wind up his watch upon a sinking ship. 'It is better,' we are told in *Aes Triplex*, 'to lose health like a spendthrift than to waste it like a miser. It is better to live and be done with it than to die daily in the sick-room. By all means begin your folio; even if the doctor does not give you a year, even if he hesitates about a month, make one brave push and see what can be accomplished in a week. It is not only in finished undertakings that we ought to honour useful labour. A spirit goes out of the man who means execution which outlives the most untimely ending. All who have meant good work with their whole hearts, have done good work, although they may die before they have the time to sign it. Every heart that has beat strong and cheerfully has left a hopeful impulse

165

behind it in the world, and bettered the tradition of mankind.' Nothing that Stevenson ever wrote came more
direct from his heart than that, unless perhaps it was this,
concerning Walt Whitman: 'He treats evil and sorrow
in a spirit almost as of welcome; as an old sea-dog
might have welcomed the sight of the enemy's topsails
off the Spanish Main. There, at least, he seems to say,
is something obvious to be done.'

It might be imagined that in his usage the principle of
immediacy has little to do with morality or religion,
and that what it has to do with them is mostly wrong.
He has a word of praise for impudent daring and instant
retaliation; he almost forces sympathy for Deacon Brodie,
who 'felt it great to be a bolder, craftier rogue than the
drowsy citizen'; he has something approaching admiration
for the tattooed white man of Ua-pu, who had so unhesitatingly obeyed his love for an island princess as to
submit to the torture of tattooing that he might have her
for his wife. Mr. Loudon Dodd commits himself to enter-
prises which on the large scale are mischievous, quieting
his conscience with the thought that he is doing it for
his poor friend Jim Pinkerton; 'this is a poor, private
morality, if you like,' he truly confesses, 'but it is mine,
and the best I have.' Yet in all such instances there is an
underlying quality which is good, and from which much
goodness springs. It is the quality which Browning im-
mortalises in *The Statue and the Bust*, and without which no
man may enter the heaven of 'the soldier saints who, row
on row, burn upward each to his point of bliss.' The
quality of immediacy has thus a certain claim to virtue in its
own right, dangerous and uncertain though its action may
often be. It at least saves a man from the tamer immor-
ality of accepting the universe without thinking about right
or wrong at all. It saves a man from the opposite
166

temptation, yielding to which 'the ingenious human mind, face to face with something it downright ought to do, *does something else.*' It never, even at its worst, approaches the level of those who give themselves solemnly to dissipation 'with a perverse seriousness, a systematic rationalism of wickedness that would have surprised the simpler sinners of old.' On the other hand, enlisted on the better side, it guides men to the right course in many a situation. 'He who temporises with his conscience is already lost,' he warns us; and a golden rule of his was, 'When you are ashamed to speak, speak up at once.' We see in Carthew, how the broken gentleman finds himself again when in the squad of navvies he is face to face with work that must be done instantly, with no time left for asking whether it were necessary. In Christian ethics there is ever a double duty. Christianity trains men's eyes upon the far-off ideal, and yet commands them to lay hold upon the nearest duty. Either, if alone, gives but faulty and imperfect result. Of Stevenson it certainly cannot be said that he neglected the long results of conduct; but in a time of many theories and much speculating by people who do not commit themselves to action, he has done a still higher service by calling attention in so clear a voice to what another has called 'the commanding immediacy of life.'

It was largely this delight in immediacy which developed in Stevenson his interest in war, and that soldier spirit which is so remarkable in him. True, he does not seem, at first sight, a likely type of military man. That weak body, which kept so many of his days in silence and inaction, might have seemed to close for him all chances of active service, and to turn him to quieter thoughts. Yet in this region he claimed his inheritance all the more imperiously because it seemed beyond his reach. The lifelong fight with illness and weakness of body became in his hands an

167

accepted campaign and warfare. In early childhood we find him girded with a little sword. When made to wear a shawl above the sword, he was distressed by the unsoldierly uniform, until a new interpretation comforted him—'Do you think it will look like a night-march?' That was exactly the problem of life for him—to translate the careful and darkened journey of the invalid into a night-march, the shawl into a martial cloak. The metaphor remained. When he is nearing forty he writes that the ill-health with which he has to struggle is 'an enemy who was exciting at first, but has now, by the iteration of his strokes, become merely annoying and inexpressibly irksome.' Still nearer the end he writes to Meredith: 'For fourteen years I have not had a day's real health. . . . I have written in bed, and written out of it, written in hemorrhages, written in sickness, written torn by coughing, written when my head swam for weakness; and for so long, it seems to me, I have won my wager and recovered my glove. . . . The battle goes on—ill or well, is a trifle; so as it goes. I was made for a contest, and the Powers have so willed that my battlefield should be this dingy, inglorious one of the bed and the physic bottle.'

His spirit of soldierhood was, however, by no means confined to any one campaign. His whole heart was in soldiering, and there are few of his romances in which he does not fight battles vicariously in the persons of his heroes. Those are always brilliant passages in which fighting is described. Sometimes, as we have already seen, they are gruesome and sanguinary, but always they are full of gusto, and the sheer delight in fighting for fighting's sake. His theory of the brave deeds of the English admirals is that they fought their actions because they had an inclination that way, and it is a theory which he counts true and wholesome.

168

# THE INSTINCT OF TRAVEL

Thus it came to pass that the whole of life to him wore a military aspect, and in that aspect we have both brilliance and immediacy at their keenest. Life, in his view of it, was 'an affair of cavalry'—'a thing to be dashingly used and cheerfully hazarded.' He lived, and cried aloud to us all to live, to the music of bugles, and on the point of instant engagement. It was in this sense that he welcomed 'the harsh voice of duty,' and watched for 'the bright face of danger.' In his one touch of actual warfare, when in Samoa he rode for the first time to a field where troops were gathered for battle, his spirits rose to a wild exhilaration—'War is a huge *entraînement*; there is no other temptation to be compared to it, not one. . . . We came home like schoolboys, with such a lightness of spirits, and I am sure such a brightness of eye, as you could have lit a candle at.'

As in the treatment of the general subject of immediacy, so in this particular phase of it, there may or there may not be any definite ethical quality. The disreputable Deacon Brodie asks, 'Shall I have it out and be done with it? . . . to carry bastion after bastion at the charge—there were the true safety after all!' There is nothing very lofty in that. But the immediacy of war has given him some passages than which nothing that he has done is more characteristic of his faith. The first is from *Our Lady of the Snows*:

'Forth from the casemate, on the plain
 Where honour has the world to gain,
 Pour forth, and bravely do your part,
 Oh knights of the unshielded heart!
 Forth and forever forward!—out
 From prudent turret and redoubt,
 And in the mellay charge amain,
 To fall but yet to rise again!
 Captive? ah, still, to honour bright,
 A captive soldier of the right!
 Or free and fighting, good with ill?
 Unconquering but unconquered still!'

169

The second, given only in the *Life*, is there entitled *Envoy to No. XXV. of Songs of Travel* ('God, if this were enough'):

> '*Wanted Volunteers*
> *To do their best for twoscore years!*
> A ready soldier, here I stand,
> Primed for thy command,
> With burnished sword.
> If this be faith, O Lord
> Help Thou mine unbelief
> And be my battle brief.'

Precious as the doctrine of immediacy is, it is yet the easier part of life to which it guides us. At the moment, there is always 'something obvious to be done.' To do that gallantly, so as to bring picturesqueness to the aid of action, is a great thing. But there is a greater thing still awaiting us in the longer and quieter tasks which demand patience as well as attack. It is not enough to start the journey with brilliant occasional rushes. We have yet to learn to live and labour strenuously and with hope. Thus the Instinct of Travel leads on to a further stretch of practical doctrine.

The great word for this as for the former travel-doctrine is Vitality. 'Everything's alive,' shouts Archie in *Weir of Hermiston*, 'thank God, everything's alive'; and Stevenson is with him there. In Michael Angelo's art, it is 'the latent life' that he admires, 'the coiled spring in the sleeping dog,' the marble that 'seems to wrinkle with a wild energy.' He prefers life to art, or even to ease and pleasure, and delights in poignant experience of any kind. He prefers, as one of the *Letters* has it, peril to annoyance, and fear to ill-humour. Even in revolt, so long as a man is a '*vital* sceptic' it is well; and indeed it was to this that he owed his own deliverance. Of all maladies he counts that of *not wanting* the worst; of all men he is the most pitiable

170

who is 'born disenchanted,' and for whom there seems not to be 'even one thing needful.' In *Aes Triplex* and *Crabbed Age and Youth* he protests against paralysing life and its present desires by brooding on the thought of death, or checking the energies of youth by too minute a preparation for the days of age. Let a man take the risk of living while he is at it; let him wade deep in the tide of life. Sooner or later age and death will have their way with him, meanwhile there is the glowing hour. 'By managing its own work, and following its own happy inspiration, youth is doing the best it can to endow the leisure of age. A full, busy youth is your only prelude to a self-contained and independent age; and the muff inevitably develops into the bore.' 'Every bit of brisk living, and above all if it be healthful, is just so much gained upon the wholesale filcher, death.' In this fashion does the image of life as a road on which it is man's business to travel from the cradle to the grave, lead to the dominating principle 'Live while you live.' It is, as he understands it, a very different maxim from that with which the fool encourages his heart to its destruction—'Let us eat and drink, for to-morrow we die.' For Stevenson life is far more than meat and drink:

> 'Since I am sworn to live my life
> And not to keep an easy heart,
> Some men may sit and drink apart,
> I bear a banner in the strife.'

'Vital, that's what I am at, first: wholly vital, with a buoyancy of life.'

The principle of 'living while we live' may be applied in either of two apparently opposite senses. It may be a plea for idleness or a plea for work. With Stevenson it was both. Just as it is only those who have travelled far that can appreciate the wayside rest upon a mossy bank, or the evening by the fireside of the inn, so he knew the delight of idleness as none know it who are not also strenuous. Yet it was not only for the pleasure of it, but as a real department of vitality, that he advocated idling. People who cannot idle miss something of the meaning of life. 'We are in such haste to be doing, to be writing, to be gathering gear, to make our voice audible a moment in the derisive silence of eternity, that we forget that one thing, of which these are but the parts—namely, to live.' To such persons 'something to do' has become the enemy of joy, business habits a menace to the soul, and hurry but a token of their lack of faith. 'Extreme *busyness*, whether at school or college, kirk or market, is a symptom of deficient vitality; and a faculty for idleness implies a catholic appetite and a strong sense of personal identity.' To imagine that the world demands unremitting labour, and that duty allows of no relaxations, is to take ourselves far too seriously. 'Atlas was just a gentleman with a protracted nightmare! And yet you see merchants who go and labour themselves into a great fortune and thence into the bankruptcy court; . . . and fine young men who work themselves into a decline, and are driven off in a hearse with white plumes upon it.'

The *Apology for Idlers*, from which some of the passages just quoted have been taken, goes further, and discourses with great insight and wisdom upon the positive virtues of idleness. The idler is a healthy-minded person. 'He has had time to take care of his health and his spirits; he has been a great deal in the open air, which is the most salutary of all things for both body and mind.' He has acquired a peculiar kind of wisdom, not elsewhere to be found. 'While others behold the East and West, the Devil and the Sunrise, he will be contentedly aware of a sort of morning hour upon all sublunary things, with an army of shadows running speedily and in many different directions into the great daylight of eternity. The shadows and the

172

generations, the shrill doctors and the plangent wars, go by into ultimate silence and emptiness; but underneath all this a man may see out of the Belvedere windows much green and peaceful landscape; many firelit parlours; good people laughing, drinking, and making love as they did before the Flood or the French Revolution; and the old shepherd telling his tale under the hawthorn.'

Yet the other way of living while you live was essentially his way. This, we take it, is what he means by saying that he was never 'very fond of (what is technically called) God's green earth.' If the choice were between work and idleness as that which gives its essential meaning to life, he would unquestionably have chosen work. No prayer seems to come more directly from his heart than this: 'Give us to go blithely on our business. Help us to play the man; help us to perform the petty round of irritating concerns and duties with laughter and kind faces; let cheerfulness abound with industry.' Any kind of labour was precious in his sight. In Vailima we see him toiling with equal eagerness in a dozen different directions, from politics to pig-rearing, and from bush-clearing to writing poetry. 'The tenacity of many ordinary people in ordinary pursuits is a sort of standing challenge to everybody else. If one man can grow absorbed in delving his garden, others may grow absorbed and happy over something else. Not to be upsides in this with any groom or gardener is to be very meanly organised. A man should be ashamed to take his food if he has not alchemy enough in his stomach to turn some of it into intense and enjoyable occupation.' In this spirit it is man's first duty to fight on until he dies; and the gallant fighter will die young, however old he be when death shall overtake him. 'Death has not been suffered to take so much as an illusion from his heart. In the hot-fit of life, a-tiptoe on the highest point of being, he

173

passes at a bound on to the other side. The noise of the mallet and chisel is scarcely quenched, the trumpets are hardly done blowing, when, trailing with him clouds of glory, this happy-starred, full-blooded spirit shoots into the spiritual land.'

A man's view of labour must be gathered chiefly from the manner in which he faces the chosen work of his life. In Stevenson's case we have copious materials for studying his methods of literary work and his feelings regarding it. On this he is more communicative than most writers; and his letters, especially the *Vailima Letters*, are full of references to the subject. He makes no pretence of underrating his diligence. Indeed, to vindicate it, he will even underrate his natural gifts. 'I frankly believe (thanks to my dire industry) I have done more with smaller gifts than almost any man of letters in the world.' 'The work I have been doing the last twelve months (1892), in one continuous spate, mostly with annoying interruptions and without any collapse to mention, would be incredible in Norway.'

First, there was the apprenticeship. Literature has to be a trade before it can become an art, the student working indefatigably at the mechanical technique of style before he thinks of matter and creation. Stevenson, full from the first of matter calling for expression, bowed his neck and set himself to learn the trade of writing. Furnished with two books, one to read and one to write in, he 'played sedulous ape' to an incredible number of authors, forcing himself to imitate their style, until he had caught the secret of each. It was a sure instinct that guided him to this, for no amount of reading will so impress a style upon one as even a little writing in imitation of it will do. But there are not many writers who have patience for such toil, and the result is a mastery of rhetoric which many will envy who

174

little dream that it is in large part the reward of long drudgery. While still an apprentice he tried again and again to get his work published, and had it refused. Even the *Essay on Roads* was returned. Back he went to penny note-books and drudgery once more, determined that if he had not yet learned to write, he would learn. 'Never mind,' says he in 1875, 'ten years hence I shall have learned, so help me God.'

Apprenticeship over, the labour was in no measure relaxed. There is an almost envious admiration in his verses to Doctor John Brown who, 'didnae fash himsel' to think':

> 'Ye stapped your pen into the ink,
> An' there was Rab!'

With Stevenson it was very different. *The Wrong Box* begins with a graphic account of the labours involved in writing a work of fiction, which after all will serve but to while away an hour for the reader in a railway train. Having attained to the mastery over style, there is still the matter which must be mastered afresh for each new book. 'Neither clearness, compression, nor beauty of language come to any living creature till after a busy and prolonged acquaintance with the subject.' Even in fiction he cannot make another end to a story, however distasteful the natural end may turn out to be. 'That's not the way I write; the whole tale is implied; I never use an effect, when I can help it, unless it prepares the effects that are to follow; that's what a story consists in. To make another end, that is to make the beginning all wrong.' So much for his literary conscience concerning the matter of his work. But his troubles with style were not over when he had learned the art. There are times when he 'breaks down at every paragraph,' and has to 'wring one sentence out after another.' Few things, even in the *Vailima Letters*, are more pathetic than this: 'I must own that I have

175

overworked bitterly—overworked—there, that's legible.
My hand is a thing that was, and in the meantime so are
my brains.' His work discourages and disgusts him. He
took a month to two chapters of *In the South Seas*; twenty-
one days to twenty-four pages of *The Ebb Tide*; four days
to his preface to *An Inland Voyage*. He rewrote some
passages of his work four times over: he burned the entire
first draft of *Dr. Jekyll and Mr. Hyde*, lest it should tempt
him, when a criticism by his wife had revealed a fundamental flaw in it. The Parable of the Talents was a
favourite Scripture with him, and all this was what he
understood that parable to mean.

'Of making books there is no end,' Stevenson quotes from
the ancient; and he puts the passage in a new light by
adding that the preacher 'did not perceive how highly he
was praising letters as an occupation.' Certainly he himself
had abundant opportunity of testing his loyalty to the profession for which he had risked everything. When those
trials were over which beset the entrance of all aspirants in
literature, writing became one of the chief joys of his existence. It is true that during the last months we have an
undertone of melancholy, and occasional acute fits of despond-
ency; but that was when the breaking strain was on him, and
even then they are not the characteristic mood. Previously,
for many years, there had been growing a record of work
done under difficulties which it would be hard to parallel in
any literary biography. His health compelled him to travel,
and no one who has not had experience of it knows the
dead lift that writing comes to be when the mind is distracted and the body disturbed by strange surroundings and
constant change. Yet he worked on steadily, and every sort
of uncouth place served him for a study. The fight against
ill-health has been already described to us by himself[1] in

[1] Page 168.

words modelled upon those of St. Paul when he tells the story of his past conflicts. As blow after blow descends, we watch anxiously, expecting to see him succumb and cease to strive. But after each he rises, fighting against still more impossible odds, with undiminished valour, and with ever finer skill. When a temporary illness lays him on his back, he writes in bed one of his most careful and thoughtful papers, the discourse on *The Technical Elements in Style*. When ophthalmia confines him to a darkened room, he writes by the diminished light. When, after hemorrhage, his right hand has to be held in a sling, he writes some of his *Child's Garden* with his left hand. When the hemorrhage has been so bad that he dare not speak, he dictates a novel in the deaf-and-dumb alphabet. The final touch is added when we find that at the age of thirty-nine, scrivener's cramp came upon him in addition to all the rest, and forced him to write by proxy, utilising the devoted and unfailing help of his step-daughter, Mrs. Strong. After all this we must allow his claim to have 'done perhaps as much work as anybody else under the most deplorable conditions.' Scott himself, after the crash, has not left behind him a more inspiring example of indomitable strength of purpose. The two men stand together and they stand almost alone, as types of that splendid ignorance of the meaning of defeat on which British men most pride themselves. Each new assault of outrageous fortune they understand only as a challenge, never as a doom. Destiny has ceased to be an external force for them. They lay hands upon their doom and hold it prisoner to their will within, while they push forward in travel every step of which is heroic. In such circumstances the journey has become a forced march through a dangerous and distressful land. But they drive on undiscouraged, with an unconquerable energy which shows the instinct of travel at its bravest.

M        177

The principal expositions of his gospel of work are to be found in *Lay Morals*, and the *Addresses* to the Polynesian students and chiefs. In the first of these he expounds his favourite doctrine that the negative virtues are as nothing in comparison with the positive. 'Acts may be forgiven,' he used to say, 'not even God himself can forgive the hanger-back.' He did not admire the virtue of those who merely stood still and refrained from evil. 'We are content,' he says, 'to avoid the inconvenient wrong and to forgo the inconvenient right with almost equal self-approval, until at last we make a home for our conscience among the negative virtues and the cowardly vices.' It is when protesting against this that he gives us his boldest moral teaching, and at the same time comes into close and conscious unison with Jesus Christ. It was perhaps for this that Christ meant most to him; and it may even be said that it was by this that Christ saved him. For it was on this doctrine that Christ spoke many of His most strenuous and most heroic words— words which never failed to appeal to Stevenson. If he missed Christ as poet, he certainly found Him as hero, and in no part of his work does he so frequently lay claim to his share in Christ as in this. He refuses to be 'magnetised by the ten commandments,' but he does not mean by that anything of the decadent sort. On the contrary, he disparages them rather because they are not sufficiently drastic. He hardly admits that class of virtues to be virtues at all, nor does he 'care a straw for all the *nots*.' 'We are not damned for doing wrong, but for not doing right; Christ would never hear of negative morality; *thou shalt* was ever his word, with which he superseded *thou shalt not*.' So he tells us in his *Christmas Sermon*, and goes on to dwell at length on the dangers of defiling our imagination, and introducing into our judgments of sinners a secret element of gusto, when we make our thoughts on morality centre in forbidden acts.

Quoting Christ elsewhere he writes, '"Thou shalt not" is but an example; "thou shalt ' is the law of God.' 'The sins of omission are in my view the only serious ones; I call it my view, but it cannot have escaped you that it was also Christ's.' 'A kind of black, angry look goes with that statement of the law of negatives. "To love one's neighbour as oneself" is certainly much harder, but states life so much more actively, gladly and kindly, that you can begin to see some pleasure in it; and till you can see pleasure in these hard choices and bitter necessities, where is there any good news to men? It is much more important to do right than not to do wrong; further, the one is possible, the other has always been and will always be impossible; and the faithful *design to do right* is accepted by God; that seems to me to be the Gospel, and that was how Christ delivered us from the Law. . . . It is your business, (1) to find out what is right in any given case, and (2) to try to do it; if you fail in the last, that is by commission, Christ tells you to hope; if you fail in the first, that is by omission, his picture of the last day gives you but a black outlook.'

That is the moral aspect of Stevenson's gospel of work. To him, as to Thomas Carlyle, it was a gospel indeed; and while Carlyle's labour was generally a severe and sombre ideal, Stevenson's was for the most part a source of gladness and uplifting. It is true that one of the most perfect pieces of portraiture he has given us is that of Weir of Hermiston —'On he went up the great bare staircase of his duty, un-cheered and undepressed.' But that is by no means all he has to say upon the subject. A story is told by his grandfather in *A Family of Engineers*, which might stand as a parable of the grandson's faith. On a foggy day, a ship, laden with stones for the Bell Rock Lighthouse, was steering straight upon the rock, and would inevitably have been destroyed, when the sailors heard the sound of the smith's hammer and anvil right ahead, and in the nick of time put the helm about and saved her. In like manner did work save Stevenson's ship of life, and it saved his faith as well. Faith ever came to him essentially as faithfulness. Like James the Apostle, he found his faith better expressed in works than in theories. To exercise his powers to the full, to live at the utmost stretch and tension for such right ends of living as were clear to him, that was his way of approaching religion. Vitality and whole - heartedness in one's attack upon the practical problem of life—so far he could always see plainly.

But to see plainly so far is to be on the way to see more. To the end of time the great words remain true: *If any man willeth to do His will, he shall know of the doctrine.* There is no hope of a man's finding a faith that will satisfy him until he is prepared to do the nearest duty that he knows. There are some who seem to think that faith in God is a special faculty, wholly disconnected from the rest of life, so that a man may be a good student, or an able merchant, or an intelligent craftsman, and yet lack the power to be a religious man. It is even supposed that one may be faithful in morals and may succeed in obeying the demands of conscience, while still he is doomed to spiritual ineffectiveness and darkness. Nothing could be more untrue to facts. There is no such thing as a religious faculty which men highly gifted in other departments of life may wholly lack. The religious faculty is identical with the faculty for study or for any other kind of work. If a man have proved that he can succeed in any of them, he may take it for certain that he can, if he will, succeed in the religious life also. His capacity for success in religion is but the application of his ordinary human powers to another set of facts. He who has it in him efficiently to serve his employers, or his conscience—or for that matter the devil—

has it in him also to serve God. No man who does his daily work strenuously and effectively as Stevenson did his, is debarred from a strenuous and effective religious life. We may go further, and say that he who does his daily work in that fashion is already serving God. He may indeed be unconscious of the fact, but if he remain faithful, and if no perverse theory of life be allowed to warp his conscience and dim his spiritual vision, he shall sooner or later discover the higher service. Of Stevenson this was magnificently true. Taking for his rule of life the Parable of the Talents, he could not but be aware of a Lord who had committed them to his charge. It was not his part to speculate about God, but to obey Him—to think and act so that He would approve. Thus, behind the energies of his life there was the consciousness of the unseen Master of life; behind his faithfulness there was faith. It is true that none of God's servants always realises the presence of the Master. To all of them, too often, He is as a man journeying in a far country. But the realisation of God near and not far off is ever possible; and the test of faithfulness, in the religious sense, is the constancy and vividness of that realisation. Stevenson certainly wrought out his life-work under a high and solemn sense of the great Taskmaster's eye. Often he realised it so keenly as to enter into that divine fellowship of labour in which a man can say *my Father worketh hitherto and I work*. It is this that he expresses in the song which is at once the most bracing and the most religious of all his utterances:

> 'O to be up and doing, O
> Unfearing and unshamed to go
> In all the uproar and the press
> About my human business ! . . .
> For still the Lord is Lord of might ;
> In deeds, in deeds he takes delight ;
> The plough, the spear, the laden barks,
> The field, the founded city, marks ;

181

# THE FAITH OF R. L. STEVENSON

He marks the smiler of the streets,
The singer upon garden seats ;
He sees the climber in the rocks :
To him, the shepherd folds his flocks . . .
Those he approves that ply the trade,
That rock the child, that wed the maid,
That with weak virtues, weaker hands,
Sow gladness on the peopled lands,
And still with laughter, song and shout,
Spin the great wheel of earth about.'

About such an Instinct of Travel, and its consequent
association with wandering vagabonds and gipsies, ordinary
folk who bide at home at ease are likely to feel a certain
sense of homelessness, both in regard to its physical and its
moral aspects.   It is very breezy and healthful, but there is
a bleakness about the open air if there be no fireside to
return to at nightfall.   We may admit that 'to travel hopefully is a better thing than to arrive'; and yet, if there never
is any arriving, it grows difficult to travel hopefully.   Must
we then consider this spirit of wandering as part of an
unhomely and fantastic strain in his nature, which so far
keeps him aloof from us ?   To some extent it is true that
he professes no desire to arrive, and cherishes no thoughts
beyond travelling for travel's sake.   In his intellectual
point of view this is entirely the case.   To try to pin him
down to any closed and final theory of life would be to
show oneself incompetent to write a line about him.   In his
thinking he is always aware of a further place to which the
road is leading, and he plainly leaves himself open for
advance.   The theories he may express are but the wayside
inns where he tarries till he must start again on new
adventures.   This is why it is so impossible to allocate for
him a defined and classified place among the doctrines.   He
is essentially a traveller, and our conception of his faith is
that of one upon whom the Spirit of the Lord has come

182

while he presses forward, and who travels as one of the company of the sons of God.

Yet there is another side to his character, in virtue of which he feels the discomfort of the open, and longs for the warmth and kindliness of the chimney-corner. In many passages of great tenderness this sentiment of home appears, even in connection with physical travel. At the close of the voyage he too grows weary of dipping the paddle, and ready for home. 'You may paddle all day long; but it is when you come back at nightfall, and look in at the familiar room, that you find love or death awaiting you beside the stove; and the most beautiful adventures are not those we go to seek.' How passionately the longing could possess him, is familiar to all those who have read the thoughts of home from abroad in *Songs of Travel* and *Vailima Letters*. In a deeper sense, as it concerned the inward life, the same thing is true. Apparently an unresting traveller in the spiritual country, he yet had come to rest upon certain great convictions, in which his spirit had its home. These he expresses often with an evident sense of relief and the comfortable peace of assurance. In the longest journey of all, the lifelong journey, the same shadowy but hospitable and firelit sweetness awaits its close. The Covenanters pass the dark river amid a 'storm of harsh and fiercely jubilant noises' which add a tenfold peacefulness to the shores which they had reached. For himself, who does not know the *Requiem* which, written seven years before his death, was inscribed upon his tombstone at the last:

'Under the wide and starry sky,
Dig the grave and let me lie.
Glad did I live and gladly die,
And I laid me down with a will.

# THE FAITH OF R. L. STEVENSON

This be the verse you grave for me ;
*Here he lies where he longed to be ;*
*Home is the sailor, home from sea,*
*And the hunter home from the hill.'*

Such words imply more than they express ; perhaps they
mean more than the speaker knows. In them we hear
echoes of a great voice that calls home the thinker to faith,
the struggler to achievement, and the dead from dying to a
new life. And so there is arrival as well as travel, after
all. Indeed the two are combined in regard to faith, and
achievement, and that dimly seen but beautiful country
beyond the grave. In all these, the true life is at once
making for a land that is very far off, and yet at the same
time it is ever coming home.

184

# CHAPTER XI

## SYMPATHY AND APPRECIATION

WE have endeavoured to depict a personality whose fundamental faculties were vision and travel, and to show how
these expressed themselves in life, both physical and
spiritual. The task which now remains for us is that of
following the same faculties up into the ideals which chiefly
guided and ruled his character. How did they define for
him the chief duties of man? What was the message
which he proclaimed to the world by his teaching and his
life? In a word, what did life essentially mean to him,
as vision and travel wrought out its meaning?

First of all, as it concerned others, the meaning of life,
and the message he learned and delivered, may be summed
up as sympathy and appreciation. We have seen how
strongly the spectacle of the world appealed to him. Life,
at his command, becomes pageantry at times, and the figures
of history or of experience march past our wondering eyes
at the bidding of a consummate master of spectacle. We
have noted also the geographical sense, which feels the
width of the world, delights in sky-room and sea-room, and
the broad stretch of the peopled lands; and which keeps
him in every place aware of his relation to all other places.
Every one must have noted those frequently recurring
catalogues in which he brings together things and persons
apparently unrelated. Now it is 'Books, and my food, and

summer rain'; again 'the State, the Churches, peopled empires, war and the rumours of war, and the voices of the Arts.' On the world's great floor we see with one sweep of the eye troops swaying hither and thither in battle, astronomers finding new stars, actors performing in lighted theatres, and people being carried to hospitals on stretchers. In one of his prayers he contrasts the handful of men on the island with the myriads of trees and the teeming fishes, and prays that we may understand the lesson of the trees and the meaning of the fishes: 'Let us see ourselves for what we are, one out of the countless number of the clans of Thy handiwork. When we would despair, let us remember that these also please and serve Thee.' Thus does he move about the crowded world, 'catholic as none but the entirely idle can be catholic,' yet busy with all the interests of which his versatile nature is capable: sitting loose for any wind to play upon, yet always ready to devote his whole soul to the pursuit which has chanced to take his fancy.

This catholicity was due first of all to the many-sidedness of his own nature. It was not merely that he was tolerant of many different phases of life, and hospitable to all sorts and conditions of interests, whether of occupation or of companionship. He was himself alive at so many points, that each new appeal to his interest awoke a whole-hearted response. To travel about in the world was to pass through a constant succession of congenial experiences, and to discover that there was hardly anything between north and south which was really alien to him. He had little patience with the cramping and narrowing devotion to any specialism, whether in science or in nationality. He cherished no reverence for the man who is above all others 'in the classification of toad-stools, or Carthaginian history'; and in the *South Seas* he repudiated the narrowness of British prejudices, and gloried in the fact that his brotherhood with

186

the natives had given him the right to pronounce himself a man of two civilisations. It is no idle curiosity, but the extraordinary richness of his nature, which gives such world-wide range to his interests, and such intensity to each as it possesses him for the time being. As a youth, he writes as if he were an aged man; in middle age he expresses the heart of a little child. Braxfield the man of iron, and Prince Otto the man of shadows, claim an equal share in his appreciation.

Catholicity is confessedly a dangerous principle in morals. Those whose wide sympathies send them voyaging on many seas need an unusually clear judgment to steer their vessel past rocks. Stevenson's sanity and soundness are nowhere more remarkable than in this. His catholic habit of mind enables him to detect the one-sidedness of much popular morality. He understands the error of those who denounce any excess of natural appetite, but have a quite different standard 'for all displays of the truly diabolic—envy, malice, the mean lie, the mean silence, the calumnious truth, the backbiter, the petty tyrant, the peevish poisoner of family life.' This he has undoubtedly learned of Christ, in whose treatment of moral questions there is a standing protest against just that one-sidedness in moral judgment, a protest which Christendom has not yet laid to heart. He perceives, too, the relativity of morals, although he does not allow that perception to blind him to the seriousness of the issues involved. 'There is no quite good book without a good morality,' he says regarding D'Artagnan, 'but the world is wide, and so are morals. . . . Of two readers, one shall have been pained by the morality of a religious memoir, one by that of the Vicomte de Bragelonne. And the point is that neither need be wrong. We always shock each other, both in life and art.' He is equally alive to the change and development in moral ideals which goes

187

on with the passing of time. Every student of history knows how true this is of successive periods, one age having strenuousness for its ideal virtue to the disparagement of compassion; another, kindliness to the neglect of purity. In the individual life it is the same: 'What was the best yesterday, is it still the best in this changed theatre of a to-morrow? Will your own past truly guide you in your own violent and unexpected future?' This variableness of conscience in its view of moral values appears most clearly in the unceasing rivalry of Greek and Hebrew ideals—the humane and gracious, as against the severe and ascetic. The attraction of one or other of these depends upon the point of view of the age or individual; and the point of view is determined by a thousand details of heredity, education, society, and circumstances. The bigot takes none of these into account in his harsh and damnatory judgment; the moral trifler pronounces one way as good as another, and loses all sense of reality in moral distinctions. From the former danger Stevenson was saved by his catholicity, from the latter by his moral earnestness. He sets himself against the injustice of sweeping condemnations by those who see only one side of the question and make no allowance; but he insists upon the reality of right and wrong in a man's obedience or disobedience to the light he has. Above all he falls back upon certain general principles, which remain for our guidance through all perplexities and dilemmas—chiefly the spirit of magnanimity and the spirit of harmony. It can never be wrong in any circumstances, he would have us believe, to choose the greater instead of the meaner course; and if we find ourselves able to look beyond the immediate demand for action in the moment, let it not be to reward that we turn our eyes, but rather to the relation of the proposed action to the general purpose and balanced harmony of the life.

## SYMPATHY AND APPRECIATION

In religion, catholic sentiments are receiving a wider and more sympathetic audience to-day than the conditions of the past allowed. It is to be hoped, that as the smoke of battle clears away, many of the soldiers may find that their supposed enemies are but other regiments in one great army, and that the difference between them is rather one of uniform than of loyalty. So Stevenson most heartily believed. In the tenderness of *A Lowden Sabbath Morn* there is a wide catholicity. The tears are not far away while he writes of the bell swinging in the steeple, that calls the scattered family to their meeting among the graves of the churchyard, and

> 'Just a wee thing nearer brings
>   The quick an' deid.'

There is a great love for them all—the weary ploughman 'perplext wi' leisure'; the serious-faced congregation, with their peppermints and southernwood, 'fisslin' for the text'; the 'auld precentor hoastin' sair'; ay, and the 'minister himsel'.' Yet he cannot resist the chance of saying his say about the sermon :

> 'Wi' sappy unction, how he burkes
> The hopes o' men that trust in works,
> Expounds the fau'ts o' ither kirks,
>   An' shaws the best o' them
> No muckle better than mere Turks,
>   When a 's confessed o' them.
>
> Be thankit ! what a bonny creed !
> What mair would ony Christian need ?—
> The braw words rumm'le ower his heid,
>   Nor steer the sleeper ;
> And in their restin' graves, the deid
>   Sleep aye the deeper.'

It is the same in France. When the parish priest would have converted him to the Roman faith, he defended himself

189

with the plea that they were all drawing near by different sides to the same Friend and Father. 'That, as it seems to lay-spirits, would be the only gospel worthy of the name. But different men think differently.' The most interesting and the finest of all such pleas is told in the story of his meeting with a Plymouth Brother in the Cevennes :—

'A step or two farther I was overtaken by an old man in a brown nightcap, clear-eyed, weather-beaten, with a faint excited smile. A little girl followed him, driving two sheep and a goat; but she kept in our wake, while the old man walked beside me and talked about the morning and the valley. It was not much past six; and for healthy people who have slept enough, that is an hour of expansion and of open and trustful talk.

'"*Connaissez-vous le Seigneur ?*" he said at length.

'I asked him what Seigneur he meant; but he only repeated the question with more emphasis and a look in his eyes denoting hope and interest.

'"Ah," said I, pointing upwards, "I understand you now. Yes, I know Him; He is the best of acquaintances."

'The old man said he was delighted. "Hold," he added, striking his bosom; "it makes me happy here." There were a few who knew the Lord in these valleys, he went on to tell me; not many, but a few. "Many are called," he quoted, "and few chosen."

'"My father," said I, "it is not easy to say who know the Lord; and it is none of our business. Protestants and Catholics, and even those who worship stones, may know Him and be known by Him; for He has made all."'

The last sentence reminds us of the great reception-hall of his Samoan house. There a broad staircase led up from the centre of the hall to the upper floor, and on either side of it, by the great posts which sprang from the bottom steps to the roof, sat two Burmese idols, their hands folded as in prayer. It was there that the family prayers were conducted, and the thought of these Asiatic deities of former days watching the prayers of the islanders, who had but yesterday turned from their own idolatries to the worship of Christ, is curiously symbolic. Stevenson had indeed 'a great and cool allowance for all sorts of people and opinions.' In this, as in many other matters, he has sometimes used unguarded and absolute expressions from which something must be deducted. Yet when he speaks of a deeper and essential unity beneath the surface differences in the opinions of honest men, he utters a profound and most precious truth. If in the present age there be one thing which becomes daily more evident than any other, it is that earnest thinkers who have counted themselves far apart from each other in the past, are really very near at hand; they often speak words that seem to differ, while essentially they mean the same thing.

Interested in all the aspects of life, and catholic in his temper while judging them, it was to be expected that he should set peculiar value on the virtue of fairness in judgment. He confesses that he has never found it easy to be just, and it is a confession which every earnest man must make. Almost anything is, in fact, easier. Severity on the one hand appearing in the guise of faithfulness to conviction, lax indifference on the other under the name of good-nature, tempt us all from the straight path. Stevenson delightedly recalls Montaigne's famous question, 'Shall we not dare to say of a thief that he has a handsome leg?' But he knows how difficult many conscientious persons will find it to admit even that. Few passages that he ever wrote are stronger or more far-seeing than Chapter IV. of *Weir of Hermiston*, in which this difficulty is most finely expressed. Archie is in miserable rebellion against the brutality of his father's character. Glenalmond, that rare and delicate spirit, replies: 'We say we sometimes find him *coarse*, but I suspect he might retort that he finds us always dull ... and I sometimes wonder whether you and I—who are a

191

pair of sentimentalists—are quite good judges of plain men.'
The great difficulty is in detachment. We are, to begin
with, identified with one party-to the transaction. He tells
an amusing story of his grandmother which illustrates
our point. A pious crony of hers had fallen from an
outside stair, and Mrs. Stevenson recognised a special
providence in the circumstance that a baker had been
passing underneath with his bread upon his head. The
grandfather's remark was that he would like to know what
kind of providence the baker thought it. That was ever
Stevenson's point of view—to ask how a matter looked when
detached from the special preconceptions of one side; how,
in short, it looked to the baker.

The most familiar example of this fairness in judgment is
afforded us by his views of the Samoan natives and of the
white men who dealt with them. It is not pity for them
that he chiefly feels or pleads for, but only just judgment.
He regards them as perfectly competent to stand their trial
by any fair-minded man, and for the last four years of his
life-time he proclaimed this unceasingly. He insisted on
'the vast amount of moral force reservoired in every race,'
and entreated all white men to study and encourage that in
natives. This was no mere opinion accepted without
investigation to buttress an adopted theory. It was the
result of minute and interested observation of a race which
he loved ever better as he knew it more intimately. Nothing is more striking than his methods of pursuing savage
psychology—a science which he vigorously champions. He
drew out native tales by the bait of Scottish ones which he
told the Samoans; for in truth the parallel is often close,
and the one great secret of his success with the natives and
of his interest in them is simply this, that he found them so
remarkably like our Scottish selves. It is almost amusing
to note how all his South Sea work is written on the defen-

sive, and with what evident enjoyment he turns the edge of criticism by reminding Europeans that they are as bad or worse than the Polynesians. The Islanders' devil-work, their *tapu*, and a good many other ways of theirs, have counterparts near home. Their honour and their simple goodness are sometimes held up as models for the whites. It is the same in his treatment of Europeans. Whatever may be said of his furious defence of Father Damien, this at least is certain, that it was prompted by a burning desire to right the memory of one whom he believed to have been grossly slandered. He refused to receive any emolument for it, since it was a personal attack, and his share of the profits was sent direct from the publisher to the funds of the leper settlement. The *Footnote to History* is a still greater instance. In it he sacrificed not money, but what was more precious to him, literary effect and careful expression. He wrote it not as literature but as a plain appeal for justice to an ill-governed people. In the course of it he had to say many hard things about European officials in Samoa, but the book is a standing monument of fairness. Personal bitterness is singularly absent. He observes with rare fidelity the rule of separating the points in dispute from the rest of his relations with those concerned. Some of them had been, and remained, his personal friends through all the contest. The Chief-Justice, for instance, he likes, and even loves—'No, sir, I can't dislike him; but if I can't make hay of him it shall not be for want of trying.' Altogether the *Footnote* is a singularly good and great book. Where wrong was being done to the native race, he risked everything that he might right it. Yet he did so without any touch of spite or any slightest indulgence in the meaner passions of controversy. It does not surprise us when he asserts that it had proved 'a means of grace' to him; for indeed it is the Christian way of writing history.

The secret which underlies all fairness of judgment and true sympathy and appreciation, is that of putting oneself in the place of others, and appropriating the situation so as to conceive it from within and not from without. He pleads for this in the instance of the Samoans, and characteristically adds, 'It is the proof of not being a barbarian, to be able to enter into something outside of oneself, something that does not touch one's next neighbour in the city omnibus.' He lays it down as an essential duty of the poet, that he shall be able to enter into the minds of others, and express for them ideals which are already there, though unexpressed. In all this we see how far removed his view of his fellow-men is from a cold and dispassionate study of human nature. All his keen powers of psychological and moral insight, and his immense energy of imagination, are bent on the task of estimating justly the acts and motives of the lives around him.

For this his writing gave him a wide and open field, and it is because of his extraordinary power of putting himself in the place of others that the characters are so natural and the situations so impressive. He felt the mortification of men doomed to bear grotesque names, as if he himself had been called Pym or Habakkuk. He writhed in impossible moral and social situations, in the person of the wife of Durrisdeer and Archie Weir. He thought of the lives of those who crossed his path, whether they were civilised or savage, as if he had to live them himself, and traced out their inner experience and outward adventure with a personal anxiety and excitement. It is probable that there is in the language no finer piece of sympathetic interpretation of another's life than his essay on *Nurses*, whose insight had been quickened by much love and gratitude. You feel there the affection for successive children twining itself round a woman's tender heart, only to be broken off, when the friend becomes again

194

the servant, until in the end 'the neighbours may hear her sobbing to herself in the dark, with the fire burnt out for want of fuel, and the candle still unlit upon the table.' Even the most alien departments of life tempt him to enter that he may understand and sympathise. He knows how it must feel to be overwhelmed and rendered useless by the very greatness of a sudden opportunity, and he understands the heart of him who has been made a coward from his mother's womb. He has thought of the homelessness of many great people whose wealth and social position deprive them of some more precious gifts; he has realised how one-sided an affair gentlemanliness looks to the outsider who would fain be and be accepted as a gentleman. Bigotry of any kind is an abomination to him, yet he has been able to enter into the soul of Du Chayla as well as that of Pierre Séguier. He has shown us the facts of human conscience and heart that are ignored in some popular ideas of the iniquitous South Sea trader, and he has been at great pains to point out the many and perplexing moral difficulties of his situation. The interview between the trader Wiltshire and the missionary Tarleton in *The Beach of Falesá* is a notable instance of fair-minded valuation of men and gentlemen. The cold-blooded conduct of the wreckers on the Shetland Islands he has traced to its source, not in wickedness so much as in the sense of isolation, and apathy to the concerns of others, which is characteristic of feeble races. Even for cannibals he has a word to say, when they are judged, as they ought to be, by savage and not by civilised standards. In all such cases as these, he who would judge fairly, and therefore truly, must remember the surroundings in which the man is placed, and the standards to which he has been educated. 'Not the nature, but the congruity of men's deeds and circumstances damn and save them.'

The same principles apply to more ordinary and familiar

195

questions. With his sense of the difficulty of moral problems we shall deal by-and-by : meanwhile their complexity
demands a moment's notice. From several points of view
this fact appealed to Stevenson. It tempted his curiosity as
a puzzle, and his sense of the picturesque as a vivid piece of
moral spectacle. It also called forth his sympathetic insight
into the evident bewilderment of many lives around him.
Some of them are perplexed by the fact that 'there are
many kinds of good'; honour, generosity, truth, gentleness,
appearing as equally imperative aspects of duty, and confusing
the mind with their rival claims. Others are so overstrung
by the excitement of critical moments that they have lost
all sense of the proportion of things. Some who have
formulated general principles for action, but never related
these into any kind of a system of conduct, are running to
and fro distracted among their own ideals. Many are in-
adequately equipped in respect of conscience, having
consciences void of all refinement in good or evil; or being
unable to keep a whole conscience except by winking now
and then; or finding conscience perversely scrupulous
about trifles, while it perceives no evil in serious faults
until, when it is too late, it turns and rends the sinner.
The plain lesson of all this is that of charitable judgment,
and it is a good lesson, though not without its danger.
He who applies it to his own morality may find it lead
him far astray. Accordingly Stevenson reminds us many
times that 'it is the business of this life to make excuses
for others, but none for ourselves.'

His appreciation of others is that of a great and generous
spirit. He is well aware that every one has good and evil
in his nature, but his confident belief is that it is the part
of all who judge to dwell rather on the good than on the
evil. Whatsoever things are lovely and of good report, he
will think by preference on these things. Accordingly we

find that his bitterest invectives are reserved for those who
have been harsh judges of their neighbours.   It is this
character that he satirises in *A Portrait*, where the slanderer
speaks in the guise of an ape, swinging by his irreverent tail
all over the most holy places of human life.

> ' I am "the smiler with the knife,"
> The battener upon garbage, I—
> Dear heaven, with such a rancid life,
> Were it not better far to die ? '

He hates those who ' have an eye for faults and failures,
who take a pleasure to find and publish them, and who
forget the overveiling virtues and the real success.'   He
condemns the satirist, who ' has learned the first lesson,
that no man is wholly good ; but he has not even suspected
that there is another equally true, to wit, that no man is
wholly bad. . . . He does not want light, because the darkness is more pleasant.   He does not wish to see the good,
because he is happier without it.'   The temptation of the
satirist is to be amusing at the expense of others, but
Fleeming Jenkin taught Stevenson that Christ would not
have counselled that.   Without further question Stevenson
accepted the lesson and broadened it into the sweeping
statement that ' There is no more sure sign of a shallow
mind than the habit of seeing always the ludicrous side of
things.'   In one who had at his command such powers of
wit, and such a literary gift for its expression, this sentiment involves much self-denial : but the biographer of his
Edinburgh Days has told us that he seldom spoke unkindly
of any one, and that if others did so in his presence he at
once became the champion of those attacked.   He resents
Thoreau's saying that we are always disappointed in our
friends, and replies that ' We are ninety-nine times disappointed in our beggarly selves for once that we are

197

disappointed in our friend.' Of his own early essays he asserts—unnecessarily as it appears to some—that he had been too grudging of praise.

Thus Stevenson systematically turns from the evil to the good side of men and things, except where the purpose of his work demands another course. He knows well that all dealings between man and man must proceed upon the understanding that certain differences are to be first recognised and then ignored in favour of the points which they have in common. His canon for the study of great periods of literature and history is, ' Be sure you do not understand when you dislike them; condemnation is non-comprehension.' More and more he turns from the business of the runner-down to that of the crier-up. The former has the easier thing to do, but a strong man scorns to do it, and ' the Abstract Bagman will grow like an Admiral at heart, not by ungrateful carping, but in a heat of admiration.' This was no theoretical principle with him, but a real part of himself, most intimate and living. He frankly enjoyed being appreciated, and he paid back the debt most lavishly in his appreciation of others. His principle is that men are generally better than they appear to be, better than their manners, or the words they utter, or even the deeds they do. He delights in competence wherever it is found, and even in the dark pages of the *Master of Ballantrae*, some of the strongest and most congenial work is their portrayal of sheer ability. He believes enthusiastically in man in general, and many individual men in particular. He knows the greatness of the Mighty Dead, and he knows the worth and goodness of the living. His letters to his parents and to his old nurse, his thoughts and memories of absent friends, and his dealings with the people immediately about him, form an extraordinary series of studies in appreciation. His references to contemporary and rising authors are not only marked by a rare generosity, but a positive delight in their good work. With his publishers it is the same—he only 'wishes all his publishers were not so nice.' He never fails to notice any good deed or to acknowledge any touch of kindness that has come his way. In the emigrant train he is grateful to a station lad for speaking a civil word to him; at Vailima he lingers over the pleasure which it gives him when the black boys working on the estate value his 'Good-morning!' Wherever any one about him is trying, with however much of failure, to act manfully and do his duty, Stevenson is ready with his word of encouragement and appreciation, whether it be a little child managing cattle, or a native king fighting for his kingdom.

Among the many instances which prove this, his judgments of professedly religious people would form an interesting study. If we except those which belong to the embittered period of revolt, we shall find the same catholicity and the same power of seeing essential truth rather than eccentric error, good intention rather than indifferent performance. Whether it were Roman priest, or Protestant missionary, or Plymouth brother, it was the same. Sheriff Hunter, the fearless and gentle believer of the old style, has a soul 'like an ancient violin, so subdued to harmony, responding to a touch in music'; but 'the two young lads, revivalists,' are not censured.

We shall, however, refer at greater length only to the one fact of his relations with missions and missionaries in the South Seas. It would be an insult to the reader's knowledge of public facts to cite a traveller's appreciation of mission work as anything wonderful or specially creditable. Yet from a man like Stevenson we expect prejudice or at best aloofness. Foreign Mission interests and enthusiasm are still too much within an inner circle of our British church-life. They are expected of those deeply identified

with the church, but are still looked upon by only too many
as counsels of perfection rather than essential parts of
Christianity; while there are yet others who openly confess
to a prejudice against them. Prejudiced Stevenson was,
according to his own showing: 'I had feared to meet a
missionary, feared to find the narrowness and the self-suffi-
ciency that deface their publications, that too often disgrace
their behaviour.' Whether anything that he had actually
seen in missionaries had been such as to justify these words
may be doubted. But the fact that so strong a prejudice
was there renders his conduct all the more striking, as we
now know it. His bearing towards the missionaries was
such as to win them to him in a quite astonishing manner.
Claxton translated his *Bottle Imp* into Samoan; Whitmee
acted as his interpreter; Clarke read the funeral service at
his grave. Missionaries consulted and trusted him concerning difficult points in their work. They received from
him advice in which they recognised as fully the sympathy
of the fellow-worker as the shrewdness of the skilled critic
of men and things. His opinion of them in the main may
be judged by the fact that it is to missionaries that he
has paid some of the highest of his many appreciations of
noble character and work. He defends them from the
charge of meddling, and he testifies to the reality and value
of the work they have done in Christianising the natives.
In the Samoan political troubles he made common cause
with them, consulted them, understood them, appreciated
them, until whole-hearted co-operation ripened into mutual
trust and love. Even his adverse criticisms show how much
he was impressed with the reality of their work: had he
not been so, his judgments regarding it would not have been
so painstaking and so thoughtful. He knew its temptations, its difficulties, and its discouragements; the thank-
lessness of much of it, and the demand for long patience in

200

it all. He realised also its splendid opportunities, and recognised ungrudgingly its success.

Before passing on, it may be worth while to put together one or two of his estimates of missionaries, for they are very remarkable even among the sayings of one so liberal in praise and so outspoken in appreciation as he. 'Those who have a taste for hearing missions, Protestant or Catholic, decried, must seek their pleasure somewhere else than in my pages. Whether Catholic or Protestant, with all their gross blots, with all their deficiency of candour, of humour, and of common sense, the missionaries are the best and the most useful whites in the Pacific.' 'The best specimen of the Christian hero I ever met was one of [the] native missionaries.' Of Clarke he writes: 'The excellent Clarke up here almost all day yesterday, a man I esteem and like to the soles of his boots; I prefer him to any one in Samoa, and to most people in the world; a real good missionary, with the inestimable advantage of having grown up a layman. Pity they can't all get that!' He calls another 'a hero, a man who took me fairly by storm, for the most attractive, simple, brave, and interesting man in the whole Pacific.' The late James Chalmers of New Guinea he refers to as 'a man I love,' and asserts that he would hardly change with any man of his time, 'unless perhaps it were [General] Gordon or our friend Chalmers. . . . You can't weary me of that fellow; he is as big as a house and far bigger than any church.' It would be easy, if space permitted, to bring together an equally enthusiastic set of the sayings of missionaries about him.

Altogether, the general impression left on the mind after reading his work is that of a most kindly and generous spirit. No doubt there are passages of deep horror and ugliness on the one hand, and on the other hand the praise is sometimes exaggerated until it almost loses its sense of reality.

Yet in reading him we find ourselves among an uncommonly rich assembly of delightful things and admirable people. Competent men are thinking and acting competently: blunderers are after all meaning well. Writers are writing, preachers preaching, labourers labouring, and on the whole the work is done honestly and not in vain. Behind us stand the glorious dead, around us are the noble living. It is a heartening world, and one well worth living in, and its whole atmosphere braces us to do our best, that we may not shame so gallant a company of our fellow-mortals.

We have been, however, as yet but in the outer court of the temple. A man may school himself to just and appreciative criticism, while remaining naturally and persistently apathetic. How about the inner life of actual needs and desires? Of this, in Stevenson's case, there can be no question. He was by nature and by habit the most companionable man known to the public of his time. 'A man,' in his opinion 'who must separate himself from his neighbours' habits in order to be happy, is in much the same case with one who requires to take opium for the same purpose.' For himself, he frankly admits that he loves to be loved and hates to have any one angry with him. His power of winning affection was phenomenal, and its secret lay to a large extent in his felt need of affection. One friend, writing when he had received the news of his death, says: 'So great was his power of winning love that, though I knew him for less than a week, I could have borne the loss of many a more intimate friend with less sorrow. One of the strongest impressions left on the mind by his biography and his letters is that the landmarks and milestones of his life were the successive friendships which he formed. Fleeming Jenkin, Sidney Colvin, and others who came afterwards, marked the critical points in life for

202

him, and each added some contribution to the development of his individuality.

He values the most casual and slight acquaintance with a fellow-mortal. In towns he is delighted with the pleasant faces of men and women seen in passing. In the country, to see some one before him on the road, is enough to make him quicken his steps. In unfrequented districts ' a meeting is an affair of moment; we have the sight far off of some one coming towards us, the growing definiteness of the person, and then the brief passage and salutation, and the road left empty before us for perhaps a great while to come. Such encounters have a wistful interest that can hardly be understood by the dweller in places more populous.' So he goes along, finding pleasure in ' waving a handkerchief to people he shall never see again,' at home with all the world on easy terms. For ' the knowledge that another has felt as we have felt, and seen things, even if they are little things, not much otherwise than we have seen them, will continue to the end to be one of life's choicest pleasures.' When there is no human companionship—so great is his need of company—he will create it. Imagination comes to the rescue, and the fascinating Dick Turpin rides down the empty lane to meet him. He was a lover of animals: to him a stray dog was ' God's dog,' and therefore his friend. Even inanimate things would serve his turn. He knew the exquisite sympathy that exists between the engineer and his machine. Breakers on a reef, the great company of the mountains, even the very road itself, became at need his companions, and in their fellowship he was well attended.

Yet friendship is not with him a light matter worn upon his sleeve. The passing acquaintance is pleasant, but there is more in friendship than that. ' In this world of imperfection we gladly welcome even partial intimacies. And

203

if we find but one to whom we can speak out of our heart freely, with whom we can walk in love and simplicity without dissimulation, we have no ground of quarrel with the world or God.' That deeper sort of friendship he knows, and he has proclaimed its worth :

> 'For the dearest friends are the auldest friends,
> And the young are just on trial.'

The deeper friendship is not a matter of how much one can get, either of instruction, or sympathy, or any other sort of mutual improvement. 'I cannot,' he exclaims, 'count that a poor dinner, or a poor book, where I meet with those I love.' It is a matter of faith and love. 'When we have fallen through storey after storey of our vanity and aspiration, and sit rueful among the ruins, then it is that we begin to measure the stature of our friends; how they stand between us and our own contempt, believing in our best; how, linking us with others, and still spreading wide the influential circle, they weave us in and in with the fabric of contemporary life.' A curious proof of the seriousness with which he took his friendships is the diffident and self-excusing way in which he broke the news to them from the South Seas, that he would not return at the expected time. It would not occur to many voyagers in search of health to dispute their right to another year of sunshine. But with him friendship meant that he was not his own, and he had to borrow his year from those he loved.

A nature so rich in love is never far from the Kingdom of Heaven. The aged John has told us that 'love is of God; and every one that loveth is born of God and knoweth God.' It is difficult to conceive what these words mean if it be not that in all pure and unselfish love there is an element of real religion. Now and then we find love declaring its hidden meaning to Stevenson in terms of

204

a more than usually clear faith. Thus 'to love is the great amulet which makes the world a garden; and hope, which comes to all, outwears the accidents of life, and reaches with tremulous hand beyond the grave and death. Easy to say: yea, but also, by God's mercy, both easy and grateful to believe.' Yet it was not so much on the theoretical as on the practical side that love led Stevenson to faith. As has been already stated, vision is with him the signal for travel, and the quick.foot goes with the clear and far-seeing eye. Thus his love not only quickened his own life with a glow of happiness, and drew out his various powers to their utmost of enjoyable and healthful exercise; it also sent him forth among men in helpfulness and service. He was no mere paragon of glad life, whose love had kindled his ideals and kept them shining brightly for men to see and envy. All that he has is for the sake of those who need it. Like Herakles in *Balaustion's Adventure*, he

> 'held his life
> Out on his hand, for any man to take.'

Thus is love twice blessed in his experience. Intrinsically, and for its own dear sake, it is the best thing in all the world. But in its uses also it is blessed. We run to those who love us when we are mortified with failure, 'not to hear ourselves called better, but to be better men in point of fact.' 'So long as we love we serve; so long as we are loved by others, I would almost say that we are indispensable; and no man is useless while he has a friend.' 'The essence of love is kindness; and indeed it may be best defined as passionate kindness; kindness, so to speak, run mad and become importunate and violent.'

Stevenson's love for his fellows is never shown so keen and strong as in those cases where there is nothing to be gained by it in the way of service or of intellectual return—

nothing but such return of gratitude and affection as only love prizes. His whole work is full of compassion for the multitude, and for the individual men and women who compose it. His heart is open to all who are helpless and miserable, and in a man's mere pitiableness he recognises a claim upon himself. He realises how the banished Samoans must loathe the rough food and brackish water of the coral reef to which civilised rulers had sent them; his soul is touched by the horrors which runaway blackboys must suffer at night, as they hide in the homeless, devil-haunted bush; his heart burns as he sees the sufferings of the wounded in the hospital. That was toward the close, among the islanders to whom he paid out so much of his heart. Yet for them he had so strong an admiration, that, as we have already said, it was rather justice than pity which Samoa called forth. But a deep compassion goes to men and women in all parts of the world, who are entangled in the toils of the inner life and struggle. The hopeless faithfulness of love that meets with no response, whether it be in Lord Durrisdeer's son or in the disfigured wife of a heartless artisan in the Portobello train; the homelessness of those who have by their own fault alienated friendship; the hapless plight of all 'sinful men walking before the Lord among the sins and dangers of this life'—all these fill his heart with tears. Still more does he feel, and make his readers feel, the pity of it, when a good man has degenerated from his former character, and we remember the brave fight he once made against the temptations he no longer resists—'Was not this a thing at once to rage and to be humbled at? . . . I was overborne with a pity almost approaching the passionate, not for my master alone, but for the sons of man.'

In these, and countless other examples of his compassion for individual fellow-mortals, the reader is startled by the intimacy of his understanding—he has imagined so exactly how it must feel to be in such a case. And the last quotation reminds us of the fact that his sympathy was not only drawn forth by known cases of individual suffering, whose picturesqueness might move the artistic man to emotion. In imagination he went out among the painful facts of the world, with the same great-hearted compassion. At the time of the Franco-Prussian war, he was travelling among the Western Isles, and he tells us how he could *hear* the shots fired and feel the pang of the bullets striking his breast. 'It was sometimes so distressing, so instant, that I lay in the heather on the top of the island, with my face hid, kicking my heels for agony.' 'In that year,' he writes elsewhere, 'cannon were roaring for days together on French battle-fields, and I would sit in my isle (I call it mine after the use of lovers) and think upon the war, and the pain of men's wounds, and the weariness of their marching. And I would think, too, of that other war which is as old as mankind, and is indeed the life of man; the unsparing war, the grinding slavery of competition; the toil of seventy years, dear-bought bread, precarious honour, the perils and pitfalls, and the poor rewards. It was a long look forward; the future summoned me as with trumpet-calls, it warned me back as with a voice of weeping and beseeching; and I thrilled and trembled on the brink of life, like a childish bather on the beach.'

Sympathy, such as he so eloquently expressed both in theory and in practice, is in itself a great moral force. Apart from its definite outgoings in acts of helpfulness, if it pervade the spirit of a man it will instinctively solve many problems and lead to just and useful decisions. Yet it is possible to substitute sympathy for kindness, and to bring to the thirsty lips of men the empty cup of sentiment instead of the water of life. Stevenson knew the temptation and repeatedly described it, but it never was his own danger. That tenderness of sentiment which shrank from giving pain to ants, which led him to give up even the sport of fishing, and which found vent in fierce anger against any one who ill-treated an animal, guaranteed that sympathy should find a practical outlet. 'Kind deeds and words,' he says—'that's the true blue of piety; to hope the best, and do the best, and speak the best.' The code by which he guided his whole life, and arranged its relations to those most intimately connected with him, had kindness as one of its first principles. His relations to the members of his family, both before and after marriage, are full of kindness, which mellows and increases as years advance. Professor Colvin has borne testimony to 'the charm of his talk, which was irresistibly sympathetic and inspiring'; and, knowing him with an intimacy which very few were privileged to enjoy, he tells us that his was 'one of the bravest and tenderest of human hearts.' He refused to accept the ordinary trade conceptions of his relations to workmen he employed, or the ordinary domestic standards for the treatment of the servants of his household. It has been supposed that the feudal relations which existed between him and his dependents in Vailima arc traceable wholly to his love for the picturesque and striking. We have already admitted that this element was present in much of what he did, but it is difficult to see why we should hesitate to admit the more direct and simple motive. He treated his people kindly because he liked to be kind. It was impossible for him ever to regard the living persons about him in any other light than as human beings, or to school himself into any other than the natural human attitude toward them.

Nor did his kindness stop short in attitude and affection; it passed over into deeds such as are prompted only by the

208

most complete unselfishness and the heroic love of man.
The real value of a man's life, and the reason why he
should cling to it, is that 'he, as a living man, has some to
help, some to love.' The test question for a life is 'what
difference has it made to this world and our country and
our family and our friends, that we have lived. The man
who has only been pious and not useful will stand with a
long face on that great day when Christ puts to him his
questions.' Thus the needs of others and their pitiable
situations were for him not merely a vivid spectacle but a
clamorous and exacting conscience. His enthusiasm kindles
to every piece of real and conscientious work that has been
done for others. Describing the *Norah Creina's* fight with
the storm, he says: 'God bless every man that swung a
mallet on that tiny and strong hull! It was not for wages
only that he laboured, but to save men's lives.' Two of the
greatest poems which he wrote, distinguished from the rest
by their stately and solemn loftiness, are those in which he
commemorates the lighthouse-building of his fathers and
claims to be himself a lighthouse-builder of the spirit:

'Say not of me that weakly I declined
The labours of my sires, and fled the sea,
The towers we founded and the lamps we lit,
To play at home with paper like a child.'

'These are thy works, O father, these thy crown
Whether on high the air be pure, they shine
Along the yellowing sunset, and all night
Among the unnumbered stars of God they shine;
Or whether fogs arise and far and wide
The low sea-level drown—each finds a tongue,
And all night long the tolling bell resounds:
So shine, so toll, till night be overpast,
Till the stars vanish, till the sun return,
And in the haven rides the fleet secure.

This thou hast done, and I—can I be base?
I must arise, O father, and to port
Some lost, complaining seaman pilot home.'

The ideal of service to man, which these verses express so well, was the rule of his life. In little things, where men occupied with great service are often selfish, he carried it out as conscientiously as in great things, and there is nothing which better proves the sincerity of his altruism. His devotion to children was unwearied. Whether it was 'taking charge of a kid' to let its mother sleep on the emigrant train, or nursing a sick one, or racking his brains to find something for a letter that would interest a little boy, or patiently teaching any children who happened to be in his neighbourhood, it is the same delight in serviceableness that we find. In all places he seems to have been drawn into some local tussle or other, and impelled to champion the cause of the weak and wronged. He was only restrained by the utmost pressure from going at the risk of his life to occupy an Irish farm where the occupant had been murdered. In California it was the same. In the Samoan troubles he spent his last years in the defence of the natives against the unsympathetic and blundering government of Europeans. He wrote incessantly on their behalf—letters, articles, and a book which cost him infinite labour. He fought for them in meetings to which he went through storm and rain while sick with colic or in the intervals of hemorrhage. He did this at the risk of trial, prison, and banishment. He had to quarrel with all the officials on the island, and was attacked by a 'pretty scurrilous' article in the local newspaper week by week. And all this was service rendered in a department alien to his tastes. Politics was but an interruption to literature with Stevenson, and it is hardly possible to exaggerate the sacrifice of his natural inclinations which such politics involved. It is no wonder that the natives loved him, accepted him as a chief among them, and built 'the road of gratitude' to his house. For a man of his temperament

210

and in his health to do so much from pure love of helpless and half savage fellow men is surely a very honourable record on the roll of heroic self-sacrifice and service.

All this must be considered in the light of the fact that no one believed less in self-sacrifice for its own sake than he. His ideal was the fulfilling, not the denying, of the instinctive desires of human nature. Asceticism had no attractions for him, except those which love and service lent it. It is peculiarly significant that his two finest stories of self-sacrifice are stories of native life in the South Seas. *The Feast of Famine* and *The Bottle Imp* are as great morally as they are in point of literary merit. The latter rises to a simple eloquence in the words of Kokua, the wife of Keawe, which in its own line could hardly be surpassed. She had doomed her soul to eternal torment that she might rescue her husband from a like fate: 'But now at least I take my soul in both the hands of my affection. Now I say farewell to the white steps of heaven and the waiting faces of my friends. A love for a love, and let mine be equalled with Keawe's. A soul for a soul, and be it mine to perish.'

Of course the Samoan period was very picturesque and romantic. 'Tusitala,'[1] in his various capacities of patriarch, demigod, missionary, and bard, is a charmingly theatrical figure. But all this may be true and yet may never have touched the real truth of the situation. No kind of criticism is more unworthy than that which selects some striking but insignificant detail, and explains the whole of a man's conduct in its terms: it is the cheapest way of disparaging obviously noble character. In Stevenson's case, one who has rendered such self-sacrificing and effective service may well be permitted to do it in what manner he prefers. The essential truth of such actions lies simply in

[1] Tusitala was the name given to Stevenson by the natives in Samoa.

his love of men; and the thing most obvious about them is
their likeness to the character of Jesus Christ, whose spirit
breathes through them all. That Stevenson, in such conduct,
sought to follow in His footsteps, we are not left in doubt.
'The truth of his (Christ's) teaching would seem to be this:
in our own person and fortune, we should be ready to accept
and pardon all; it is *our* cheek we are to turn, *our* coat
that we are to give away to the man who has taken *our*
cloak. But when another's face is buffeted, perhaps a
little of the lion will become us best. That we are to
suffer others to be injured, and stand by, is not conceivable
and surely not desirable.' In acting as he did, Stevenson
was but trying to obey his own favourite verses in Isaiah:
'Is not this the fast that I have chosen? to loose the bands
of wickedness, to undo the heavy burdens, and to let the
oppressed go free, and that ye break every yoke? Is it not
to deal thy bread to the hungry, and that thou bring the
poor that are cast out to thy house? when thou seest the
naked, that thou cover him; and that thou hide not thyself
from thine own flesh?' In Tusitala, as in any other man,
self-sacrifice for others is a Christ-like thing. To believe
in life and to rejoice in it, yet to be always ready to lay it
down that we may save others by bearing the burden of
their sufferings with them and for them—surely that is
faith in an intimately Christian sense. Such faith is worth
more to God and to the world than many abstract beliefs.
Browning's Herakles again comes back to memory as we
think of the Samoan years:

> 'Gladness be with thee, Helper of our world !
> I think this is the authentic sign and seal
> Of Godship, that it ever waxes glad,
> And more glad, until gladness blossoms, bursts
> Into a rage to suffer for mankind.'

# CHAPTER XII

## MANLINESS AND HEALTH

IT was natural to look for the resultant message of Stevenson's vision and travel first as it concerned those among whom he walked and whose lives he saw. We turn now to the reaction of these faculties upon himself, as they determined the management of his own life and his conception of what a man's own life ought to be. Had he been asked to state in two words his ideal for life and character, it may be conjectured that the definition would not have been very different from the title of the present chapter.

Manliness for him meant first of all strength. 'Quit you like men, be strong,' was a command he never failed to hear and answer, preferring always in himself and others what he called 'the manly virtues.' With weakness accepted and offered as an excuse for failure, he had little sympathy. 'Those who go to the devil in youth, with anything like a fair chance, were probably little worth saving from the first; they must have been feeble fellows—creatures made of putty and packthread, without steel or fire, anger or true joyfulness, in their composition; we may sympathise with their parents, but there is not much cause to go into mourning for themselves; for, to be quite honest, the weak brother is the worst of mankind.' For himself, strenuousness was ever a welcome demand upon life. It was with no suspicion of complaint, but rather with a sort of not unnatural boastfulness, that he wrote of himself as 'facing

213

as stoutly as I can a hard, combative existence, full of doubt, difficulties, defeats, disappointments, and dangers.' He delights in hard tasks, for the very hardness of them. He often presents life to himself and others in its most difficult aspects, that he may tempt us all to heroism. He does not count that life a high calling whose main part is pleasure, but that which confronts many uncongenial tasks and dangerous adventures.

In one whose bodily health was so weak and precarious as his, this is perhaps not surprising, for it is usual for the weak to realise the value of strength and covet it as the best of gifts. Yet it is none the less heroic, when we think how much effort and pain it must often have cost him to carry it out in practice. And he is entirely free from the harshness that sometimes characterises those who live strenuously against great odds. True manhood is not only strong—it is strong graciously, delicately, and sanely. The Greek element in life must be added to the Hebrew, the lighter facts must balance the darker and more sombre. This kind of manhood, with its all-round balance and harmony, Stevenson achieved. As he conceived of it, normal human life was something clean and healthy as well as robust, lived in the open air, freshened by a breeze; and this frank and natural ideal dominated all departments of his thought. It gave their tone to his moral and spiritual judgments, and it culminated in that Gospel of Happiness which is at once his highest and his most characteristic message.

In all true strength there is the consciousness of another and greater Power in the universe before which man's strength is but weakness. This is but one instance of the universal truth that in order to really know any part of the world a man must take into his reckoning that which is beyond the world. So incomplete is this life of ours, so literally a broken arc, that none who confine their attention

214

to what they see upon the earth can by any possibility understand even that. Not for beauty only, nor for hope, must we look beyond the world, but for truth also—for anything but a mistaken conception of the world itself. This is especially true in the matter of strength. He who thinks proudly of his human strength, who exults in that and is satisfied, has, like Samson of old, let his strength lead him into blindness. From him the world need look for neither permanent heartiness nor truly valuable service.

Accordingly we find that there is an element of fatalism, in one form or another, in all really great thinkers, and Stevenson is no exception. Sometimes, as in *Olalla*, this appears in a sense of the dread physical forces of the world, whose play is seen in natural law in general, and in heredity in particular. We have already discussed this in connection with the double aspect of Nature—'the beauty and the terror of the world.' In *Olalla* the woman is for the man who loves her 'the link that bound me in with dead things on one hand, and with our pure and pitying God upon the other: a thing brutal and divine, and akin at once to the innocence and to the unbridled forces of the earth.' It is dangerous for a fatalist to have so strong an imagination as Stevenson's, and *Olalla* is a standing tribute to a faith which could look with steady and undaunted eye upon the Sphinx-like mystery of the world. Seen vaguely, the great powers of the universe are only awe-inspiring and sublime: seen in detail, they are often too terrible for any but the most indissuadable faith. A somewhat different aspect of destiny is presented in those curious fragments where the characters of his fiction come out from their places and discuss the story, and the purpose of their author. Thus, in the first fable, John Silver and Captain Smollett, two of the puppets from *Treasure Island*, converse. The miscreant Silver is confident that if there be such a thing as an author,

he himself is his favourite character; while the Captain is
equally certain that the author is on the side of good, and he
needs to know nothing more. It is a cunning device, and
extraordinarily effective as a commentary upon some of the
common arguments about Calvinism, for and against. In
other passages the treatment of the subject is more solemn
and the teaching plain and weighty. Rebellion against
the established order of the universe is exhibited in all
its futile irrationality on the one hand; God's slow but
irresistible designs are manifest on the other. 'The
world, the universe, turns on vast hinges, proceeds on a
huge plan; you, and we, and—and all, I potently believe
it—used for good; but we are all—and this I know—as the
dust of the balances. The loss or the salvation of the
*Lübeck* was weighed, and was decided, in the hour of birth
of the universe.'

> 'The child, the seed, the grain of corn,
> The acorn on the hill,
> Each for some separate end is born
> In season fit, and still
> Each must in strength arise to work the almighty will.
>
> . . . . . .
>
> So from the sally each obeys
> The unseen almighty nod ;
> So till the ending all their ways
> Blindfolded loth have trod ;
> Nor knew their task at all, but were the tools of God.'

Fatalism, taken as a doom, is the death of energy and
hope alike, and one of the strongest entrenchments of sin
against goodness. In the persons of those characters in his
stories whom Stevenson has marked out for evil, we see
this repeatedly. Markheim, the unwilling criminal, protests
that ever since his birth the giants of circumstance have
dragged him about by the wrists. Mr. Archer, in *The Great
North Road*, sets the pieces of a broken rush to float upon a

stream, and accepts the path of evil because two out of the three go down a certain channel.[1] In such cases the agents have persuaded themselves that nothing they may do at the prompting of reason or conscience is of any avail—it is written otherwise. No theory of fate could be more convenient and consoling for the sinner, whose plea is that he cannot help his nature and must be excused for gratifying it. Meredith has spoken of this kind of fatalism as 'regarding the Spirit of Life as a remote externe, who plays the human figures, to bring about this or that issue.' With that external view of destiny he has contrasted another—'beside us, within us, our breath, if we will; marking on us where at each step we sink to the animal, mount to the divine.'

The distinction between the outer and the inner view of destiny is, as regards its practical effects, one of the most important points in ethical controversy. It was the latter aspect that braced the life of Stevenson. Destiny was constantly present to his imagination, yet its effect was always quickening and tonic. The man's mind and will sprang to the great alliance with the mind and will of the universe, and wrought out actions and character as in a veritable sense inspired and chosen of heaven. No soul is ever great without the sense of this alliance. To explain even the most commonplace experience wholly in terms of one poor little human life, is to show that one has never realised the meaning of life at all. There is always the *surd*, the unexplained and inexplicable element beyond all that. The recognition of this is the first requisite of true manliness, and a belief in predestination of some sort is the necessary basis for any healthy view of life. Thus does the thought of destiny perform at

[1] Yet it is significant that he does not launch them evenly, declaring that 'no man can put complete reliance in blind fate; he must still cog the dice.'

217

all times a double function in the world : the bad it commits
to badness, slackening all their powers of resistance, and
thrusting them ever deeper into the evil of their choice;
the good it braces for action, until, claiming it for their
own, they are competent to face and conquer anything that
life may set before them. The latter was Stevenson's course,
summed up with even more than his usual appositeness in
the phrase, 'to waylay destiny and bid him stand and
deliver.'

The result in character was one of the most brilliant
records of human courage which are to be found anywhere
in the biographies of British men. Courage is not one of
the highest or most delicate virtues. It is closely connected
with the physical life, and even moral and intellectual daring has its roots among the nerves of a man. Yet even so,
it is, in Stevenson's phrase, 'the footstool of the virtues,
upon which they stand,' and therefore it is 'the principal
virtue, for all the others presuppose it,' so that 'no man is
of any use until he has dared everything.' It is a noteworthy fact that in almost every one of his recorded prayers
there is a petition for courage, for it will generally be found
that a man's most distinguishing characteristic is that for
which he has oftenest prayed. That the circumstances of
his life demanded an unusual fortitude will be denied by
none who have any knowledge of the facts. In Vailima the
demand became excessive. *Vailima Letters*, from this point
of view, records a continuous succession of troubles. The
incessant worries with the native servants—who seem always
to be reverting to savage madness, or breaking down with
illness, or relapsing into moral weakness and failure—were
of themselves enough to discourage any ordinary man.
They were met with a constant compassion, an unfailing
effort to please and help. We have already written of the
part he played in the political situation and the difficulties
218

under which he did his literary work. The courage displayed in these is eclipsed only by the still more splendid courage with which he met his many illnesses. We have seen how, in the words of Mr. Graham Balfour, 'his sufferings did not dull the kindliness and sympathy which largely formed the fascination of his character.' Yet the inner victory over trouble was even more brilliant. As we read of the incessant returns of prostrating illness and blindness; pain in the head, the back, the limbs; wakefulness, and its sense of ruin; fever, racking cough and bleeding lungs; we can but thank God for a creature able to meet them all as he did. Dr. Robertson Nicoll has somewhere said very memorably that to understand Robert Louis Stevenson one *must have put up a little blood.* Yet even those who cannot thus know to its depth the meaning of that splendid courage, may well perceive that here there is the record of no ordinary heroism. He met it all with a gallant defiance, often whimsical, always good-natured and exhilarating. The hemorrhage he nicknamed 'Bluidy Jack,' and fought it as an admiral might engage a three-decker of the enemy. After two of its attacks, in his last year, he writes: 'No good denying that this annoys, because it do. However, you must expect influenza to leave some harm, and my spirits, appetite, peace on earth and good-will to men are all on a rising market.' When at one time nature had been too much for him, and he had written some pages of 'the wailings of a crushed worm,' he destroyed them and sent a fine piece of fooling instead. Stevenson's *St. Ives*, like Scott's *Count Robert of Paris*, is the work of a dying man. With a pathetic intuition he likens his book to the other, and the most enthusiastic lover of Scott will own that *St. Ives* does not suffer in that comparison. Thus he constantly flung off depression and turned again to his task with a glorious laughter, until he had fairly turned the tables upon calamity.

219

# THE FAITH OF R. L. STEVENSON

Long before the Vailima days he had written of Scotland: 'Poverty, ill-luck, enterprise and constant resolution, are the fibres of the legend of this country's history. The heroes and kings of Scotland have been tragically fated; the most marking incidents in Scottish history—Flodden, Darien, or the Forty-Five—were still either failures or defeats; and the fall of Wallace and the repeated reverses of the Bruce, combine with the very smallness of the country to teach rather a moral than a material criterion for life.' In another of his earlier books he quotes the words of Thoreau: 'Make your failure tragical by courage, and it will not differ from success.' In his closing years all this came home to himself, and found him prepared with an unflinching intrepidity, so that his other words were never more explicitly proved true than in his own experience: 'A high measure of health is only necessary for unhealthy people,' and 'true health is to be able to do without it.'

The conjunction of fatalism and courage prepares us to expect a serious view of moral life. The noble life is never easy, and was never meant to be so. It is a kingdom of the strenuous, and its gates open for them alone. Its gospel may begin with thoughts about birds of the air and lilies of the field, and the promise of an easy yoke; but when it comes to the actual grapple of experience, it is a narrow way and a strait gate by which men must enter, not without an agony of striving. Every book of Stevenson's shows how well he knew this. The difficulty of life's task and the height of its calling are ever before him, and it was the sense of these which gave him some of his greatest thoughts.

Chief among such thoughts was that of dual personality, which found so speedy and world-wide a recognition in *Dr. Jekyll and Mr. Hyde.* Popular religion adopted the allegory partly because it was a modern echo of St. Paul's words to the Romans, in which the apostle describes himself as leading the double life of unwilling sin and unfulfilled desire for holiness. But still more must the popularity of *Jekyll and Hyde* be attributed to its ghastly truthfulness as a rescript of common experience. In this mysterious twofoldness of the inner life it was felt that Stevenson, like St. Paul before him, had exposed the root of all our moral difficulties. It is because of the war of the carnal man against the spiritual man within them that the best men, though they may approach the great task and adventure of life with light hearts, grow grave and stern as they advance. For Stevenson this was a dominant type of ethical thought, and it is never absent from any of his delineations of character. It corresponds with the duality which he finds in nature—that ' beauty and terror of the world ' to which we have referred so often. In many different lights and aspects he exhibits it. Sometimes we see the essential life in poise, ready to identify itself with either the good or the evil possible man within. In other cases, described with equal power, each of the two alternately claims the soul for its own. Now it is selfishness and generosity that are pitted against each other; again it is a just reason against nerves quivering with petty spite. In *Deacon Brodie* the tragedy is represented as it wrought itself out in an actual history; in many of the novels it is invented to bring out various aspects of the same dread warfare. Dr. Desprez exclaims to Jean-Marie: ' I am in the black fit: the evil spirit of King Saul, the hag of the merchant Abudah, the personal devil of the mediæval monk, is with me, is in me (tapping on his breast). The vices of my nature are now uppermost; innocent pleasures woo me in vain; I long for Paris, for my wallowing in the mire,'—and he hands over to the boy the money in his pockets and beseeches him rather to wreck the train than to let him go. The *Master of Ballantrae* is another instance, in which the refined sensitiveness of the exterior serves but

221

to throw into darker relief the impudent grossness within. It is the personal note of deep and sore experience that makes all such descriptions of the double life and its warfare so wonderfully telling. 'I send you,' he writes to Mr. Low, in a letter accompanying the newly written *Dr. Jekyll and Mr. Hyde*, 'I send you herewith a Gothic gnome for your Greek nymph; but the gnome is interesting, I think, and he came out of a deep mine, where he guards the fountain of tears.' We are left to conjecture what inner struggles gave the suggestion for that dream which took its final form in the allegory.

Our double nature is the radical difficulty in morals, yet it is but the beginning of the trouble. In every department the detail of goodness is far more difficult than it seems. Any course in life, looked at thoughtlessly, seems to offer us not only a possible but an easy career of goodness, if only we were set free from the present, which always appears to be handicapped. Yet the easy aspect is but an illusion, and we only need to enter on the career to find that out. The most typical instance of this is the case of honesty, to which he very often reverts. People in one rank of society view with envious eyes those in another rank, thinking that for them 'honesty is no virtue, but a thing as natural as breathing.' Even for themselves most people consider honesty a virtue which they may take for granted, and which they find 'as easy as Blind-Man's Buff.' Stevenson thinks otherwise. In legal and commercial questions he shows by many illustrations scattered throughout his books that honesty is 'a more delicate affair than that; delicate as any art.' It is in this that he finds the difficulty of moral life most pressing, and he devotes much labour to working out the detail of his contention. As regards possession, for instance, he is very explicit, whether the possession be great or small. 'It is not enough to take off your hat, or to thank God upon

your knees for the admirable constitution of society and
your own convenient situation in its upper and more ornamental stories. Neither is it enough to buy the loaf with
a sixpence, for then you are only changing the point of the
inquiry; and you must first have *bought the sixpence.*
Service for service: how have you bought your sixpences?'
Again, as regards labour, the same principles apply. He
who undertakes to forge a knife, to cultivate a farm, to
write a book, to hold an office, is accepting a certain portion
of the material or intellectual property of mankind on trust.
That he shall produce good workmanship is not a matter
which concerns himself alone. In no department can he
produce bad workmanship without abusing the trust confided in him, and fraudulently wasting material which is in
no sense his own. In all employments 'the slovenly is the
dishonest,' and the careless workman has by no means settled
his score with the universe when he is punished by personal
want of success. He has still to answer for abuse of trust
property.

This instance of honesty is but one out of many examples
which might be chosen. We have called it the typical example, because it sets the point of view for Stevenson's theory
of the whole active service of human life. In his view of
duty there is nothing slavish, as of those who cringe before
a master, and act under the lash; neither is there much of
the free and comprehending spirit of love to God, in which
all theorising is lost in the desire to please One who is very
dear to our hearts. His attitude is rather that of a man
passionately endeavouring to be honest and to pay his debt
so far as he may. It is not the fully developed Christian
doctrine; yet it is exactly modelled upon many sayings of
Christ. The parables of the Pounds and the Talents are
with him in this teaching, and that far-reaching and seldom
realised word to the disciples, 'When ye have done all, ...

223

say, We are unprofitable servants: we have done that which was our duty to do.' There was much unexpressed love behind Stevenson's service, as there is behind that of many another reticent disciple.

This, however, is but a specimen. The difficulty of forgiving injuries is almost as pointedly stated as that of being honest. Truth is difficult, so is good temper, so is purity; and passages might be quoted which show every one of the cardinal virtues in an arduous and trying aspect. The difficulty is increased by circumstances. Heredity in some, natural taste and disposition in others, marriage, the necessities of business, the condition of one's health, all help to complicate the situation. Altogether the art of living is very hard to learn, and this is a supremely difficult world to be good in. To many these constantly repeated warnings may appear disconcerting and unintelligible. But all those who have any experience of earnest struggle against evil, and any consequent knowledge of their own hearts, will find in them a wonderfully companionable and helpful message. It is much to know, when we are tempted and discouraged, that there are others by our side who feel the same difficulties. It is far more when these difficulties are expressed as Stevenson has been able to express them. In his lucid words they stand out in such clearness that we feel we have seen them in their final form, and that the vague burden of a general sense of demand which we cannot fulfil is exchanged for a set of definite encounters with life on fields which he has made plain to our eyes.

All teaching which emphasises the difficulty of high ideals runs the risk of ending in laxity. Professor Masson has cited Milton as a standing exception to the common rule that poets and artists generally 'are and ought to be distinguished by a predominance of sensibility over principle, an excess of what Coleridge called the spiritual over what

he called the moral part of man.' How shall Stevenson
stand in this judgment? His sensibility and spirituality
are beyond question, and we have already shown that
these qualities were reinforced by a catholic appreciation
of all sorts and conditions of men, and by a kindly interest
in all the phases of life. We might therefore expect his
strong sense of the difficulty of being good to end in a
general amnesty, with no place left in it for condemnation
or even for moral earnestness. He has praised in a friend
'his pious acceptance of the universe': how much, ethically,
does that involve? Does it mean that we are to refrain
from attempting to change the universe in any part, or is
there still room left for aggression in the moral domain?
He, more than almost any other writer, has helped us to
realise plainly the extreme difficulty of a noble life, and he
has, like many humane thinkers of our time, insisted on the
gentleness of God in judgment. 'He who shall pass judgment on the records of our life is the same that formed us
in frailty'; and while men know only, in regard to flagrant
acts, our exceptional sins, God knows and allows for our
exceptional excuses. Yet with all this he does not succumb
to that nerveless and maudlin compassion which some have
mistaken for charitable judgment. The God of such weaklings has good-humour for His distinguishing attribute
instead of holiness; and Stevenson is well aware that
without holiness no man shall see the Lord. It is because
of his consuming sense of the reality of moral character
that he feels its difficulty so keenly. His interests and his
sympathies are wide, and he has seen that sterling virtue is
widely diffused in the world. Accordingly he falls back
from the sense of difficulty not upon slackness as a thing
inevitable in so impossible a world, but upon courage and
strenuousness that may, at worst, rescue what we can from
the wreck. His elaborate and frequent exposition of the

difficulties is not of the nature of a sentimental sigh, which
is really an excuse for failure; it is a challenge sent out
into the battle by a willing soldier.

Thus we come again to that moral earnestness in him of
which our past studies have afforded us so many examples.
It is true that no writer of our time has introduced a more
quaint humour into serious considerations. Thus in *The
Black Arrow,* Joanna laments her forced wearing of men's
clothes, ' which is a deadly sin for a woman; and, besides,
they fit me not.' In the children's rhymes and *Moral
Emblems* there is much in this vein. The whole duty of a
child is to behave himself well in various specified situations, ' at least as far as he is able.' In the emblem
attached to a woodcut of one man pushing another over
a cliff, we are invited to

> 'Mark, printed on the opposing page,
> The unfortunate effects of rage,'

which turn out, however, to consist mainly in the uncomfortable reflections which are likely to annoy the murderer. A
more elaborate engraving of a beggar asking alms in vain
from a gentleman in a tall hat, has a verse opposite it
which ends in the lines:

> 'He from the poor averts his head. . .
> He will regret it when he 's dead.'

The comicality of these is irresistible, and it is the comicality
of the Scottish Stevenson rather than of the French. It
does not mean that he judged moral questions simply from
the artistic standpoint, as ultimately matters of good or bad
taste; but only that in all Scotsmen there is that grim
humour with which Carlyle has familiarised the world, and
which is never more effective than when it plays on moral
problems.

To convince ourselves of his moral earnestness we need
226

only recollect the exaggerated condemnation of reward as a motive to good deeds. Whether in the shape of money, or of glory, or even of seeing some result of our labour, we noted how he utterly repudiated the notion of payment for virtue, and considered it the enemy of piety. It is by no means necessary to agree with him in that view in order to see the moral earnestness which lay behind it. The main reason for his antagonism was that in his opinion morality was far too serious a matter to allow any such consideration to enter. 'The world must return some day to the word duty, and be done with the word reward. There are no rewards and plenty duties. And the sooner a man sees that and acts upon it like a gentleman or a fine old barbarian, the better for himself.' Another illustration is found in his views as to the nature and value of money. Pressing the well-known principle of political economy to its detailed applications, he finds that a certain amount of money is necessary, 'but beyond that, it is a commodity to be bought or not to be bought, a luxury in which we may either indulge or stint ourselves like any other. And there are many luxuries that we may legitimately prefer to it, such as a grateful conscience, a country life, or the woman of our inclination.' Without soul, with its appetites, aspirations, appreciations, the rich man remains miserably poor—'bankrupt of desire and hope, there, in his great house, let him sit and look upon his fingers.' For his own part, Stevenson tells us he wants but little money, 'and I do not want to be decent at all, but to be good.'

This desire to be good involves more than appears. He knows the cost of goodness in anxious carefulness of life, and in 'the daily expense of spirit.' Every situation in life is a dangerous and critical post. Those who are married have doubled the ideals which they must serve: they have 'domesticated the Recording Angel,' and 'their witness is not only the

227

judge but the victim of their sins.' Yet even for the unmarried the demands of conscience are searching and severe beyond men's ordinary ideas of morality, for they are dealing with a divine and eternal criterion in every act. Every day brings to every man new opportunities; and one of the things on which Stevenson lays great stress is the critical nature of the question whether a man shall prove worthy of his opportunities. The doctrine of positive as contrasted with negative virtue still further proves our point, for 'as we must account for every idle word, so we must account for every idle silence.' And then, to fail is a desperate matter, because evil is so hateful. If our reading of his portrayal of the sinfulness of sin[1] be the correct one, we have already shown how bitterly in his heart he hated evil. This must, of course, be gathered not so much from direct statements or tirades against wickedness, as from the general tone of his treatment of moral questions. No one thinks of inveighing against evil in the abstract, because it is taken for granted that every man, if he be not reprobate, is on the side of good. A man's moral attitude is to be judged rather from the sincerity and spontaneousness of his shrinking from what is evil and his unconscious influence in leading his readers to shrink from it, as from a thing loathsome and abhorrent. That Stevenson has done with a power which has seldom been surpassed. It is needless to multiply examples, when they are to be found in almost everything he wrote. Yet the one touch in Markheim, where he describes for us a man in whom the hatred of evil survives the death of all love of good, is itself a conclusive proof that in him we have one whose earnestness, as well as his insight, is assured. To most men, in this world where the finer spiritual and moral life grows slowly from the primitive soil of coarse and animal instincts, hatred is a principle hardier and more

[1] P. 145.

inalienable than love, whether for evil or for good. Browning knew this well when he wrote his great lines:

> 'Dante, who loved well because he hated,
> Hated wickedness that hinders loving.'

Stevenson could not have loved the good so well, had there not been in him a bitter hatred of the evil.

We have already noted his power of depicting the moral tragedy of life. It must now be added that apart from all considerations of the picturesque and vivid by which that tragedy may have tempted him, the real secret of his success in this department lay in moral earnestness. In some of his more violent work, such as *The Bottle Imp*, we see the tragedy at its most exciting point of horror; or, as in *The Great North Road*, the criminal, growing insane in the recklessness of crime, finds that it has now come to the question whether he 'minds for God.' Yet it is not in such passages as these that Stevenson's moral earnestness is most impressive, but rather in his calmer work. Near the close of *The Black Arrow* there is a passage which it would be hard to match for quiet power of this kind, where Dick, at the expense of his own favour with the Duke, saves the life of Captain Arblaster, upon whom he has unwittingly brought ruin.

'Arblaster,' said Dick, 'I have done you ill; but now, by the rood, I think I have cleared the score.'
But the old skipper only looked upon him dully and held his peace.
'Come,' continued Dick, 'a life is a life, old shrew, and it is more than ships or liquor. Say ye forgive me; for if your life is worth nothing to you, it hath cost me the beginnings of my fortune. Come, I have paid for it dearly; be not so churlish.'
'An I had had my ship,' said Arblaster, 'I would 'a been forth and safe on the high seas—I and my man Tom. But ye took my ship, gossip, and I'm a beggar; and for my man Tom, a knave fellow in russet shot him down. "Murrain!" quoth he, and spake never again. "Murrain" was the last of his

words, and the poor spirit of him passed. 'A will never sail no more will my Tom.'

Dick was seized with unavailing penitence and pity; he sought to take the skipper's hand, but Arblaster avoided his touch.

'Nay,' said he, 'let be. Y' have played the devil with me, and let that content you.'

The words died in Richard's throat. He saw, through tears, the poor old man, bemused with liquor and sorrow, go shambling away, with bowed head, across the snow, and the unnoticed dog whimpering at his heels; and for the first time began to understand the desperate game that we play in life, and how a thing once done is not to be changed or remedied by any penitence.'

The moral earnestness which this passage and many others reveal might well have led him into an austere morality and given us our last glimpse of him trudging, in the wake of Hermiston, 'up the great bare staircase of his duty.' He cultivates a solemnising and sometimes terrifying seriousness in dealing with grave moral subjects, and insists that it is part of true manhood to be able to be serious when occasion requires it. Remembering the morbid passages in *Memories and Portraits*, and the exceptional power he had of lowering his lights until the darkness of his work grew altogether depressing, one watches for the end and the final verdict with anxious curiosity. He has a Hebrew conscience and a Greek imagination, a Scottish sense of sin and a French delight in beauty. Austerity might conceivably claim such a spirit for its own, and send him eventually forth in sackcloth, a prophet of pessimism. On the other hand, by sheer force of reaction from his sense of the tragic in human life, he might have left the bitter problems alone and turned to lightness.

As a matter of fact, he took neither of these courses, but one better and more true to himself than either of them. In him duty and pleasure were both imperative and he

230

managed to retain them both. A passing sentence in a letter to Mr. Edmund Gosse may serve to illustrate this. He is counselling his friend regarding style: 'And in a style which (like yours) aims more and more successfully at the academic, one purple word is already much; three—a whole phrase—is inadmissible. Wed yourself to a clean austerity; that is your force. Wear a linen ephod, *splendidly candid.*' The words which we have italicised are delightfully significant. Both are Latin words, obviously intended to be understood in their Latin sense. With this shining whiteness, this brilliance of raiment white and glistering, a writer assuredly needs no purple. But the austerity which has reached such effulgence has almost ceased to be austere, and this was his only sort of austerity either in art or in morals. Life was painted for him in high lights and deep shadows, and neither the light nor the darkness had it all its own way. In the brightest hour there is a shadow, in the darkest a gleam.

Nor do the two moods alternate in a broken and fitful life. Rather, the impression which grows as we watch the advancing years is that of sanity and balanced thought. If there is less of exuberance, there is more of quiet certainty. He retains his enthusiasm. Sanity never means with him a deadening of vitality, nor yet does he ever return even for a moment to the prison-house of the conventional from which he broke loose once for all in youth. Only there is an assured and confirmed healthfulness and an all-round naturalness of view, which are increasingly marked and always bracing and inspiring. 'I am,' so he tells us at the age of thirty-eight, 'very glad to fight out my battle, and see some fine sunsets, and hear some excellent jests between whiles round the camp fire.' Thus do the affectations of youth pass more and more into a harmonious naturalness of thought and character. He knows himself, and what he

231

is fit for, and what he prefers. He is no longer either aggressive or on his defence, but calm and smiling even while he makes his most startling announcements. Pagan in the frank delight in pleasant and bright things, Puritan in the austerity of his moral judgments, he appreciates the strength of rude elemental virtues and also the delicacy of spiritual refinements. But ever it is naturalness, truth to himself and his nature as he finds these, that is his guiding principle. He recognises the fact that each man has, for any given period of his life, a certain normal level, on which alone he can lead a healthy moral life. There are some who allow themselves to sink below that level, and these are they who dwell in darkness, lit by no ideals : others have been taught by conventional morality to aspire to high-flown virtues which are entirely out of their present reach, and these, blind to the fact that the ideals they claim to live by are for them no more than words, are the unconscious and well-meaning hypocrites. For himself, he knows his limitations and his reach, and lives up to the stretch of his present strength and light, knowing that the only way to gain the sunlit heights is by patiently climbing shoulder after shoulder of the mountain-side.

*Health* is, above all other words, the distinguishing and appropriate word for him. Cynicism he hates as an acute and disastrous form of morbidness. He will allow just a touch of it, as a tonic 'in cases of advanced sensibility,' or to keep people from a silly extravagance of optimism in moral affairs. 'So much of cynicism to recognise that nobody does right is the best equipment for those who do not wish to be cynics in good earnest.' For the fashionable cynic he cannot find words too scornful. He knows the perverse modern delight in misery, and the books in which 'young gentlemen with three or four hundred a year of private means look down from a pinnacle of doleful experience on all the grown and hearty men who have dared to say a good word for life since the beginning of the world.' He knows that sort of book, and he abominates it. 'I hate cynicism a great deal worse than I do the devil,' says he, 'unless perhaps the two were the same thing!' In contrast with all such morbidness we turn to his descriptions of heroes and to those casual lists of ideals in which a writer betrays without premeditation his own preference and admiration. Here are a few of them, typical of many others. 'Fire, thrift, and courage—a creature full-blooded and inspired with energy.' 'Never to set up to be soft, only to be square and hearty, and a man all round.' 'A fine face, honourable rather than intelligent, strong, simple, and righteous.' 'Strong, healthy, high-strung and generous natures.' 'Very, very nice fellows, simple, good, and not the least dull.' Such estimates prepare us for the more deliberate summary of human virtue which is now one of the most familiar of his sayings: 'To be honest, to be kind—to earn a little and to spend a little less, to make upon the whole a family happier for his presence, to renounce when that shall be necessary and not be embittered, to keep a few friends but these without capitulation—above all, on the same grim condition, to keep friends with himself—here is a task for all that a man has of fortitude and delicacy.' The closing words may be taken as the best possible summary of his ideals, and the best account also of his achievement. Fortitude and delicacy—in these is the fulfilling of the Law according to R. L. S.

One other instance of his general healthfulness must be mentioned. It is the spirit of purity which everywhere breathes in his work. It would be difficult to find any writer of so many books who has penned so few lines that leave a stain upon the memory. Not that there is the slightest suspicion of prudery about him. He is realist enough to insist upon facts when he has to deal with unpleasant characters and situations, and he resents interference in such matters. Indeed they are safe in his hands. In reading his broadest delineations of ugly vice or savage roughness of manners, there still remains the undefinable sense that we are in the presence of a man of delicate and clean instincts. He has described men's houses as the little clean spots which they create to dwell in; and one feels, in all his books, that he has built for the imagination many such houses. There is nothing obtrusive about this, it is simply part of his healthiness of mind, and we owe him all the deeper debt for it on that account. In a good deal of the literature of our time this phase of healthiness has been conspicuous by its absence. The demand of the age is for what is interesting; *ennui* threatens many, and to combat it several devices have been employed. Anything (within certain limits of course) will be forgiven a writer nowadays—any grossness, or falsehood, or unpleasantness— so long as he is not dull. To meet this demand one easy expedient is, by suggestion and allusion at least, to utilise the impure facts of life. Not that the morals inculcated are bad—the modern conscience is not robust enough, or rather perhaps it is not honest enough, to permit of that. The moral is generally excellent; but a real impurity is possible, and it is quite as interesting, in attacks upon certain vices as in defences of them—a secret well known to some of our writers of problem novels. From any suspicion of this, Stevenson is free. He succeeded in the task of being interesting without the help of sensuality. He has sent a clean and fresh breeze blowing over us, like that which we feel in Scott's work; and for this service alone our literature and our public morals owe him much.

As a final illustration of Stevenson's health of mind, let us take his view of the future and of the past—regions of

234

thought in which a man has perhaps a greater chance of growing morbid than any other. The spirit in which a man looks forward to the future is perhaps the most obvious test of his health of mind in the present. For Stevenson the future essentially means a new chance. The meaning of life itself is progress, and the thought of what we yet may be is the inspiration of the present. 'If we are indeed here to perfect and complete our own natures, and grow larger, stronger, and more sympathetic against some nobler career in the future, we had all best bestir ourselves to the utmost while we have the time. To equip a dull, respectable person with wings would be but to make a parody of an angel.' For the strenuous, the future wears but one aspect. For them there is no fearful looking for of judgment nor yet resignation in view of an approaching doom. Theirs it is to go bravely into the thick of the fight,

'And in the mellay charge remain,
To fall but yet to rise again.'

Fall they will, no doubt, as they have fallen in the past, but God, who sent them their opportunity and who also set for them the impediment through which they missed it, will act in a manner worthier and more Godlike than that of one who is quick to mark iniquity. Rather will He

'Diviner vengeance take—
Give me to sleep, give me to wake
Girded and shod, and bid me play
The hero in the coming day.'

It is, however, in regard to the past that the questions of moral earnestness and health are most severely tested, and demand the most careful balance. On the one hand, the sick soul is tempted to despair; on the other, the healthy-minded are led off into too light-hearted and shallow a view of sin. Stevenson's course is steered between the two, and there is no part of his theory of life more easy to formulate with

235

definiteness than his doctrine of repentance. His prayers afford the clearest examples, though there is a great deal besides that might be cited. We have seen his views of the evil of sin and of its hatefulness, and to these passages we would again refer the reader.[1] The prayer quoted on p. 146 is itself sufficient evidence of the importance of the place which he found for repentance in his moral system. But repentance is, in his estimate, a very different thing from 'the unclean passion of remorse,' and for that he found no place. In his *Prayer for Self-blame*, after the request that we may feel our offences with our hands, see them great and bright like the sun, eat and drink them for our diet, he goes on to pray: 'Help us at the same time with the grace of courage, that we be none of us cast down when we sit lamenting amid the ruins of our happiness or our integrity; touch us with fire from the altar, that we may be up and doing to rebuild our city.'

In a word, without energy, repentance is disease. He who can find nothing to do but weep for his sins, will end by weeping because he has nothing to eat. Like Mackellar, he 'knows nothing less respectable than the tears of drunkenness, and turns his back impatiently on this poor sight.' He is not afraid of the application of his principles to individual cases, and says plainly of Robert Burns: 'He was still not perhaps devoted to religion, but haunted by it; and at a touch of sickness prostrated himself before God in what I can only call unmanly penitence.' It is in the light of these and other such statements that we must read his assertion that we all think too much of sin. 'Never allow your mind to dwell on your own misconduct: that is ruin. The conscience has morbid sensibilities; it must be employed but not indulged. . . . Shut your eyes hard on the recollection of your sins. Do not be afraid, you

---

[1] P. 145.

will not be able to forget them. . . . Not every action
should be higgled over; one of the leading virtues therein
is to let oneself alone. But if you make it your chief
employment, you are sure to meddle too much.' Taken by
themselves these latter statements are no doubt startling.
But nothing could be healthier than their teaching, if we
understand them in the sense which he intended. There is
all the difference in the world between a sensitive conscience
and a scrupulous one. And in these sentences he is also
combating a more serious evil—a frame of mind in which
men are meanly grovelling before God. In doing this he is
but echoing the words which the prophet heard when he
fell upon his face by the river Chebar, stunned and terrified
by his vision, and the Voice said to him, 'Son of man, stand
upon thy feet and I will speak unto thee.' So, in Stevenson's
view, should life even at its worst be taken standing.
Otherwise remorse can only lead to uselessness, and the
sense of one's own sin to the stern and unfeeling condemnation of the trespasses of others.

To save us from such inert and profitless discouragement
he reminds us that even sin has its uses in the great and
mysterious design of human life. 'To any but the brutish
man his sins are the beginning of wisdom,' he protests, and
God warns men by their crimes. If life be progress to all
the strenuous, then the past, at its worst, is yet a stage on
the way to better things. He tells the story of a former
friend which remains with all who have read it as a hopeful
and inspiring memory. 'The tale of this great failure is,
to those who remained true to him, the tale of a success.
In his youth he took thought for no one but himself; when
he came ashore again, his whole armada lost, he seemed to
think of none but others. . . . He had gone to ruin with a
kind of kingly *abandon*, like one who condescended; but once
ruined, with the lights all out, he fought as for a kingdom.'

And so we come to the moral of it all, which may be expressed in the one phrase, 'Cling to what is left.' It is a phrase illuminated by its association with that accident to the canoe, when Stevenson, in imminent danger of his life, still clung to his paddle, and chose this record for a fitting epitaph to be inscribed upon his tomb. The incident is a not unfitting allegory of his whole view of the way in which a man should deal with character. It is a tragic affair, this human life of ours, beset with dangers and foredoomed to many failures. Even the victors in its contest shall assuredly, every one of them, enter into life maimed. In many a moral crisis there will be much that is lost, and what is lost in that warfare is lost for ever. But, apart from what may be actually gained, there is always at least something that remains not yet lost. In judging others it is well to remember this, and 'boldly make up your mind that you can do perfectly well without the rest; and that ten thousand bad traits cannot make a single good one any the less good.' In meditating over our own past, it is important, with all our regret and shame, still to be 'thankful that we are no worse.' 'Honour can survive a wound,' he writes in his discussion of Dumas' novel; 'it can live and thrive without a member. The man rebounds from his disgrace; he begins fresh foundations on the ruins of the old; and when his sword is broken he will do valiantly with his dagger. So it is with Fouquet in the book; so it was with Dumas on the battlefield of life. To cling to what is left of any damaged quality is virtue in the man.' In this there is the hope and the spring of renewed activity. There is no conceivable situation in life which does not offer a man one right course to follow at the moment. We have seen how he describes as the saddest and most miserable feature in the plight of Robert Burns this, that he is condemned to the choice of two evils, and whichever way he chooses he will still be wrong. That, however, is but the appearance of the case. In reality there is always a way which will be right. 'Conceive a man,' says Mr. Archer, 'damned to a choice of only evil—misconduct upon either side . . . naught before him but this choice of sins. How would you say then?' 'I would say that he was much deceived, Mr. Archer,' returned Nance. 'I would say that there was a third choice, and that the right one.' It is true that in this case there was no apparent fault behind the man driving him to the dilemma. Yet even if there had been, Nance's was the true answer. Life never absolutely commits any man to crime; there is always set before every man an open door.

It is thus that Stevenson's moral earnestness is the inspiration not of a morbid but of a supremely healthy view of life. To some of his detailed statements we may take exception, and it is true also that there is another side to all this teaching, without due consideration of which it is not without its dangers. There are depths of moral experience which it has never sounded, and the sick soul will sometimes touch bottom in a despair far below its range of helpfulness. Yet still his doctrine retains its truth and value. It is not a wise, though it is only a too common, principle of criticism, which judges a man by what he has has left unsaid. For that silence there may be various motives, and his experience may have gone at times too deep for any attempt at expression. So far as it goes, this part of his faith is Christian, full of a courage, a resoluteness, and a hope which Christ Himself approved. In some of those to whom He said, 'Go and sin no more,' there can have been but a very halting faith, so far as intellectual understanding went. In all of them there was the forsaking of the broken and wasted past, to face the future with that which remained. The power to do this certainly lay in Him who inspired them with new courage and offered them the new chance. But when we see a man, obviously inspired for duty, undismayed by failure, facing the future as Stevenson ever faced it for himself and urged his fellows to face it, may we not discern behind the gallant figure of the human combatant the form of the Son of Man? At least we may be sure of this, that there are very many persons whose moral condition needs exactly this message. With faith confused and dim, with the irrevocable past filling all their souls with discouragement, it cannot but be well for them to hear the voice that calls to them to hold fast that which remains. If they will take heart and obey, sooner or later the Master will reveal Himself to them; for it was Himself who said that many acts done strenuously and lovingly by those who knew not that they were serving Him would prove at the last to have been done unto Him.

# CHAPTER XIII

## THE 'GREAT TASK OF HAPPINESS'

THE faith which expressed itself in sympathy and appreciation, and in manliness and health, led up to one great truth in which it culminated. The duty of joy, the ethical value of happiness, is *par excellence* the message of Robert Louis Stevenson. This, more than any other ideal, was the light of his vision, and the inspiration of his travel. It touches every part of his experience, from physical pleasures, up through the delights of intellectual and moral life, to the most exalted spiritual joys; and its proclamation is the distinguishing feature of his life-work.

The idea of enjoyment cannot be mentioned in connection with ethics, without at once suggesting the utilitarian doctrine that the end of action is happiness, which thus becomes the ultimate motive and test of conduct. We must hasten at the outset to dissociate Stevenson from any such doctrine. Much as he has praised happiness and inculcated it, there is nothing further from his faith than this, nor anything which he has more explicitly disowned. Fleeming Jenkin had said to one who announced that she would never be happy again: 'What does that signify? We are not here to be happy, but to be good.' Stevenson, who recorded the saying, heartily endorsed it, correcting it, however, by a significant addition: 'We are not here to be happy but *to try* to be good.' This sentiment he repeats in some of his most serious letters, and he adds the further assertion that happiness is not only not the end of our life, it is not even our deepest desire. 'We are not put here to enjoy ourselves: it was not God's purpose; and I am prepared to argue, it is not our sincere wish.' 'Men do not want, and I do not think they would accept, happiness; what they live for is rivalry, effort, success.' The relation of all this to his doctrine of reward is obvious, and it is plainly stated in another letter: 'Nor is happiness, whether eternal or temporal, the reward that mankind seeks. Happinesses are but his wayside campings; his soul is in the journey.'

So far Stevenson is at one with Carlyle, and would readily subscribe to the immortal words of *Sartor Resartus*: 'What is this that, ever since earliest years, thou hast been fretting and fuming, and lamenting and self-tormenting, on account of? Say it in a word: is it not because thou art not HAPPY? Because the THOU (sweet gentleman) is not sufficiently honoured, nourished, soft-bedded, and lovingly cared for? Foolish soul! What Act of Legislature was there that *thou* shouldst be Happy?' But he soon comes to a practical dilemma, at which he parts from Carlyle. So far as the man himself is concerned, he can repudiate happiness. 'In his own life, then, a man is not to expect happiness, only to profit by it gladly when it shall arise.' But where the happiness of others is involved, the case is different. Stevenson feels that 'somehow or other, though he cannot tell what will do it, he must try to give happiness to others. And of course there arises here a frequent clash of duties. How far is he to make his neighbour happy? How far must he respect that smiling face, so easy to cloud, so hard to brighten again?' And besides, if happiness be indeed no right end of conduct for oneself, how can it be the proper thing to aim at for one's neighbours?

This is one of the few instances in which there appears to

be some inconsistency or at least confusion in Stevenson's
thought. He is aware of the dilemma, and he escapes from
it not by working out a theory, but by committing himself to
a practical principle of action. *Solvitur ambulando;* and
the solution is as satisfactory as any that the most subtle
logic could have offered. In the Carlylian mood he states
in strong terms the opinion that happiness is by no means a
certain accompaniment of right conduct. 'Happiness and
goodness, according to canting moralists, stand in the
relation of effect and cause. There was never anything less
proved or less probable: our happiness is never in our own
hands; we inherit our constitution; we stand buffet among
friends and enemies; we may be so built as to feel a sneer
or an aspersion with unusual keenness, and so circum-
stanced as to be unusually exposed to them; we may have
nerves very sensitive to pain, and be afflicted with a disease
very painful. Virtue will not help us, and it is not meant
to help us. It is not even its own reward, except for the
self-centred and—I had almost said—the unamiable.' Thus
does he cast aside the doctrine of the happiness of duty as
it has been generally held. Happiness, considered from the
point of view of ethics, he defines as nothing but an internal
harmony—a harmony between our conduct and our conviction, whether the conduct be in itself right or wrong.

We might naturally expect, as the sequel, a final dis-
missal of all considerations of happiness in the moral life.
Nothing could be further from his mind. The doctrine of
the happiness of duty is only cast aside in favour of the
less familiar one of the duty of happiness. The theoretical
perplexities are left to settle themselves; the facts of life
present him with the practical exit from their coil. To a
man of sympathy and strong human affection, the happiness
of those around him, so far as that lies in his power, cannot
fail to be imperative. Accordingly we come atonce to the

243

duty of making others happy, and of being happy ourselves
that we may be able so to do. These principles are stated
with his usual absoluteness, in epigrams which, taken by
themselves, are sometimes startling. 'Pleasures are more
beneficial than duties, because, like the quality of mercy,
they are not strained, and they are twice blest. . . .
Wherever there is an element of sacrifice the favour is
conferred with pain, and, among generous people, received
with confusion. There is no duty we so much underrate as
the duty of being happy.' 'No man was ever anything but
a wet blanket and a cross to his companions, who boasted
not a copious spirit of enjoyment.' 'A happy man or
woman is a better thing to find than a five-pound note.
He or she is a radiating focus of good-will; and their
entrance into a room is as though another candle had been
lighted.'

Once canonised as a duty in its own right, the duty of
happiness soon takes the place of honour and precedence.
'Gentleness and cheerfulness, these come before all
morality; they are the perfect duties. . . . If your morals
make you dreary, depend upon it they are wrong.' 'Noble
disappointment, noble self-denial, are not to be admired, not
even to be pardoned, if they bring bitterness.' In a word,
we have no right to be gloomy upon any pretext. The
poem in which this sentiment finds fullest expression is
*The Celestial Surgeon*, in which he contemplates the possibility of lapsing into a condition of joyless apathy and
sullen gloom, and prays for anything that may arouse him,
whether it be a pleasure, or a pain, or even a killing sin.
This poem has been frequently quoted by writers who are
alive to the spiritual dangers of the time, and it has
quickened not a few whose spirits were flagging. Although
to many readers it is familiar, we copy it entire from
*Underwoods*:

244

# THE 'GREAT TASK OF HAPPINESS'

'If I have faltered more or less
In my great task of happiness;
If I have moved among my race
And shown no glorious morning face;
If beams from happy human eyes
Have moved me not; if morning skies,
Books, and my food, and summer rain
Knocked on my sullen heart in vain:—
Lord, thy most pointed pleasure take
And stab my spirit broad awake;
Or, Lord, if too obdurate I,
Choose thou, before that spirit die,
A piercing pain, a killing sin,
And to my dead heart run them in.'

For that one phrase of the fourth line, a 'glorious morning
face,' we owe him much. It was one which was evidently
very attractive to himself, for we find it again in one of his
prayers, in *The Black Arrow*, and elsewhere. Had he done
nothing else than to set these bright words in the hearts
of his readers, he would have still been a man with a
message to his generation.

The phrase 'duty of happiness' is rather suggestive of
happiness at the sword's point, and there were times when
it needed all the determination and courage at his command.
Yet it was reinforced by an abundant spring of natural
gaiety and joy which he preserved unchanged from his
childhood. Mr. Gosse says that gaiety was his cardinal
quality—' a childlike mirth leaped and danced in him; he
seemed to skip upon the hills of life.' Such continued
childhood was evidently a favourite type of character with
him. No one who has read his *Memoir of Fleeming Jenkin*
can ever forget the charming picture of the last days of the
Professor's father, Captain Jenkin, a chapter breathing the
sweetest spirit of the child, and one which could have been
written only by a man possessed of the rarest genius for
such work. The Captain's request for a device to be hung
below the trophy in his dining-room is significant of the

whole : ' I want you to work me something, Annie. An anchor at each side—an anchor—stands for an old sailor, you know—stands for hope, you know—an anchor at each side, and in the middle THANKFUL.' Stevenson must surely have had the Captain in his mind, when, in the year following the publication of the Memoir, he wrote in *A Christmas Sermon*: 'And the kingdom of heaven is of the childlike, of those who are easy to please, who love and who give pleasure. Mighty men of their hands, the smiters and the builders and the judges, have lived long and done sternly and yet preserved this lovely character; and among our carpet interests and twopenny concerns, the shame were indelible if *we* should lose it.'

It was in his own childhood that he learned the secret of gladness. The glee of children is partly a matter of physical vitality : it is as inevitable as childhood itself—

> ' Happy hearts and happy faces,
> Happy play in grassy places—
> That was how, in ancient ages,
> Children grew to kings and sages.'

From his earliest days he never found it hard to 'make himself cheerful,' and his imagination transformed the sick-bed into 'the pleasant land of counterpane.' The same exuberance of animal spirits is to be seen in children even more handicapped than he, as we perceive from the wonderfully fine picture he has drawn of two ragged little girls dancing barefoot on the Edinburgh pavement in the teeth of an east wind. But the secret of his childlike gladness was more than animal spirits. It was a sense of the opulence of the world in interesting and delightful objects. Some of his happiest verses are inspired by this thought, especially those entitled *A Thought* and *Happy Thought*:

# THE 'GREAT TASK OF HAPPINESS'

> ' It is very nice to think
> The world is full of meat and drink,
> With little children saying grace
> In every Christian kind of place' ;

and

> ' The world is so full of a number of things,
> I'm sure we should all be as happy as kings.'

Besides his sense of the opulence of the world, the child's joy kindles at the thought of anything which makes him feel his own importance and significance in it. The gladdest thing for a boy, is to be made to feel that he is somebody and counts for something. This conviction is the same as that interest in himself, that sense of his own personality, which we have already found so strong in Stevenson. The essay in which it finds its most perfect expression is 'The Lantern-bearers,' in *Across the Plains*. Of that essay Professor James has said, in one of his *Talks to Students*, that it deserves to become immortal. He quotes it at great length, but for our present purpose the following extracts will be enough :—

'Toward the end of September, when school-time was drawing near and the nights were already black, we would begin to sally from our respective villas, each equipped with a tin bull's-eye lantern. The thing was so well known that it had worn a rut in the commerce of Great Britain ; and the grocers, about the due time, began to garnish their windows with our particular brand of luminary. We wore them buckled to the waist upon a cricket-belt, and over them, such was the rigour of the game, a buttoned top-coat. They smelled noisomely of blistered tin ; they never burned aright, though they would always burn our fingers ; their use was naught ; the pleasure of them merely fanciful ; and yet a boy with a bull's-eye under his top-coat asked for nothing more. . . .

'When two of these asses met, there would be an anxious 'Have you got your lantern?' and a gratified 'Yes!' That was the shibboleth, and very needful too ; for, as it was the rule to keep our glory contained, none could recognise a lantern-

247

bearer, unless (like the polecat) by the smell.  Four or five would sometimes climb into the belly of a ten-man lugger, with nothing but the thwarts above them—for the cabin was usually locked—or choose out some hollow of the links where the wind might whistle overhead.  There the coats would be unbuttoned and the bull's-eyes discovered; and in the chequering glimmer, under the huge windy hall of the night, and cheered by a rich steam of toasting tinware, these fortunate young gentlemen would crouch together in the cold sand of the links or on the scaly bilges of the fishing-boat, and delight themselves with inappropriate talk.  Woe is me, that I may not give some specimens—some of their foresights of life, or deep inquiries into the rudiments of man and nature, these were so fiery and so innocent, they were so richly silly, so romantically young.  But the talk, at any rate, was but a condiment; and these gatherings themselves only accidents in the career of the lantern-bearer.  The essence of this bliss was to walk by yourself in the black night; the slide shut, the top-coat buttoned; not a ray escaping, whether to conduct your footsteps or to make your glory public; a mere pillar of darkness in the dark; and all the while, deep down in the privacy of your fool's heart, to know you had a bull's-eye at your belt, and to exult and sing over the knowledge. . . . For to miss the joy is to miss all. In the joy of the actors lies the sense of any action.  That is the explanation, that the excuse.  To one who has not the secret of the lanterns, the scene upon the links is meaningless.'

When he became a man, there were some childish things which, happily for himself, he did not put away.  The glee of childhood remained with him as a constitutional optimism, a natural tendency, like that of his mother, to look upon the bright side of things.  He highly appreciates the sentiment of D'Artagnan's old servant, ' *Monsieur, j'étais une de ces bonnes pâtes d'hommes que Dieu a faits pour s'animer pendant un certain temps et pour trouver bonnes toutes choses qui accompagnent leur séjour sur la terre.*'  In this full-grown optimism we perceive the development of that sense of opulence in the world which the child had already

248

felt. His world is full of pleasures for him, 'so that to see the day break or the moon rise, or to meet a friend, or to hear the dinner-call when he is hungry, fills him with surprising joys.' His prayers are full of such catalogues of blessings, thanking God for work and friends, for food and laughter. He tells us he used to sit at night on the platform of his house in Silverado, and listen to the song of the crickets, 'and wonder why these creatures were so happy; and what was wrong with man that he also did not wind up his days with an hour or two of shouting.'

The keenness of his senses made all the physical world minister to his pleasure. He was not one of those who profess to despise the pleasures in which they nevertheless continue to indulge. We have all met the man who says he smokes because he cannot give up the practice, but speaks sententiously about its evils. If such had been his sentiments, Stevenson would, like any other man of sense or principle, have given it up at once. He smoked because he enjoyed smoking, and he smoked hard. On the wider field of Nature, his susceptibility to joy remained keen and strong throughout. 'O my beautiful forest,' he exclaims at Vailima, 'O my beautiful, shining, windy house, what a joy it was to behold them again! No chance to take myself too seriously here!' 'Some very violent squalls came as we sat there, and every one rejoiced; it was impossible to help it; a soul of putty had to sing.' In Silverado 'A rough smell of resin was in the air, and a crystal mountain purity. It came pouring over these green ocean slopes by the oceanful. The woods sang aloud and gave largely of their healthful breath. Gladness seemed to inhabit these upper zones, and we had left indifference behind us in the valley. "I to the hills will lift mine eyes." There are days in a life when thus to climb out of the lowlands seems like scaling heaven.'

249

While his disposition made happiness natural to him, the circumstances of his life were such that the inclination had often to be reinforced by a sense of duty. It is a mixed world, and even the lightest-hearted will find at times that he has to make a deliberate choice of the brighter things, and to ignore the darker, if his heart is to remain light. It is for lack of any sense of duty in the matter of good spirits that many naturally happy persons either end in alternating between high spirits and hopeless gloom, or sink into a deepening distrust of life and cease to be their former selves. Their mistake is to trust to nature for everything, something being always left for will to do. Many a man, on the other hand, gets little credit for his indomitable good cheer, because it is supposed that this is but his natural inclination. But a virtue is still a virtue, even though it be congenial; and those who have diligently kept their lamp of joy alight are not the least worthy of God's faithful ones. As for Stevenson, he deliberately drew upon and encouraged all the available sources of gladness. He carried with him into manhood, not only the glee that comes from physical vitality, and the sense of the world's opulence, but also the spirit of the Lantern-bearer, who carefully kept alive his inner light. His natural optimism is unquestionable, but it should be remembered that he needed it all, and that, if his strenuous choice of it had flagged, pessimism would not have been far to seek. It is a great and potent secret, that of fostering our own peculiar enthusiasm as a sacred flame. Regard yourself, as you face the simplest duty of to-morrow, as tending within your soul's temple the fires of God, and you shall find the bright parable true. Both these sources, the outward and the inward, were largely drawn upon by Stevenson.

This involves, first of all, a deliberate selection of the brighter things for attention. Nothing could be blither

250

than those sudden glances across the world which, in the *Child's Garden* and elsewhere, show its inhabitants rejoicing far and near:

> 'Of speckled eggs the birdie sings
> And nests among the trees;
> The sailor sings of ropes and things
> In ships upon the seas.
>
> The children sing in far Japan,
> The children sing in Spain;
> The organ with the organ man
> Is singing in the rain.'

In the character of the French especially he is delighted with the 'clear unflinching recognition by everybody of his own luck. They all know on which side their bread is buttered, and take a pleasure in showing it to others, which is surely the better part of religion.' He compares the French Camisards with the Scottish Covenanters, and prefers the spirit of the former, because they had only bright and supporting visions, while the latter were much in conflict with the devil, and 'though they might be certain of the cause, could never rest confident of the person.'

In every situation there are pleasant things for a man to attend to if he will. 'I saw the sea,' he says, 'to be great and calm; and the earth, in that little corner, was all alive and friendly to me. So, wherever a man is, he will find something to please and pacify him: in the town he will meet pleasant faces of men and women, and see beautiful flowers at a window, or hear a cage-bird singing at the corner of the gloomiest street; and for the country, there is no country without some amenity—let him only look for it in the right spirit, and he will surely find it.' So it is in judging the characters of our fellow men; there is always something that is lovely and of good report in them. So it is in judging of one's own experience. If much have gone from life,

251

there is still something left. Even if the worst come to the worst, there is some compensating element in the very fact that one has now at last touched bottom. 'This is life at last,' he may tell himself; 'this is the real thing. The bladders on which I was set swimming are now empty; my own weight depends upon the ocean; by my own exertions I must perish or succeed.' But the worst does not, as a matter of fact, come to the worst nearly so often as we fear, either in our fortunes or in our character. 'It is a commonplace that we cannot answer for ourselves before we have been tried. But it is not so common a reflection, and surely more consoling, that we usually find ourselves a great deal braver and better than we thought.'

But Stevenson's deliberate optimism, in which happiness is a great task as well as a natural disposition, involved more than selection of the brighter elements in life. There are for every man seasons when no element seems bright, and in such dark times the brightness has to be created by the would-be optimist. Professor James, who has many things in common with Stevenson, has brought into prominence of late a startling and most suggestive theory of the emotions. It is usually supposed that immediately after perceiving the exciting fact, the emotion follows, and then, third in the order of time, the bodily expression. Thus, to use the great psychologist's own illustrations, 'we lose our fortune, are sorry and weep; we meet a bear, are frightened and run.' His theory reverses the order of the latter two statements, and makes the bodily effect follow directly on the perception, to be followed in its turn finally by the emotion. Under this view it is our weeping that causes sorrow, our trembling and running that induce the emotion of fear. This is no place to discuss the theory upon its merits, or to judge for or against its psychological value and sufficiency. Its claim

252

upon our attention here is that it has given the key to a large number of actual problems in practical life, in which by forcing the body into certain expressions we may lead the mind to follow suit, and so may, by the help of the flesh, produce certain spiritual conditions which are otherwise wholly beyond our reach. It is this that lies at the root of much that we have already said of acting.[1] In the present connection it means that a darkened life may often be recalled to a sense of the brightness of the world by a determined effort. By resolute smiling, so to speak, we may become glad; and our world will eventually respond to our determined policy of taking it as if it were brighter than for the time it appears. By a deliberate pretence that the world is fairer than it looks, we can see the miracle of a world actually becoming fair under our eyes. This is another phase of that victory of faith which overcomes the world; it overcomes the world by forcing it to assume the aspect it desires. The secret was well known to Stevenson. Not only did he diligently seek out the encouraging and bright aspects of experience as he actually found them. Jesus Christ once said to a doubting apostle, 'Blessed are they that have not seen and yet have believed.' Stevenson believed through many an hour when he had not seen, and so was blessed. When all was dark, he pointed his telescope right into the blackness, and found a star. It is thus that faith may imitate the Master's work, calling things which are not as though they are, and find that the dark world has no power to resist faith's command when it boldly says, Let there be light. Many a happy fact, insignificant and easily forgotten amidst prevailing difficulties and trials, he emphasised and isolated, and let his thought play round it until it had assumed such proportions as to dominate his view of life, and command the spirit

[1] Cp. p. 43.

to rejoice. It is in the light of all this that we must remember his advocacy of boastfulness, which is one way of making the most of what good a man finds in his situation: 'If people knew what an inspiriting thing it is to hear a man boasting, so long as he boasts of what he really has, I believe they would do it more fully and with a better grace.'

It is the element of duty in it that saves optimism from being one of the worst of things and makes it one of the best. There is a cheap and impertinent optimism, which consists in not looking at the facts of life, but nursing a pleasant mood without reference to them. From this Stevenson was singularly free. He prayed to be delivered from all cheap pleasures, and refused to cheat himself into any blindfold light-heartedness. He found some good things actually there, and concentrated on them—a very different matter from the brainless optimism of the blindfolded. His action, when no good could be seen, was founded upon a faith that in the depths

'This world's no blot for us,
Nor blank ; it means intensely and means good'

—a faith which he found experience abundantly to confirm. It is one thing to live in a fool's paradise of our own imagining; it is a very different thing to trust life and to find it reveal its trustworthiness in return for the venture of faith. Whether optimism shall be mere vanity, or whether it shall be the discovery of God, depends almost wholly upon how much it is cherished on the one hand as a form of selfishness, or on the other as a matter of duty He believed in life because he found that only in that belief could a man be true to himself and serviceable to others. And life justified his faith, for to the strenuous and the unselfish it is always true that 'experience worketh hope, and hope maketh not ashamed.'

254

Such were his principles, and if the question be asked, how far he realised them in actual life, there need be no fear as to the answer. He was, indeed, a man of many moods, and it would be vain to attempt to hold him down to any one of them. He was also a man whose physical health must have rendered it absolutely impossible for him to maintain an unbroken cheerfulness. In the latter years, when health seemed in an unhoped-for degree to have been restored, the complications and responsibilities of his life must often have rendered peace an impossibility and gladness a triumph. From these years, and from times of specially bad health before them, when he was 'far through,' there come confessions of gloom and even protests against circumstances such as any reasonable onlooker would expect. It would be quite possible, and yet it would be entirely misleading, to gather from such passages the impression of a deepening pessimism. They certainly forbid us to think of him as a thoughtless or feather-brained optimist, but their presence beside the courageous belief in life, and the cheerfulness and enjoyment which alternate with them even at the worst, only serve to give the impression of a sober and chastened joy, and to keep his happiness from frivolity.

Under the burden of ill-health or overwork, his cheerfulness does occasionally give way. He speaks of having known what it was to be happy once, long ago, at Hyères, while now he knows only pleasures, plentiful, indeed, but none of them perfect. Again he tells us that he is gay no longer. His literary work becomes painful and burdensome. He is not strong enough to do his best, and work tires him, so that when it is done he does not know whether it is good or not, or is positively disappointed with it. In such hours of depression a constitutional distrust of the future possesses him, in spite of the hopefulness he had inherited from his mother. He will never write well again, he fears. He views the future as a heavy task from which all zest and interest have departed. He thinks he has lost his chance by not dying sooner. Within a few months of the end he fears that there is no hope of his dying soon and cleanly, and 'winning off the stage.' He will 'have to see this business out, after all.' This sense that he had outlived his life was the saddest point he reached. The quality of the work he was doing at the time entirely belied it; but sometimes his life ran too low to allow him to appreciate the joy of that labour which had reached as near perfection as it is almost ever given to man to reach. *Weir of Hermiston* was written *after* he had penned these lines:

> ' I have trod the upward and the downward slope ;
> I have endured and done in days before ;
> I have longed for all, and bid farewell to hope ;
> And I have lived, and loved, and closed the door.'

It is but just to record these depressions and misgivings, for we desire to know the man as he was, and it may be that they bring him nearer to some of us than any unbroken record of good spirits could have brought him. Without them, the victory might have seemed so complete as to be unhelpful to those—and they are the most of men—who cannot be always shouting for joy.

Yet, even in the darkest times, the victory was wonderfully near completeness. He had many varieties of gladsome moods with which to confront the forms of darkness in his Valley of the Shadow. There is no need for us to labour at the distinction between what is called happiness and what may be better designated as joy, or at any other definitions of a similar kind. Such distinctions are never exact, and then he knew all the phases without analysing them, so that we may be pretty safe in assigning to him whatever phase of gladness appeals to us. Roughly speaking, it may be said that in him we see (1) natural gaiety affording much happiness, and (2) that happiness settling down upon the life in an optimism which may be called contentment, and (3) finally passing over into a deep and strong joyfulness of soul.

1. The gaiety is bright and daring. It is what we naturally expect in strong and well-developed spirits, as a natural reaction from the gloom. The twinkle of humour that plays about all his work, even the most serious, must have been apparent to every reader of the extracts we have quoted. The fun and banter of his letters are kept up to the last, and there are passages in many of them whose comicality is irresistible. Remembering how hard pressed he was by many troubles, our heart is glad for him when we find Professor Colvin writing: 'To those about him, whether visitors or inmates, he remained the impersonation of life and spirit, maintaining to the last the same charming gaiety as ever, the same happy eagerness in all pursuits and interests; and fulfilling without failure the words of his own prayer, "Give us to awake with smiles, give us to labour smiling; as the sun lightens the world, so let our loving-kindness make bright this house of our habitation."' In the thick of the political fight which brought with it so many vexations, he still writes that 'it's capital fun.' One of his last letters ends: 'Literally, no man has more wholly outlived life than I. And still it's good fun.' In such utterances there is doubtless a certain element of defiance, and their gaiety is a little forced, reminding us of that hero of our younger days who

'Played a spring and danced it round
Beneath the gallows-tree.'

In one morning prayer there are two petitions for laughter that may help in the performance of 'the petty round of irritating concerns and duties.' Yet the buoyant gaiety did not need much forcing. It was part of his nature; and if the old pathetic words might well have been applied to him, 'Werena my heart licht I wad dee,' it is consoling to remember that his heart was indeed light enough to carry him through the trials of his life. When all else died down within him and his life ran low; when hope had lost its glamour and even courage itself seemed to be shaken; the strained and doubtful situation is relieved by a burst of ringing laughter, and when that subsides we find the air clear again. '"Be sure we'll have some pleisand weather, When a' the clouds has blawn awa'."' Verses that have a quite inexplicable attraction for me, and I believe had for Burns. They have no merit, but are somehow good. I am now in a most excellent humour.'

2. Mr. Chesterton has said that 'the supreme and splendid characteristic of Stevenson was his levity; and his levity was the flower of a hundred grave philosophies. The strong man is always light: the weak man is always heavy. . . . His triumph was, not that he went through his misfortunes without becoming a cynic or a poltroon, but that he went through his misfortunes and emerged quite exceptionally cheerful and reasonable and courteous, quite exceptionally light-hearted and liberal-minded. . . . Stevenson was characterised by a certain airy wisdom, a certain light and cool rationality, which is very rare and very difficult indeed to those who are greatly thwarted or tormented in life. . . . It may not be impossible or even unusual for a man to lie on his back on a sick-bed in a dark room and be an optimist. But it is very unusual indeed for a man to lie on his back on a sick-bed in a dark room and be a reasonable optimist: and that is what Stevenson, almost alone of modern optimists, succeeded in being.'

These are words of rare insight and analysis, perhaps as near the mark as anything that has been said about him. Nothing could be more exact than that 'levity of the strong

man,' that 'light and cool rationality of the much thwarted
and tormented.' This leads us down from the sparkling
peaks of gaiety to the far more difficult optimism of the
valley and the foot-hills. To defy life's worst with loud
laughter is often a wise and good thing to do: it is always
heartening to those who hear the shouts. Yet its exhilaration is not assured victory over life, and its excitements are
apt to be followed by reaction. It is good to mount up
with wings as eagles, but there remains the harder task of
learning to walk and not faint. This task also he achieved.
With all the inequalities of Providence, with all the
iniquitous and savage cruelty of Nature, with all the
incomprehensible obstacles thrown across his own path, he
still accepted the universe, not so much in resignation as in
acquiescence. In a sense, every sane person accepts the
universe—there is nothing else to do, and those who rail
against the universe make the preposterous assumption that
they have understood it, and found it out. But there are
some who accept it only in the sense of taking what comes,
with silent tongue and hard-set teeth. Stevenson not only
did not grumble; he also appreciated to its full the intelligible and kindly elements in the mystery of things. 'Sick
or well,' he writes, 'I have had a splendid time of it, grudge
nothing, regret very little.' It will probably be a long
while before a parallel passage can be written to the following, in which Mr. Graham Balfour tells the story of an
illness in the Riviera in 1884 :—

'Recovery was very slow and attended by numerous complications, less dangerous, but even more painful than the
original malady. The dust of street refuse gave him Egyptian
ophthalmia, and sciatica descending upon him caused him the
more pain, as he was suffering already from restlessness. The
hemorrhage was not yet healed, and we now hear for the first
time of the injunctions to absolute silence, orders patiently
obeyed, distasteful as they were. In silence and the dark, and

in acute suffering, he was still cheery and undaunted. When the ophthalmia began and the doctor first announced his diagnosis, Mrs. Stevenson felt that it was more than any one could be expected to bear, and went into another room, and there, in her own phrase, "sat and gloomed." Louis rang his bell and she went to him, saying, in the bitterness of her spirit, as she entered the room: "Well, I suppose that this is the very best thing that could have happened!" "Why, how odd!" wrote Louis on a piece of paper, "I was just going to say those very words."'

3. It is one thing to announce, in loud and oft-repeated assertions, that one's experience of life is all very good; it is another thing actually to rejoice in life. Without involving ourselves in any intricate analysis, it may be asserted that while happiness is possible upon less exacting terms, true joyfulness is possible only to those who have accepted it as a duty. The joyfulness of Stevenson was no surface optimism; it lay rich and deep beneath the gaiety and the contentment alike. He was not content either to laugh through his life, or merely to tolerate it; he enjoyed it. This is obvious in the feelings with which he regarded his art. Like all art, it had to be learned painfully; yet he found that 'No other business offers a man his daily bread upon such joyful terms.' He frankly asserts the highest function of Art to be the diffusion of joy. 'In my view, one dank, dispirited word is harmful, a crime of *lèse humanité*, a piece of acquired evil; every gay, every bright word or picture, like every pleasant air of music, is a piece of pleasure set afloat; the reader catches it, and if he be healthy, goes on his way rejoicing; and it is the business of Art so to send him, as often as possible.' Yet that can only be true of Art if it be in the first place true of Life itself. If Life, at the heart of it, is joyless, the joy of Art is but a pleasant lie. Stevenson, like all wise artists, had gone deeper than Art for the foundations of his joy. He was

'one that delighted in life,' and who was able to sing from
an honest heart:

> 'I know not how it is with you—
> *I* love the first and last,
> The whole field of the present view,
> The whole flow of the past.'

We have now arrived at a point from which it is but a
step to religious faith. In a letter which we have already
quoted, Stevenson expressly rejects Optimism in favour of
Faith. His words are: 'There are only three possible
attitudes—Optimism, which has gone to smash; Pessimism,
which is on the rising hand, and very popular with many
clergymen who seem to think they are Christians; and
this Faith, which is the Gospel.' This distinction between
optimism and faith he insists upon at greater length in
*Virginibus Puerisque*, optimism appearing under the name
of Hope. 'Hope, they say, deserts us at no period of our
existence. From first to last, and in the face of smarting
disillusions, we continue to expect good fortune, better
health, and better conduct; and that so confidently, that we
judge it needless to deserve them.' Later on, however, we
read that 'Hope is the boy, a blind, headlong, pleasant
fellow, good to chase swallows with the salt; Faith is the
grave, experienced, yet smiling man. Hope lives on
ignorance; open-eyed Faith is built upon a knowledge of
our life, of the tyranny of circumstance, and the frailty of
human resolution. Hope looks for unqualified success; but
Faith counts certainly on failure, and takes honourable
defeat to be a form of victory. Hope is a kind old pagan;
but Faith grew up in Christian days, and early learnt
humility. In the one temper, a man is indignant that he
cannot spring up in a clap to heights of elegance and
virtue; in the other, out of a sense of his infirmities, he is

filled with confidence because a year has come and gone,
and he has still preserved some rags of honour.'

With his description of faith we have no quarrel, nor yet
with the high place he assigns it. In his own words,
'whether on the first of January or the thirty-first of
December, faith is a good word to end on.' But his conception of hope, and his consequent depreciation of optimism,
do not appear to be equally warranted. When he speaks
of hope, is he not thinking of Prometheus, and really meaning blind hopes? There is a kind of hope which is founded
on faith, or, to be more accurate, which is but a higher and
bolder exercise of faith, so that optimism itself is in a sense
identical with faith, and is but a fully developed belief in
life. It must be this, indeed, if it is to be held worthy of
any serious consideration; for no sane man, judging by the
present appearance of things apart from faith, would say
that the world is even passable. The only possible optimism
which is without faith is that which shuts its eyes to the
suffering and failure that it may selfishly enjoy the rest—
a course which must in all cases be immoral.

In a word, what Stevenson called faith is the only
worthy optimism, and we are justified, in spite of his own
disclaimer, in applying the word optimist to him after all.
Let us look for a moment at that faith of his, as it is
expressed, let us say, in *Pulvis et Umbra*. Unfortun-
ately quotation is almost useless, for the exposition must
be taken as a whole, and indeed, it must be taken in
connection with other essays, so that no fragment could
justly convey his view. It is a description of the world, of
physical life in brute and man, and of man himself with his
moral and spiritual strivings. The writer stands off from
the 'rotatory island' of earth, and sees it, humid and fertile,
groaning and travailing through all its substance with the
myriad birth of life. The realism is crude and, in parts,

intentionally disgusting: the unrestrained imagination is put forth with a power and a daring at which we stand aghast as we read. Yet, as it turns out, all this is but the terrific background against which man's courage, the inalienable remnant of his honour, the unquenchable ardour of his struggle after nobleness, stand out in desperate relief. Nothing could be more tragic than such a picture, and from one point of view nothing could be more exact. If this writer be an optimist, certainly he has faced facts which might make men pessimists on a far less candid and unflinching view of them. Yet the practical outcome of the essay is not courage only but joyfulness; not a forced acceptance of the inevitable, but a whole-hearted acquiescence in the situation, and a glad belief in life. 'In the harsh face of life,' he tells us, 'faith can read a bracing gospel.'

In such a case the real question is one as to the ultimate facts. Do these facts, hidden in so tragic a darkness, correspond with the man's faithfulness, or with the pitiless and conscienceless play of natural forces? In a word, Does the universe back him, or does it not? Now it is quite true that Stevenson is not given to concerning himself much with theories about the ultimate facts. Faith, with him, is a practical affair, concerned with the immediate demands that life makes upon a man. Yet let us be plain here. Without the conviction that the universe backs his faith, that his attitude corresponds with the ultimate facts, such faith as his, and the joyfulness it produces, are mere folly and dishonesty. Various courses are open to a man who holds no such conviction, but this course is not open to him. He may reasonably adopt the darker view, and settle down in an embittered pessimism; or he may be agnostic, and take what comes, with courage but without enthusiasm; but joyfulness or faith in life are not for him. He who retains even a joyless belief in life, can do so only

263

in the manner of Ixion, appealing against that Jove whom men call Providence (who is the ultimate fact to most men) to some unknown higher power. He who believes and rejoices can do so only in the strength of a conviction that he positively *knows* the universe to mean well by him, no matter how unintelligible his actual experience may be.

Such was Dante's conviction, when he penned the inscription for the Gate of the Inferno. Such was Francis Thompson's when he wrote the lines :

> 'Yea, and God's mercy, I do think it well,
> Is flashed back from the brazen gates of hell.'

Such, beyond all possibility of question, was Stevenson's conviction. In a playful mood he writes to Austin Strong a long account of the exorcism of an evil spirit by an old woman who had frightened the natives of Vailima by her ventriloquism. ' All the old women in the world might talk with their mouths shut, and not frighten you or me, but there are plenty of other things that frighten us badly. And if we only knew about them, perhaps we should find them no more worthy to be feared than an old woman talking with her mouth shut. And the names of some of these things are Death, and Pain, and Sorrow.' So much for his estimate of those haggard aspects of life which he has so uncompromisingly depicted at their most formidable. But there is clearer evidence that his optimism was founded on a faith that the ultimate facts were with him. From the thick of the fight in Samoa, little more than a year before his death, he writes to Professor Colvin : ' The inherent tragedy of things works itself out from white to black and blacker ; and the poor things of a day look ruefully on. Does it shake my cast-iron faith ? I cannot say that it does. I believe in an ultimate decency of things ;

264

ay, and if I woke in hell, should still believe it!' That evidence may be accepted as final. It is the faith of one who has found himself able

'To feel, in the ink of the slough,
And the sink of the mire,
Veins of glory and fire
Run through and transpierce and transpire,
And a secret purpose of glory in every part,
And the answering glory of battle fill my heart.'

There is no need, however, for one who writes of Stevenson to confine himself to such vague and general formulæ as those with which we have just been working. He himself relates his optimism most frankly to the belief in God, leading back his life to Him in thankfulness and prayer. When a man prays for cheerfulness and laughter, we may take it that he regards his brightness to be in accordance with the mind of God for men. In the height of his good spirits he shouts aloud, 'Thank God for the grass, and the fir-trees, and the crows, and the sheep, and the sunshine, and the shadows of the fir-trees'; or he writes that 'all the way along I was thanking God that He had made me and the birds and everything just as they are and not otherwise.' A recent preacher has asserted that the fundamental thing in life is not to do good, not even to be good, but to believe that God is good. There are indeed some, for whom in the meantime the goodness of God is obscured by sorrows or by doubts, and with them the order is reversed. Their stress must lie on being and doing, and the power to believe will ultimately reward them. But Stevenson's faith is of the kind which the preacher's words describe. His belief in God was so far removed from any reasoned metaphysical conclusion, that we have described it as the highest form of a spirituality which belongs rather to the Religion of Sentiment than to the Religion of Dogma. Yet that instinctive belief was none the less a part of real knowledge. It is because, in the

depths, he is sure that God is good, that he is able to face
the life of action and of character strenuously. Indeed, the
thought of God is for him so identified with hope and
brightness, that when he hears the *Miserere* performed in
Noyon Cathedral, he is constrained to say that he takes it to
be the work of an atheist. ' I could bear a *Miserere* myself,'
he goes on, ' having had a good deal of open-air exercise of
late ; but I wished the old people somewhere else. It was
neither the right sort of music nor the right sort of divinity
for men and women who had come through most kind of
accidents by this time, and probably have an opinion of
their own upon the tragic element in life. A person up in
years can generally do his own *Miserere* for himself ;
although I notice that such an one often prefers *Jubilate
Deo* for his ordinary singing.' In several places he refers
to the answer which the Scottish Catechism gives to its first
question, ' What is the chief end of man ?' The answer
is, ' Man's chief end is to glorify God and to enjoy Him for
ever.' It was an answer which went to the heart of
Stevenson's philosophy of life, for it linked on the rejoicing
man with the Eternal God. It is only those whose faith
finds its chief end in God, who may know the secret of joy
as he knew it.

One of the finest incidents recorded in that ' tall quarto of
533 pages' in which Robert Stevenson told the story of his
operations at the Bell Rock Lighthouse, may here be narrated
as it is given in *A Family of Engineers*. A great storm had
broken upon the rock and the ship *Pharos* riding at her
anchor beside it, on September 5, 1807. All the following
day it raged with unabated violence, now threatening to tear
her from her moorings, now to overwhelm and break her to
pieces as she rode. After twenty-seven hours of what
to the landsman seemed imminent peril, he made the best of
his way aft and saw the tremendous spectacle of the waves.

'On deck there was only one solitary individual looking out, to give the alarm in the event of the ship breaking from her moorings . . . and he stood aft the foremast, to which he had lashed himself with a gasket or small rope round his waist, to prevent his falling upon deck or being washed overboard. When the writer looked up, he appeared to smile.' The writer goes on to record that he had been much relieved by that 'smile of the watch on deck, though literally lashed to the foremast. From this time he felt himself almost perfectly at ease; at any rate he was entirely resigned to the ultimate result.' We offer no apology for telling the story as a very perfect allegory of the grandson's faith. His storm also was long and affrighting, and he was not only 'entirely resigned to the ultimate result,' but indeed 'almost perfectly at his ease.' The reason was that he too, looking out, had seen a smile upon a certain Face.

> 'Well roars the storm to those that hear
> A deeper voice across the storm.'

# CHAPTER XIV

### STEVENSON AND HIS TIMES

In his great essay on *Self-reliance* Emerson has written, 'Trust thyself! Every heart vibrates to that iron string. Accept the place the Divine Providence has found for you, the society of your contemporaries, the connection of events. Great men have always done so, and confided themselves childlike to the genius of their age.'

The words are no less wise than they are exhilarating. He does not, of course, counsel us to allow ourselves to be tossed about with every new wind of doctrine; nor to take for permanent truth, or even for truth at all, the vagaries of the Zeitgeist. Great men have very frequently shown their greatness by resisting rather than by following such passing fashions. But in a deeper sense there is in every time a Spirit of the Age, the creation of its needs and its aspirations, which sets the tone of its thought and points the direction of its activities. Evidently such a spirit must also determine the lines along which the age may best be appealed to. No man who lives by the light of yesterday, or who talks the language of to-morrow, will influence his generation so greatly as he who talks to the understanding of the present day. The first secret for effectiveness is always that of living in one's own time. It is along the lines of the present, feeling its deepest needs and appreciating its most valuable enthusiasms, that men generally find their best opportunities of achieving manhood for themselves and rendering service

268

to others. How does Robert Louis Stevenson stand in this respect? We have been studying his characteristics as those of an individual thinker. It is fitting that we should close our study with some attempt, however fragmentary, at a more public and typical view of him, as he takes his place among the teachers of his day. What does he stand for? What are the leading characteristics of that spirit which he represents, and what is its religious value for the new time? To answer that question it will be necessary to glance rapidly at certain aspects of the past history of intellectual and spiritual tendencies in our national literature.

Among all the complex elements of human nature, whose various combinations determine the spirit of each successive age, there runs one central line of division, which marks the main dualism both in times and in individuals. That dualism has been differently conceived and named by different writers and at different periods. Sometimes it has been understood as the division between body and soul; at others, that between intellect and conscience. It has given us the popular contrast of Puritan with pagan, and the classical one of Hebraist with Hellenist. The latter nomenclature, though in some ways far from satisfactory, is yet that which, on the whole, best suits our subject, and we shall borrow it from Matthew Arnold's *Culture and Anarchy* for the present purpose.

In another of his books, *Celtic Literature*, Arnold has insisted that in almost every living Briton there is some admixture of the blood, or at least some very distinct hereditary influence, from three separate races, viz. Celtic, Saxon, and Norman. Of these three, the Saxon elements have produced a character plain, steadfast, and practical—a character which always tends towards the Hebraic type. The Celtic, with its fire and sensitiveness, and its capacity for delight,

269

tends in the main towards Hellenism. So does the Norman, in virtue of a different set of qualities—its fastidious delicacy and its clear and rational energy. Each of the latter two, in its different way, boasts a vivid sense of colour and of beauty, each has an exalted spirituality of its own—qualities all of which tend towards Hellenism. If we could blend all these elements, so as to produce a perfect balance of character and harmony of ideals, we should indeed have achieved something very like perfect manhood, at once strong and gracious, as earnest as it would be delicate. If we must confess that the actual Briton falls in most cases far short of so excellent a creature, it consoles us to reflect that this is at least our true national ideal. Each nation follows its own lights. The spirituality of France, the practical doggedness of Germany, far excel anything that we can boast. But all their lights are also ours in a measure by inheritance, and we make up in breadth what we lack in specialised intensity.

It is but too true, however, that the blend is in no case complete. As individuals, we for ever find war in our members, with two or more than two types of manhood struggling within us for mastery. There is a pagan part of human nature to which most men occasionally revert, though they know all the while that that will never satisfy their instinct for manhood; and a Puritan element upon which they fling themselves in extreme reaction, though they are equally well aware that it will prove to be but a maimed and cheerless ideal. In some cases one or other of these moods is adopted as the normal and desirable condition. Other impulses are checked and mortified, until the character becomes intentionally and on principle one-sided. But even with the most successful discipline this result is seldom completely effected. Most of us feel more or less to the end the swinging of those spiritual tides which bear us backward and forward with their alternate ebb and flow.

It is the same with the movement of History on the larger scale. Balance is preserved on the whole, yet there never has been an epoch of perfect balance. It is preserved by the constant alternation of forces, the same tidal swing as is felt in individual lives. There is no long duration of either the Hellenistic or the Hebraistic tendencies. Celt and Saxon act and react within the national character, at longer or shorter intervals, but with unfailing alternation. The dark severity of Mediæval asceticism was followed by the glad humanism of the Renaissance; that again led on to the Puritan ascendency, which suddenly ended in the Restoration; the worldly century which carried on the traditions of the Restoration brought on at length the religious revivals of Whitefield and Wesley; these in their turn were followed by that great outburst of secular interest in literature and science which began the nineteenth century. It was not long after that until Carlyle was solemnising his times with a new Hebraism, to be followed at length by the still more recent Hellenism of to-day. Let it not be supposed that we desire exclusively to claim truth or the message of God to man for either the brighter or the sterner periods of the past. 'There are, it may be, so many kinds of voices in the world, and none of them is without signification.' God was in them all, and His Word was spoken by none of them with greater clearness than by some of those whose voices were most severe. Only we insist that the Word of God is spoken not only in the sterner voices of the generations but also in the kindlier; and that, in the main, each generation must hear that Word in its own language and find inspiration in its own spiritual ideals.

Nothing could be more pleasant than a study of those glad voices of the past which have cheered the hearts and

271

chased away the fears of successive generations. Form
after form rises before the imagination. The dim heroic
figure of the Herakles of Æschylus is there, him whom, in
Browning's poem, we have quoted twice already :

> 'The gay cheer of that great voice
> Hope, joy, salvation ; Herakles was here
> Himself o' the threshold, sent his voice on first
> To herald all that human and divine
> I' the weary, happy face of him. . . .
> The irresistible, sound, wholesome heart
> O' the hero . . . drove back, dried up sorrow at its source.'

There too is Dunbar, with his old sweet words:

> 'Be merry, man, and tak not sair in mind
>   The wavering of this wretchit warld of sorrow :
> To God be humble and to thy friend be kind,
>   And with thy nichtbours gladly lend and borrow ;
> His chance to-nicht, it may be thine to-morrow ;
>   Be blythe in heart for ony aventure,
> For oft with wise men it has been said aforrow,
>   Without gladness availeth no treasure.'

Shakespeare knew them, and the value of them, these glad
encouragers of the world. It is his own King Henry V. who
goes forth in the dark and ominous night, and walking from
tent to tent, visits the host with such 'cheerful semblance
and sweet majesty,'

> 'That every wretch, pining and pale before,
> Beholding him plucks comfort from his looks,'

under the spell of

> 'A little touch of Harry in the night.'

John Bunyan, Puritan though he be, is conspicuous for his
appreciation of this side of life. His Hopeful, Help, and a
long list of others, are prophets of the brighter truth. His
Greatheart is but a shadow, yet he lives in the town of

272

Good Confidence, and the evil workers of the darkness flee before him.

Dante is the most significant of them all. Austere and solemn, burdened with lifelong sorrow, and bearing on his heart his nation's and the world's iniquities, yet the sin he most bitterly rebukes is that of perverse gloom. By far his best work is the *Purgatorio*. The *Inferno* is subterranean, the *Paradiso* is in the air, while the *Purgatorio* is on the earth, with its breeze fresh off the sea or heavy with the scent of flowers. This for ever claims him from untempered Hebraism, which is essentially the doctrine of heaven and hell, for Hellenism which has a religion of the green earth as well.

These are but a few instances, found in this and other lands, cited at random as they came to mind from the great company of the world's heartiest and bravest spirits. Listening to them, we seem to hear that laughter of the cheerful soul of the world which the sorrows of all the centuries have not quenched. These immortal dead, smiling upon us and our perplexities from their happy stations, still cheer us by their undying health and confidence and gladness. It is to that band that the writers most typical of the new spirit of to-day belong, and Stevenson is in the front rank of them.

To return from this digression: the period immediately preceding the present was one of sombre Hebraic tone. It was indeed a time of many-sided literary activity, but the voice that dominated it was the voice of Thomas Carlyle. Born in the same year as Keats, and but three years after Shelley, he had to wait till their voices, and others of their time, were silenced. Then his solemn accents found hearing in a world ready for a period of reaction. The year after Sir Walter Scott died, when Byron had been dead nine years, Shelley eleven, and Keats twelve, appeared *Sartor*

*Resartus*—certainly the most critical and epoch-making book published in the nineteenth century. There followed that literature of which Thackeray, the Brontës, and George Eliot may be taken as representative types. Looking back, at the distance of three-quarters of a century, it would seem as if, after the age of Scott and his contemporaries, English literature had grown conscience-stricken, feeling that the earlier period had enjoyed life too well to be quite fitting in so serious a world. The succeeding period is the age of sterner prophets, whose message was a burden of the Lord. Carlyle's earth is not green nor is his heaven golden. His God is essentially a Taskmaster; and accordingly for him work is the one reality, happiness a negligible detail.

To think otherwise than reverently of that great time and its solemn message, would be as ungrateful as it would be ignorant. It seems likely that many a year will pass before a new time matches it for greatness. Yet obviously such a spirit must be but for a time. Imagine a succession of unbroken periods of similar Hebraism, and it will not be long until you shall have reduced human nature to a mere skeleton, holding nothing within it but a conscience for a soul. To the nineteenth century at least the burden grew unbearable. In the swifter and more headlong race of life many men were so wearied as to require something kindlier than even the 'Everlasting Yea.' The increasing complication of social problems, and the more enlightened sympathy with social miseries, forced all who loved their fellow men to recognise both an economic and a religious value in happiness. Owing to a great variety of causes, not a few thoughtful men and women have lost their hold upon the religious beliefs which supported the courage of their fathers; and our leading pessimist has noted the result, as a fact obvious enough to require no proof—'the chronic melancholy which is taking hold on the civilised races with

274

the decline of belief in a beneficent power.' A shrewd observer has noticed one instance in which the facial expression is already changing. In the portraits of English gentlemen of the eighteenth century, the eyebrows are usually rounded, as in men placid and at their ease. The living faces of the descendants of these gentlemen may reproduce almost exactly the features of their ancestors, but in one respect they will often be found to differ. The eyebrows are lowered to a sharper and more straightened curve. This curious detail of the falling eyebrow is surely significant. Although, as we believe, the pessimistic estimate of our time is grossly exaggerated, still there must be a considerable body of facts which have seemed to justify it. These indicate that the first necessity of the present day is for an encouraging and heartening type of faith, lest we sink to that *fin de siècle* dejection in which an age 'goes dispiritedly, glad to finish.'

When we venture to assert that Carlyle and his contemporaries have served their generation, we imply not only that, meanwhile at least, their time is past; but that in that past time they did incalculable service, for which all wise generations henceforth will call them blessed. But their time is past, and a new spirit has taken command of our literature. Nothing could prove this more convincingly than the fate of those thinkers of to-day who have remained aloof from its exhilarating and buoyant hopefulness. Stephen Phillips is gifted with a wonderfully rich and pure poetic quality, but Mr. Churton Collins utters the exact truth when he speaks of the 'monotonous dreariness' of his poems. William Watson is an unrivalled master of poetic criticism, expressed with a severe and noble Doric power, but his subjectivity tends to pass over into sheer grumbling. Thomas Hardy's strength is Titanic, but he is the master-pessimist of our time. Robert Louis Stevenson

275

wrote: 'Denunciatory preachers seem not to suspect that they may be taken gravely and in evil part; that young men may come to think of life as of a moment, and with the pride of Satan wave back the inadequate gift.' This is exactly what has happened. For here comes Thomas Hardy telling us that 'The view of life as a thing to be put up with, replacing that zest for existence which was so intense in early civilisations, must ultimately enter so thoroughly into the constitution of the advanced races that its facial expression will become accepted as a new artistic departure.' When we read further on, that 'Human beings, in their generous endeavour to construct a hypothesis that shall not degrade a First Cause, have always hesitated to conceive a dominant power of lower moral quality than their own,' we recognise in the cynical words that Nemesis which inevitably comes upon a belated Hebraism.

The note of the new spirit is health and gladness. It is true that these have had their advocates in the preceding time, and indeed in every time. All generalisations which divide the progress of thought into periods are necessarily very far from being either exhaustive or exclusive. It is by subtle changes of emphasis, by the silent and often unconscious disappearance of one set of conceptions, and the equally unobtrusive introduction of other conceptions, that each new Zeitgeist comes in place of an old. Yet in the course of years these changes, unnoticeable at the moment, grow obvious at last; and we know that we are breathing the air of a new day.

As for the present spirit, it has already asserted itself along the whole line of contemporary literature. Robert Browning and Matthew Arnold were its pioneers in the departments of Poetry and of Criticism. The robust and uncompromising optimism of Browning is now happily so familiar that any quotations in proof of it are unnecessary.

276

## STEVENSON AND HIS TIMES

The cultured Hellenism of Arnold has been leavening English thought for many years. Both writers came before their age, and had to be content with neglect and misunderstanding; but like others born out of due season, they did much to mould the spirit of the coming time. Each of them is deliberate in his reaction from the Carlylian spirit. The very boisterousness of

'God's in his heaven,
All's right with the world,'

and a hundred other verses of Browning's, is of the nature of a protest. Arnold tells us—and the words are characteristic of his habit of serene overstatement of what is nevertheless a truth—that, in his opinion, Carlyle is 'carrying coals to Newcastle, . . . preaching earnestness to a nation which had plenty of it by nature, but was less abundantly supplied with several other useful things.'

Sir John Lubbock (Lord Avebury) has given us, in his *Pleasures of Life*, a remarkable example of the invasion of Science by the same spirit. It is a collection of innumerable quotations from writers old and new, the gatherings from many years of reading, and is the cheerfullest book imaginable. All possible sources are ransacked, or rather, as the author is careful to state, not nearly all, though many, sources. The cumulative result would satisfy Mark Tapley or the Cheeryble Brothers. He rings the changes on the Duty of Happiness and the Happiness of Duty. He is prepared to make the best of everything life may have in store for him; and even death is to find him *in utrumque paratus*, and yet full of hope.

Professor William James has brought the same spirit into philosophy. He has done this not only in his well-known and much-debated Gifford Lectures, but in all his books. Some of his best work in this line is to be found in

277

those essays entitled *Talks to Students*, whose themes are 'The Gospel of Relaxation,' 'On a Certain Blindness in People,' and 'What makes Life Significant.' The splendid healthfulness of these essays, their width of sympathy and depth of understanding, and their immense practical encouragement to many hard-pressed people, rank him high among the helpers of mankind. His Gifford Lectures, apart from all controversial points they may have raised, have certainly achieved one end at least. They have constrained Philosophy to take serious account of the spirit of Healthymindedness, as a phenomenon of first importance in the life and thought of to-day. In doing this they have effectually served to fix it as a characteristic spirit of our time, and to lead to its recognition as such.

The Church, too, has her representatives. Few writings of late years are more significant than Bishop Paget's brilliant essay ' Concerning Accidie,' which forms the introduction to his volume entitled *The Spirit of Discipline*. In that essay he reviews the phases of melancholy as they appeared in past ages; and, for the benefit of the present age, he sets Fortitude against Gloom once more, as a kind of righteousness much needed to combat a deadly sin. It is pathetic to remember, as he reminds us, that Chaucer and Langland had to do the same thing so long ago. It is for us peculiarly interesting to find that he puts *The Celestial Surgeon* in a prominent position among works of contemporary authors to the same purpose, and gives to Stevenson the place of honour among them. All through his work there runs the same strain of brightness and vivacity, the same call to courageous health and gladness.

Finally, there is Robert Louis Stevenson, who, for many reasons, may be taken as the chief representative of the healthful and bright spirit of the new Hellenism. The popularity of a book or doctrine does not indeed afford any evidence of their ultimate truth, but it may be fairly said to show that they have met a felt want of their time. In this connection it is worthy of remark that *The Pleasures of Life* has, since its publication in 1887, already all but reached its two hundredth thousand. The popularity of Stevenson has long been assured, and it is still rising. To a very large number of readers he is the unrivalled favourite among the writers of his time. Many reasons may be assigned for this. We have seen how many-sided his interests were, how sensitive to every sort of influence. That in itself rendered it probable that he would call out a wide and various response. His genius is as commanding as his personality is attractive, and such a light as his could not have been hid. Yet after the fullest allowance has been made for all that, it still remains true that the deepest secret of his popularity is the need that men and women have felt for the message he has brought, and the powerful effect of it in quickening their lives. That message we have found to be the 'great task of happiness,' backed by moral earnestness on the one hand and sympathy on the other. We have sought to trace it from its sources in the gift of vision and the instinct of travel. We have seen how it, like all gospels, has passed through bitterness. From the conventionalities of his early surroundings he broke away in a revolt that for the time being was painful and dangerous in the last degree. In after-life, the physical conditions through which he had to fight his way to health of mind were such as to have silenced any preacher less resolute and less convinced. From all this he emerged on us, original and clear-sighted in thought, swift and energetic in action, and radiantly healthy in both. Finally we have seen the whole of his life and work culminate in the Gospel of health and gladness, his own especial word to his brethren of mankind. To be happy is every man's immediate task and duty—to be happy and to spread happiness around him. Stevenson meets all such lamentable prophecies as that one above quoted regarding 'the facial expression of the future,' with his often-repeated challenge that we shall present to the world a 'glorious morning face.' A princely figure, he takes his station in the front rank of those whose faith is that of the healthy mind.

It must be remembered, too, that Stevenson—and he is by no means the only one of whom this fact is true—had to fight against terrible odds his battle for the gladder faith. His victory proves that the thing can be done. All who will may make a stand against the gloom which they have seen closing in upon themselves and their time. To many who have suffered far less than he, his faith is a challenge to fling off their neurotic miseries, and to quit themselves like men. To others, strong and capable, but bewildered and discouraged, the thought of such a man may be an inspiration of priceless value.

Obviously all manifestations of Hellenism are liable to the two great dangers of moral laxity and pleasure-loving selfishness, evils which undoubtedly are a serious menace to the younger life of the present day. Against both of these dangers Stevenson has safeguarded his message.

In respect of the former, the question at once presents itself, Is it safe, this kindlier and brighter view? To which history answers promptly that that depends upon its safeguards. An indolent and selfish Hellenism is supremely dangerous, inevitably degrading and ruinous. If we were condemned to a choice between Hellenism unstrengthened by any Hebraism, and Hebraism untempered by any Hellenism, every wise man would choose the latter. Professor Butcher has found it necessary to defend Hellenism against the charge of being 'eccentricity tinged with vice.' For Hellenism, when it has appeared as a revolt from

Hebraic austerity, has sometimes rushed into that infatuation of moral laxity which prides itself on its freedom

> 'To say of vice, What is it?
> Of virtue, We can miss it,
> Of sin, We can but kiss it,
> And 'tis no longer sin.'

Even Walt Whitman, with all the exhilarating opulence of his thought, is marred by one great defect. He often seems to be incapable of realising the meaning of the word 'sin' at all. Needless to say, any so-called Hellenism such as this is neither a healthy nor a helpful thing. Stevenson owed much to Whitman, and has not been wanting in acknowledgment. Yet any one who knows Whitman's writings and Stevenson's essay on them, must feel that with all the apppreciation and gratitude, there is still a reserve, and that his catholicity has not abrogated any of his own convictions. In Stevenson's opinion, as in Professor James's,[1] Whitman's optimism 'o'erleaps itself, and falls on t' other side.' Without a considerable weight of Hebraism for ballast, the vessel of Hellenism is at the mercy of all the winds of evil. When lightheartedness means indifference to moral facts, it is no more to be called health than are the comfort and painlessness which sometimes smooth the downward course of disease.

For Stevenson, as we have seen him, there were many safeguards. His sense of the terror of the world, and his view of heredity, were themselves sufficient to sober the most fantastic 'reveller in the situation.' There were also his vitality and his human sympathy to guard against laxity. When courage and vivacity are the watchwords of the personal life, when the heart is open to a world of the disinherited who everywhere around us claim their share of gladness, it is safe to follow the bright ideal. 'Let us teach the people,' says Stevenson, 'as much as we can, to

[1] Cf. *The Varieties of Religious Experience*, p. 87.

enjoy, and they will learn for themselves to sympathise; but let us see to it above all that we give these lessons in a brave, vivacious note, and build the man up in courage while we demolish its substitute, indifference.' He retained throughout, a strong conscience of sin and a vivid sense of its disastrous and repulsive sinfulness. Aware of the reality of evil, associating beauty with goodness; sobered by an almost Calvinistic sense of the seriousness of life, assured that good and not evil lay at the heart of the universe—there was little fear of the result. He was essentially a Hellenist; but he had appropriated so considerable an amount of Hebraism of the Scottish type, as to insure his optimistic faith against the risk of licence.

The second danger of such a message as his is that it should be confounded with pleasure-loving and worldliness. This is especially the danger of a society whose increased wealth is tempting it by a thousand new opportunities of self-indulgence. It cannot be too strongly asserted that selfish pleasure-loving is not a phase of health but a disease. The belief in life is the extreme opposite of a cheap satisfaction with the world. The low ideals of worldliness are but the travesty of God's glad word for to-day, the caricature of His ideal as Stevenson beheld it. Only those, as we have already stated, who look beyond the world can really appreciate even the world itself, and worldliness is the most pathetic of follies, foredoomed to failure by the very constitution of things. It has been well said that 'earth is in darkness if it lives not in the light of heaven.'

We have had abundant opportunity of observing the exalted spirituality of Stevenson's view of earth. He was aware of a spiritual world, not so much above this world as within it, by reference to which he was constantly interpreting the daily life. Thus he was spiritual, but not with the hectic spirituality of those who have become alienated from the earthly life with its physical conditions and human interests. His spirituality was that true health of mind, in which life is seen as it is, under earthly conditions indeed, but with a secret inspiration impossible without the vision of spiritual things.

With these safeguards, Hellenism is safe, and it offers us a view of life whose conspicuous quality is that of glad health. The Religion of Healthy-mindedness is being much discussed in our time. As Stevenson advocated it, health must be understood in its etymological sense of wholeness, for it is a happy and suggestive fact that the two words are the same. The healthy eye is not that which sees all things under a rosy light, any more than that which sees all things yellow. The first condition, and indeed the essential meaning of health, is truth to the whole facts of the case. Accordingly the war of the new Hellenism is only against one-sided views of things. It is not destructive or silencing towards any set of truths, but rather reconciling and comprehensive. It looks fearlessly around the whole horizon of the world and notes all there is to see ; and its verdict is that when you have seen all, you cease to be afraid of life, for you have found that the victory lies with good and not with evil. It is only in virtue of this heartening persuasion, that Stevenson's message can be understood. Assured of this, he directs us to dwell on the pleasantness rather than on the miseries of our lot; he presses on our conscience the positive instead of the negative virtues; he lays stress on hope instead of on remorse, and trains our eyes rather on the beauty of goodness than on the ugliness of sin. In a word, he counsels us to live in the light and not the darkness, and to believe in life as an unfailing opportunity of seeing God's glory in common joys and sorrows, and doing God's work in simple duties.

It remains for us to estimate in a few last words the

value of this spirit which found in Stevenson so brilliant an exponent, in terms of Psychology and of Religion.

1. The spirit of which we speak is vitally and closely allied with Psychology. The ultimate grounds of faith are not psychological but always theological. Even the atheist is a theologian : it certainly was not the study of his own soul and its facts which gave him his conviction that there is no God. We have found that Stevenson himself rests his optimism upon a conviction of ultimate facts which are beyond the reach of unaided psychology. God's Revelation of Himself to man is manifold, and may be found both in outward facts and in inward experience; but each believer falls back on his assurance that God has *somehow* broken the silence and has spoken words of eternal life to him who will hear them. Granted the revelation, in which, however conceived, we get out beyond the psychological region and are in touch with the ultimate reality of things, the next question is how we are to relate to actual life, as our guide in thought and conduct, that ultimate truth which we have found. There has sometimes been a tendency to keep the revelation apart from life, to explain the whole phenomena of the religious experience in terms kept exclusively for themselves, or not to attempt to explain them at all. It is here that the modern spirit makes a new departure. Mr. Fotheringham, in his book of studies on Robert Browning, has said that 'the great modern view of religion' is that it is 'part of the vital study of man.' In other words, the whole play of man's mind in its various religious exercises is studied as the same in kind with its play upon the common facts of life, and its experiences are analysed by the same methods. It is characteristic of the new spirit, that its principal advocates are psychologists. Professor James is the most influential psychologist alive. Robert Browning was the greatest exponent of psychological drama in the nineteenth century.

284

The interpretation of religious experiences in terms of the general laws of psychology has given alarm needlessly, though not unnaturally, to some believers. These have fallen into the same fallacy as that to which Darwin's critics have often succumbed: they have forgotten that to explain the process of a phenomenon is not to explain its ultimate causes, or to deny to it the operation of those hidden spiritual forces with which Christianity has familiarised us. Spiritual experience would be no less divine though we were able to trace it point by point along a sequence of psychological processes to the point at which the soul of man receives from God His authentic revelation. Divineness does not consist in unintelligibility, nor is it the sole attribute of God that he hideth Himself from sight. So far from being in any way a menace to religion, psychology may be and has been among the most valuable of its allies. The worst feature about religion as it has often been understood is its aloofness from the ordinary facts of life, and its severance of the sacred from the secular. The inevitable result for the majority of men must be a deadening of the religious interest, and a more or less gloomy sense of remoteness in sacred things. The temptation to pessimism, or at least discouragement, comes to all men from the disheartening experience of their daily conflicts and defeats. But those whose religion is held apart have no defence against it, the God whom their theory has isolated from life being 'far off from helping them.' To such men the new spirit offers a God who is near at hand, a Word which is nigh them, in their mouth and in their heart. The result is immediate in the spring of quickened vital interest and enthusiasm, in an optimistic view of life and a gospel of health and gladness.

Such was Stevenson's way of dealing with the phenomena of the religious life. As we have seen, he recognised that he was essentially a psychologist. His fundamental conviction was that of personal identity and the inestimable value of the individual human soul. His doctrines of life and morals were drawn from a far-seeing and clear insight into the facts of human nature. He insisted on finding these for himself, and in various respects they differ from the commonly accepted views. One quality they all have, and that unfailingly: they are vital and not conventional. It is easy to see how this vital and direct way of dealing with the facts of human life should lead on to his great message of gladness. All worthy Hellenism is characterised by a profound belief in life and a conviction that it is worth living. True, that conviction rests ultimately among facts that are beyond life, as we have seen. Yet it can remain and grow stronger in a more and more assured optimism, only on the condition that a man's continued experience and study of life shall confirm it. And Stevenson found it confirmed.

2. The more important question, as to the religious value of Stevenson's message, remains. Is this gospel of glad healthfulness, which he and others are proclaiming, a religion at all? Can it even be said to possess any serious religious value? No doubt some of those who find it very precious as a stimulus and source of encouragement will answer that this does not concern them. So long as it quickens vitality and brightens the aspect of life for them, they will ask no more from it. To these it must be replied that they would be wiser if they did ask more. A faith in life such as Stevenson's requires foundations and it requires sanctions. We have seen how for him the foundations were laid upon the ultimate facts. To all honest thinkers there must come an hour when they have to face the investigation of the grounds on which their faith is resting. Psychology can do nothing for them then. If they have no assured

STEVENSON AND HIS TIMES

foundations beyond the region it explores, they will have to confess to themselves definitely at last that their faith is groundless, and having stated that in plain terms they will never again be able to trust life except by forgetting. It requires sanctions also, for life is sure to put the breaking strain of sorrow upon the faith of most men. A view of things at once so attractive in itself and so full of interesting associations as this of Stevenson's is a fine thing to keep about one as an ornamental part of one's mental furniture. But when it comes to fighting, it is not the chasing of the design upon the sword-blade, but the temper of its cutting edge, that concerns us. An unsanctioned faith, though it were the most charming in the world, will fail us in the evil day. Life is too difficult to be able to do without religion. To be a man, a right healthy and glad man, is a noble thought; but without the sanctions of religion none but a very few have ever persisted in even *trying* to be it. Mr. Kidd may be taken as a sufficiently unbiassed judge, and he tells us unhesitatingly that the race is growing and must continue to grow steadily more and more religious.

Returning to the main ·question, it is necessary here to remember the distinction between religion and theology. Theology is the science of which religion is the corresponding art. Stevenson's faith, if it be a religious faith, appears to wear the aspect of an art without a science. He offers us no system of new doctrines that can be set up in contrast with the old : his faith will fit into almost any theological system. In this sense it is really not a new faith at all, but only a fresh way of using the old; bringing but a change of emphasis among the various parts, and a new naturalness and nearness to the human facts.

Yet while this is true, it is true also that a faith like his is bound to react upon the theological position of those who hold it. If a man has thought either harshly or frivolously

287

of God, this will secure for him an estimate both finer and more exalted. The character of God has suffered grievously at the hands of morbid piety; those whose ideal is health may find a truer conception of Him upon less dreary terms. Further, there is nothing more likely to lead men back to a reasonable faith, and to strengthen faith where it is weak, than such a message, in an age of loosened creeds and vague, unfocussed doubt. One cause of the present decline from old beliefs is a spiritual debility, a lack of the power to take energetic hold on beliefs, even when the reason has no fault to find with them. Nothing could be imagined more likely to counteract that nerveless condition than an energetic attitude to human life. Those who gladly and enthusiastically lay hold on life are the likeliest to attain to a faith which deals robustly with that which lies beyond life.

But, when we come to the task of finding for the faith of Stevenson a place among the various forms of religious belief, a new question arises. This spirit which we are discussing may be called the Gospel of Health. But that is a claim which every phase and sect of religion makes. To revert again to etymology, the watchword of all religions is holiness. But holiness, *heiligkeit*, is the same word as wholeness, health, *heil*. Even the most austere asceticism believes itself to be healthy, and declares that it is compelled to dwell in its frozen climate because there alone can it find air bracing enough. The chief question between rival systems of religion lies in the difference between their views of what health or holiness means. What, then, shall we say about Stevenson's conception of health? How far, in particular, can it be called a Christian conception?

Christianity has been claimed by many thinkers with widely different points of view; and the only error that many

288

of these claimants have made is to insist that they alone can claim it. Christianity is a larger and more comprehensive religion than any of our little systems; it is the monopoly of none of them. Like the human spirit itself, it is 'wider than the most priceless of the forces which bear it onward.' It would be absurd, for instance, to identify it either with Hebraism or with Hellenism. It is neither because it is both. It is just Christianity, the interpretation of all the various moods and factors in human life.

As an exhaustive, or even an adequate account of Christianity, the faith of Robert Louis Stevenson is very far from complete; but that is not to say that it may not have an immense value as the exposition of a true aspect of Christianity to its generation. For each particular age there is one set of Christian thoughts and principles which is more valuable than any other. It is by successive changes of emphasis that Christianity has proved itself a religion adequate for the needs of the world, because capable of interpreting life and revealing God to man in all ages. The need of many in the present time is for a gospel of health and glad encouragement, expressed in terms rather of human life than of metaphysical discussion; and once more Christianity is found adequate to the demand. Christ said long ago all that is valuable in the most recent thought. The guiding principles of His life were strenuousness and compassion. Many of His most familiar sayings were words of courageous hope and cheerful encouragement. The great task of happiness was never preached so forcibly as when He summed up His beatitudes in words spoken in express defiance of slander and persecution, 'Rejoice and be exceeding glad.' The most characteristic word of Christ was 'My joy'—a word spoken in the midst of overwhelming calamities. So far, then, Stevenson's gospel amounts simply to this: that he took seriously, what so few of us take seriously, Jesus Christ's command that His disciples should rejoice.

It is true that Christ also preached self-denial, and laid vehement emphasis on the necessity for cross-bearing. It is true also that behind all Christianity there stands the Cross of Christ—variously understood, always mysterious, and yet always commanding. Those are happy who have understood the meaning of the Cross of Christ sufficiently to formulate to themselves its doctrine. But the healing and life-giving shadow of that Cross falls on others who cannot do this. As to the cross-bearing of the disciples, He never spoke of that as an end in itself, but only as a means towards the real ends of human life—a means rendered necessary by the perverse conditions of man's present state. Self-denial comes as a duty upon all men. But beyond it lies the region of positive virtue, and health and gladness, for the sake of which it comes.

All this Stevenson's faith implies, and indeed he has stated much of it in explicit terms. His faith was not for himself alone, and the phases of Christianity which it has asserted are peculiarly suited to the spiritual needs of many in the present time. Health and gladness, arising out of energetic and compassionate life, are essentially Christian virtues. The late Professor Seeley, in a brilliant and famous passage, has contrasted the New Athens with the New Jerusalem. He has confessed, as we all must do, that it is better to be a citizen in the latter than in the former. But the question presses for answer, Are these two separate cities after all? Are they not but two different names for the ultimate City of God, that lieth foursquare, with gates on the west as well as on the east? So long as the glory of God doth lighten it, and there entereth into it nothing that defileth, it matters not much for the name whereby it is called.

Meanwhile, as to the ideals we have been considering as characteristic not only of Stevenson's faith, but of that of many other thinking men and women, they are the ideals which the wheel of life has brought uppermost for the hour in which we are appointed to live. Doubtless their time also will one day be past, and some new Hebraism—who can tell?—will have come instead of them. So much at least may be said for them, that they have achieved a more harmonious balance of the various elements of life than most of the Hellenisms of the past, and so, perhaps, have advanced a few steps nearer to the final truth. But, in the meantime, they are here—to some men and women the clearest light of God that they can see. The task of life for each of us is to walk faithfully through the hours of our day by that day's light. And it is thus that we must estimate the Faith of Robert Louis Stevenson—to whom was given a most brilliant vision of a certain stretch of sunlit earth, and who travelled in that light joyously to the end.

# GENERAL INDEX

295

# INDEX

296

# INDEX

# INDEX

INDEX TO REFERENCES AND QUOTATIO

FROM STEVENSON'S WRITINGS

# INDEX TO REFERENCES AND QUOTATIONS
## FROM STEVENSON'S WRITINGS

301

# INDEX

Edinburgh: T. and A. CONSTABLE, Printers to His Majesty